AUDIENCE AS PERFORMER

Actors always talk about what the audience does. I don't understand, we are just sitting here.

(Audience member, New York 2013)

Audience as Performer proposes that in the theatre there are two troupes of performers: the actors and the audience. Although academics have scrutinised how audiences respond, make meaning and co-create while watching a performance, little research has considered the behaviour of the theatre audience as a performance in and of itself.

This insightful book describes how an audience performs through its myriad gestural, vocal and paralingual actions, and considers the following questions:

- If the audience are performers, who are their audiences?
- How have audiences' roles changed throughout history?
- How do talkbacks and technology influence the audience's role as critics?
- What influence does the audience have on the creation of community in theatre?
- How can the audience function as both consumer and co-creator?

Drawing from over 140 interviews with audience members, actors and ushers in the UK, United States and Australia, Heim reveals the lived experience of audience members at the theatrical event. It is a fresh reading of mainstream audiences' activities, bringing their voices to the fore and exploring their emerging new roles in the theatre of the twenty-first century.

Caroline Heim is Lecturer in Drama at Queensland University of Technology, Australia. Before entering academia she worked as a professional actor on New York and other US stages, winning a Drama League Award.

AUDIENCE AS PERFORMER

The changing role of theatre audiences in the twenty-first century

Caroline Heim

Routledge
Taylor & Francis Group

LONDON AND NEW YORK

First published 2016
by Routledge
2 Park Square, Milton Park, Abingdon, Oxon OX14 4RN

and by Routledge
711 Third Avenue, New York, NY 10017

Routledge is an imprint of the Taylor & Francis Group, an informa business

British Library Cataloguing-in-Publication Data
A catalogue record for this book is available from the British Library

Library of Congress Cataloguing-in-Publication Data
Heim, Caroline.
Audience as performer : the changing role of theatre audiences in the twenty-first century / Caroline Heim.
pages cm
Includes index.
1. Theater audiences. I. Title.
PN2193.A8H45 2015
306.4'84--dc23
2015006154

ISBN: 978-1-138-79691-1 (hbk)
ISBN: 978-1-138-79692-8 (pbk)
ISBN: 978-1-315-75756-8 (ebk)

Typeset in Bembo
by Taylor & Francis Books

Dominus illuminatio mea

CONTENTS

ACKNOWLEDGEMENTS

Foremost I would like to acknowledge all the audience members that I have encountered while researching. Without their particular insights this book would not have current significance. My gratitude also extends to the many actors and ushers I interviewed who generously shared their understandings of audiences. Thanks also to Anne Bogart, Martha Lavey, Jim Houghton, Lynne Meadow, Tim Crouch and Kevin McCollum for our conversations and the opportunities they provide for audiences to play.

Some theatre practitioners and audience members have particularly gone out of their way to assist my research: Helen Oakleigh, Sondra Lee, Trevor Danby, Marc Bonanni, Aaron Carter, Mel Miller, Joerg Bochow, Martin Bedford, Sally-Ann Djachenko and Francesca Perlman. Special thanks to my agent, the ever-congenial Bernard Liebhaber, who opened up many doors for me in New York.

My heartfelt thanks to the colleagues that read sections of my book: Joanne Tompkins for her incredible support, mentoring and astute comments from the beginning; and Veronica Kelly for her inspirational comments on my history chapters. Veronica first introduced me to the idea of an audience costume while I was still a student at The University of Queensland. As PhD supervisors and now as colleagues, Joanne and Veronica continue to model excellence and academic rigour. In addition to insightful comments on chapters of my book, Bree Hadley has provided much guidance and encouragement through the difficult road of early career research. Alan McKee's excellent feedback and support dispelled any initial doubts I harboured. My editor, Ben Piggott at Routledge, has supplied much enthusiasm and direction from the start. Harriet Affleck at Routledge has worked to make the production process seamless.

I would also like to acknowledge Queensland University of Technology for recognising that women need career interruptions to mother their children by giving me a Women in Research grant to research part of my book.

A support team was always there to encourage and strengthen. I thank my son Reuben for his many hours of transcription and keen insights into interview responses and my son Benjamin for his help with the cover and for his truth seeking which guided some of my research. Both my sons' and husband's delightful culinary arts sustained me while writing. My parents' love, strength and enthusiasm has always been boundless. Thanks also to the continuous support from the "discussion group" and particularly to my friend Joy Lawn for her words of encouragement.

Finally, this book would not have been written without the love, constancy, belief, sacrifice and inspirations of my other half, Christian. As we walked the streets of our hometown and the many cities we visited together abroad for my research, his shared insights and vital contributions breathed life into very pedestrian sections of my book. He also gave me the courage to approach and interview my first audience member in New York. I thank him for poring over multiple drafts as we edited late into the night after burdensome days at his own work. On a more personal level, I thank him for supporting and loving me unconditionally through the stormy times and for rejoicing with me through the more triumphant.

INTRODUCTION

> Normally you go and the stage is lit up but you are in the dark so you might just
> applaud at the end of the show. Here you tap your feet in time to the music, you boo,
> you coo-ee, you cheer, you sing along. It is a different kind of being an audience.
>
> (Terry 2013, Butcher, Personal Interview (PI))

These early decades of the twenty-first century are exhilarating times for audiences. Different kinds of "being an audience" are emerging in mainstream theatres in most Western capital cities. The role of audiences and their behaviour in plays and musicals on Broadway and the West End has changed dramatically in the last decade or so. Audience members often scream, hold hands, go up on the stage, take photos with their iPads, talk back to the stage, write their own reviews and customarily give standing ovations after every performance. When audience members were invited onto the stage to join actors for the first production of *Godspell* in 1971, a tentative six people braved the stage. Now, when the invitation is given in the play *The Testament of Mary* to go on the stage and take photos of the actor Fiona Shaw, audience members "bolt out of their seats" (*Testament* usher 2013, PI). Similarly in *Once* the musical, audience members eagerly clambered onto the stage to tap their feet with the cast. Some productions leave the house lights on for all or part of the performance. Compared with the last century, when most audiences were expected to sit practically comatose in the dark, the twenty-first century audience experience is a new frontier.

This book introduces the concept of the audience as performer. Through analogy with the actors' performance it explores how the embodied actions of audience members constitute a performance. Drawing from historical records I document the performative role audiences have played in nineteenth- and twentieth-century mainstream theatres. Interviews I have undertaken with mainstream contemporary audience members record the experiences of the audience in the twenty-first century.

The concept of the audience as performer stems from various roles in the theatre industry that I have played. I have spent half my career performing as an actor onstage and half as an academic researching theatre audiences. As an actor backstage I have cursed audience members for their interruptions: "Will that woman in the third row ever stop talking?" I have also praised them for their helpful contributions: "*Such* a good audience." As a theatre critic I have written about audiences: "The audience sit in their plush seats and gaze at the sitting women – fascinated, uncomfortable" (Heim 2012). As an usher I have been part of the pre-production and interval excitement in mainstream productions in several cities. As an academic I research and theorise on the role of audiences in the theatrical event. The focus of my entire career has been centred on theatre audiences: performing for audiences, watching audiences, directing audiences, listening to audiences and writing about audiences.

Do Audiences Perform?

When I first interviewed audience members for this book, I asked them what they enjoy doing at interval. The most recurrent comment that I heard was, "When I go to a play or musical I watch the audience. It is the best part isn't it?" (Mark 2013, PI). People-watching is not a new phenomenon, but, as I probed a bit further, I found that audience members watch each other because they "like to see how they respond, [they] like to see what they smile at, who they applaud, what's funny for them. It's a fascinating thing to watch" (Patricia 2013, PI). All of these behaviours – laughing, applauding, and many more – are part of the responses of a group of people who are gathered together in the communal space called a theatre auditorium. They come together to play a role – that of audience.

This role is different to roles the same people may play as a passenger on an aircraft, a guest at a hotel or a patient in a hospital. As with many roles, the role of audience has its own idiosyncrasies, prescribed gestures and spontaneous expressions. Being an audience member is a role that individuals may get the opportunity to play in life. The responses of audience members in a theatre are not only "fascinating to watch" from the perspective of the actors, the ushers or other audience members, but help to create the entire theatrical experience. The real enchantment of theatre happens in the encounter between actors and audience members. This encounter occurs in the theatre, as opposed to the cinema, because theatre is a live performance. The actor's performance influences the audience, and the audience member's responses influence the actors. The encounter and the electricity of co-creation that transpires in the theatre is what makes playing the role of theatre audience member quite distinct from other roles in life. As explored in this book, audience responses actually contribute to, inform and alter the onstage performance. In one sense I am asking the reader to gaze not at the stage, but at the audience, and consider the fascinating responses of audience members.

To explore what it means to "be" an audience, I draw on Erving Goffman's perspectives of social performance.[1] There are three terms that Goffman employs that I use to illustrate how an audience performs in the theatre: "repertoire of actions," "front" and "encounter." Goffman argues that whenever we encounter other individuals we perform a series of activities depending on the social role we are playing at the time. The series of actions performed are known as the individual's "repertoire of actions," which are "pre-formed and dramatised" into a performance (1959: 74). The repertoire of actions make up what Goffman calls our front: "[T]hat part of an individual's performance which regularly functions in a general and fixed fashion to define the situation for those that observe the performance" (1959: 22). The front is performed for an observer: "Performance is always performance *for* someone, some audience that recognises and validates it as performance" (Carlson 2004: 5). In the next chapter, I argue that the actors are one of the audience's observers.

The core of all theatre is the encounter: the encounter of the actors with the audience, the actors with each other, the audience members with each other. In Goffman's encounter, "one given set of individuals" are in the "continuous presence" of another set of individuals (1959: 15), and there is a reciprocal influence on each other's actions. This reciprocal arrangement is the heart of the live event that can actually be felt in the electric air between actor and audience member. It is the encounter with others that, I argue, initially constructs the individual as performer. In the theatre, audience members have encounters with actors and with each other, during which time they perform their repertoire of actions.

As I argue in this book, audiences are extremely versatile and adaptable performers, and their repertoires of actions are often influenced by the socio-cultural milieu. When the London audience members of Shakespeare's *Hamlet* in 1756 sat on the stage to show off their "front," their latest fashions, they were performing. When the Dublin audience members of Synge's *Playboy of the Western World* in 1907 developed a new repertoire of actions, engaging in singing contests, coughing fits, and blowing tin whistles while the play continued onstage, they were performing. When the Buenos Aires audience members of Webber's *Cats* in 1993 wore *Cats* t-shirts to the performance, they were performing. When Stuttgart audience members of Ulrich Racher's *The Choir* in 2006 yelled back at the stage "enough, enough!" during an explicit rape scene, they were, in a sense, performing. The same could be said of some Brisbane audience members of Albee's *Who's Afraid of Virginia Woolf* in 2009 who had heated encounters with each other about comedy in a post-show discussion, London audience members at Andrew's *Three Sisters* in 2012 who tweeted their responses to the production during a performance, and New York audience members of Leveaux's 2013 production of *Romeo and Juliet* who screamed at the entrance of a star actor. All audience performances in the theatre commence as responses. New concepts of what it means to perform as an audience have been introduced here that will be further explained in the proceeding chapters. This list of audience performances not only reveals how varied their performance can be, but also illustrates how an audience's repertoire of actions changes diachronically as new technologies and new opportunities for the audience to perform arise.

Performer, Performance, Audience

The word "performer" is Old French and derives from *parfournir*: to accomplish. If patrons in a theatre are playing the role of an audience, what are their accomplishments, or what is their performance? There is a fertile array of perspectives on what constitutes a performance ranging from the performance of any action, such as brushing one's hair in private, to the necessity of at least one performer and one witness performing intentional actions in a designated performance space such as a theatre. That performance involves some sort of action is understood. Richard Schechner describes performance as being made up of acting (doing) and being (2013: 28). In this bifurcation, the "action" is the performance and the "being" is the role. In Sartrean terms, I am *being* an audience member and the actions I undertake make up my performance. While there has been much research into what constitutes a performance, surprisingly little discussion has focussed on the defining traits of a performer. In this book, a performer is one who executes a repertoire of actions in a role. A phenomenon occurs in the theatre that does not happen in private while brushing one's hair making the audience performance unique: the encounter between actor and audience members. This is an important part of my definition of a performer.

This book proposes the concept that, in the theatre, there are two troupes of performers: actors and audience members. As Patrice Pavis argues, "the performer stages his[her] own self, while the actor plays the role of another" (1980: 262). In the theatre, the actors play character roles, but audience members stage their own selves. Similarly, Goffman asserts that we stage the self when playing, what he calls, different social characters called "parts" (1959: 252). The audience member stages themselves *through* a role: the role of "audience." In her seminal book *Theatre Audiences*, Susan Bennett alludes to the performative nature of the audience, noting that audiences "clearly play a role in theatre" (1997: 17). The idea of "playing" is central to performing. Jean-Paul Sartre gives the cogent example of a waiter in a café whose behaviour seems to the beholder to be a game. "He is playing," contends Sartre; one "must play *at being* a waiter in order to be one" (2010: 82). Likewise, theatre-goers, consciously or otherwise, play *at being* an audience. The first audience member I interviewed was Terry Murray, quoted above. Murray intuitively understood this concept of "being." What it means to "be" an audience became the starting point for my research.

Carlson argues that "the task of judging the success of the performance (or even judging whether it *is* a performance) is [...] not the responsibility of the performer, but of the observer" (2004: 4). From Carlson's perspective, as observers, actors should then be able to confirm whether the audience has given a performance. Backstage when actors ask "What are the audience like tonight?" they are essentially asking about the audience's performance. As illustrated in Chapter One, actors' responses in my interviews reflected this.

It is necessary here to distinguish audience performance in the mainstream theatre I focus on from participatory theatre. In the 1960s, productions of the

Living Theatre and the work of Jerzy Grotowski explored a theatre of participation in which audiences became part of the performance by playing a text-specific role in the production. Ariane Mnouchkine, Richard Schechner, Punchdrunk and Tim Crouch are some of the many practitioners that include a participatory role for the audience in their productions. Theatre of participation is limited in its application to specific written texts and productions. In one sense, an audience relinquishes their role as audience and takes on the role of actor in the onstage play. This differs considerably from the spontaneous contributions of a theatre audience in that the audience is participating under the direction of theatre professionals.

Gareth White has defined audience participation as "the participation of an audience, or an audience member, in the action of a performance," also articulating that audience participation is different from the activity performed when the audience member is playing the role of the audience (2013: 4). Audience participation, where the audience member agrees to take on a role in the onstage performance, occasionally happens in mainstream theatres in this twenty-first century. New opportunities are emerging for audiences to become part of the onstage action, if only momentarily. While I do not include what is generally called experimental, fringe, alternative or avant-garde performances in my analyses of theatre events, some of the more courageous invitations for audiences to perform that are issued from the mainstream stage have a legacy indebted to the more experimental, participatory theatre of the 1960s. As discussed in Part II, the recent emergence of immersive theatre practices in Off-Broadway and Off-West End playhouses has also influenced participatory practice in mainstream theatres. Interestingly, it is the emboldened tourist audience member that is more likely to play a participatory role onstage in twenty-first-century mainstream playhouses.

Audience theorists and practitioners tend to agree that approaching, writing about and conceptualising audiences and what they do is slippery (Kennedy 2009: 3), risky (Grehan 2009: 4), complex and full of paradox (Bogart 2006). Audiences are fascinating to watch because their spontaneous, moment-to-moment performance itself *is* complex and full of paradox: how delightful. In very simple terms, an audience is a group of individuals gathered together to watch a performance.

Along with many concepts associated with the study of audiences, the construction of audiences as both individuals and as a collective is problematic. In consideration of the audience as performers, the individual/collective incongruence can be simplified. Onstage, the actors' performance – their dialogue and actions – while most often performed individually, can also be performed as an ensemble. In the auditorium, the audience's gestural, vocal and paralingual activities can also be performed individually or as an ensemble. Their performance is, therefore, individual at times and collective at others.

It is also important to emphasise that audience members have their own unique style of performance. Sartre explains this in terms of the individual's praxis. He argues that a collective, which he interchanges with the theatrical term "ensemble," is not an ontological unity but a practical combination of individual praxis. He further argues that acting as part of an ensemble enriches the individual praxis of its members (Sartre in Boileau 2000: 115). The audience ensemble is a heterogeneous combination of individual performers each with their inimitable performance style.

Countless terms have been used to describe the individual that attends a theatrical event: onlooker, observer, participant, voyeur, witness, customer, celebrant, eavesdropper, beholder, watcher, co-creator, guest and patron. The term that has dominated contemporary criticism is "spectator." This term has been disseminated through many areas of performance analysis and has been applied to nearly all performative events including media events, sporting events, science observation and, more recently, terrorist events. For the purposes of this book, which is partly to privilege the audience voice, I employ a term that is idiomatic to attendees of theatrical events and represents the theatre-goers' understanding of their role: "audience member." When I discuss the audience members' ensemble performance, they are referred to as "audience."

Writings About Audiences

Theatre audience research has established that theatre audiences respond, make meaning and co-create (Bennett 1997; Dolan 2005; McConachie 2008; Fischer-Lichte 2008; Grehan 2009). The role of the audience as responders and meaning-makers has been explored from a wide range of psychological, phenomenological, semiotic, ethical, historical, aesthetic, gendered and socio-cultural perspectives. Authors that address "spectating" in the arts in general in recent texts include Lynne Conner (2013), Hilary Glow et al. (2013), Matthew Reason and Dee Reynolds (2012), Claire Bishop (2012), Jacques Rancière (2009), Alison Oddey and Christine White (2009) and Paul Woodruff (2008). In *The Spectator and the Spectacle*, Dennis Kennedy (2009) considers how the audience "assists" at the spectacle, promising a more performative perspective of the audience member. By his own admission, however, his theories "sidestep" some of the problematic areas of assessing audiences. In *Audience Participation in the Theatre*, Gareth White (2013) concentrates on theatre of participation in immersive theatre and introduces a theory of the invitation which is discussed in Chapter Seven. Helen Freshwater's refreshing booklet *Theatre & Audience* (2009) appeals for more in-depth study of mainstream theatre audiences often ignored in most audience texts.

In *Engaging Audiences*, Bruce McConachie (2008) introduces a cognitive paradigm for reading audience behaviour which is a comprehensive and important contribution to cognitive audience research.[2] It is important to clarify that I do not endeavour to espouse a cognitive or behaviourist approach. Numerous theoretical and empirical studies have already attempted to quantify audience cognition. Bernard Beckerman, Malgorzata Sugiera, Henri Schoenmakers and Willmar Sauter examine the particular psychological processes of the audience in making meaning. In an attempt to gauge intellectual, emotional and behavioural responses to a theatrical event, audience's reactions have been scrutinised using various psycho-physiological empirical methods. Response machines allowing audience participants to push buttons to indicate intellectual responses were used in the United States and

Germany. Galvanic skin response, cardiogram, encephalogram and "applaudimeters" measured cognitive response in studies in Germany and Belgium in the 1960s, 70s and 80s. These empirical studies provide some interesting observations of audience behaviour.

In audience research only cursory mention has been made of the audience as performer. In this book I argue that audience response is a performance in and of itself and that in the diegetic world of the theatrical experience the actors *and* the audience are performers in this world. In his phenomenological text *The Audience*, Blau argues that the audience's physical presence is easier to understand and more palpable than its emotions (1990: 379). In many ways, I am traversing an area of enquiry that is much more accessible and easier to quantify than that of the audience's meaning-making. No book, as yet, has considered the audience primarily as performer.

Listening to the Audience

Freshwater argues that audience researchers never ask "'ordinary' theatre-goers – with no professional stake in the theatre – what they make of a performance" (2009: 4). Professional theatre-goers such as theatre critics are those usually consulted.[3] For the purposes of this book, I employ "ordinary" in the sense that it represents a contemporary "everywo/man" as opposed to an "integral" audience member: critics, friends, those who have a professional stake in the production or those that work or teach in the theatre industry (Schechner 1988: 220). This latter group often attend theatre for different purposes than those of the ordinary[4] audience member, and they read the production through a different frame of reference. In mainstream theatre, the ordinary audience members far outnumber the integral audience. Integral audiences often attend opening nights, and on Broadway and the West End the remaining 223 performances[5] are predominantly filled with ordinary audience members. Because theatre is experiential, what better way to understand the audience experience than asking audience members about their experience. This book contains material from interviews I conducted with ordinary audience members during or directly after their theatre experience.

Audience researchers are perennially plagued by the fact that using the comments of ordinary audience members can seem subjective and generalised, so it is avoided. Reliable sources of information on audiences are considered to be academics, theatre critics and the authors' own perspectives. Freshwater suggests that this avoidance is deep rooted in twenty-first-century attitudes of mistrust, fear and cultural anxiety (2009: 38). This book does not avoid using the "the passions, feelings and emotions which 'ordinary' people invest in their 'ordinary' lives" (Bourdieu 1979: 4): it champions them. In many ways, audience members in my book are seen as extra-ordinary.

Audience research that precludes audience comments is similar to a twentieth-century theatre performance where the audience has conventionally been told to sit motionless in the dark and not to make a sound. The vibrant opinions of the audience members themselves have tended only to be shared in ticket lines, foyers, coffee shops, bars, cafés, taxis, coaches and in private homes in private conversations.

To borrow Jacques Rancière's term, the "emancipation" of the audience members' opinions in theatre audience research is long overdue.

In this book, the audience voice is juxtaposed with the voice of the actors. Actors are incredibly intuitive creators and co-creators, and, during my interviews with them, their insights into and understanding of audiences have often astounded me. I share some rare glimpses into the actors' world, its rituals, humour, insecurities and triumphs. I also introduce the reader to the actors' language with all its nuances, colours and quirks. Ushers often share parts of this language, living, as they do, in the liminal space between stage and audience. I have also conducted interviews with this intriguing community.

I ask the reader to comprehend the audience quotations in this book as one would listen to the comments of an actor talking about their performance in a play. The audience members' opinions included do not represent the opinions of the "ideal" audience member; just as many actors' comments do not represent the opinions of the "ideal" actor. I make no apologies that the quotations represent the audience's subjective experiences. For, as phenomenologist Edmund Husserl argues, we can only know what we experience (1962). Likewise, directors, theatre academics and critics are other subjective voices who only know what they experience. I sometimes quote these voices, but they have not been privileged in this book. As new vehicles for audience performance are opening up in this twenty-first century, it is my intention that this book fairly represents the voice of the theatre audience which is beginning to gain more authority and retrieve some of its lost influence.

To record the audience voice, I have used a combination of techniques. The audience and theatre professionals' comments are taken from personal interviews, post-show discussions and questionnaires undertaken with ordinary audience members, actors and ushers. A total of 106 in-depth interviews were conducted with audience members and 29 in-depth interviews with actors and ushers during intervals or after performances in mainstream theatres in New York, London, Sydney, Toronto, Chicago and Glasgow in 2013 and 2014. The majority were conducted in New York and London. I have chosen the latter two cities as they are considered to be the capitals of mainstream theatre in the English-speaking world. The other cities were chosen for similar purposes in that they can be seen as smaller but also representative centres of mainstream theatrical events. Toronto, for example, is colloquially known as "Broadway North."

It was important to capture the audience and actors' voices in the moment of the experience or directly after the event while they were still playing their roles, or remained "in character" in the lived experience of the event. In many ways the in-depth interviews became an extension of the audience member's auditorium performance. A small number of interviews with friends of friends were pre-arranged in the UK. Some additional interviews were undertaken after post-show discussions or after I delivered public lectures on theatre where I asked for volunteers who were regular theatre-goers, but not theatre professionals. The interviews ranged from five minutes to one hour in length. The average interview time was 20 minutes. None of the interviewees were previously known to me.[6]

Throughout the book, audience members are identified in citations by their first names and the letters "PI" (Personal Interview), while theatre professionals (actors, ushers, etc.) I interviewed are identified by their surnames and the letters "PI". This distinguishes their words (taken from my interviews with them) from those of quoted academic authors. A full list of the audience members, actors, ushers, front of house managers, merchandise managers, directors, producers and other theatre professionals I interviewed is included at the conclusion of the book.

The interviews were semi-structured, and the majority included open-ended questions. Initial closed questions such as "How many times in a year do you attend the theatre?" were followed by five standard questions. Actors are often asked about what it means to be an actor or to perform. The standard questions were devised to try and determine what it means to be an audience by asking audience members to describe their theatre-going experience:

> In what ways have you seen audiences change over time?
> What does it mean to you to "be" an audience?
> How would you describe the atmosphere of theatre?
> Do you think your reactions give something to the actors?
> What do you talk about at interval or after the performance?

These questions were followed by various others that were prompted by initial audience responses. Standard questions that were broad such as "What does it mean to you to 'be' an audience?" resulted in a wide range of responses. Audience comments are interspersed throughout the chapters but are mainly used in Part II. General summaries of the audience members' responses to all these questions can be found in Appendix 1. In the actor and usher interviews, variations of the question "What do audience reactions look like to you?" were asked. The actors were also asked if the audience's reactions influenced their onstage performance. Some further interviews, particularly for the case studies which follow each chapter in Part II, were undertaken with theatre directors, producers and merchandise managers. The case studies explore theatre companies or venues that are introducing new practices for audience performance in the twenty-first century. Further, they provide an in-depth examination of the concepts of audience performance I explore in each chapter.

Recordings of 20 post-show discussions after performances of mainstream theatre events in New York, London, Chicago, Sydney and Brisbane between 2006 and 2014 provide additional audience comments. Between 12 and 117 people attended each discussion. I was therefore able to capture several hundred more audience voices and their insights into the productions they had seen. The post-show discussions I draw from were all audience-directed, and I facilitated approximately half of these. Freshwater suggests that audience researchers ask the audience what they make of performances (2009: 4), that is, what their critical responses to the content of performances are. A small number of researchers have undertaken this.[7] While some post-show discussion audience opinions are included, documenting audience responses to content is not the purpose of this book. I focus on and have asked audiences about their theatre-going experience to determine what it means to individuals to "be" an audience in this twenty-first century.

Questionnaires were completed by audience members at mainstream theatre events in New York in 2013 and London in 2014. The questionnaires undertaken for this research usually only supplement my discussions with some statistical information. Questionnaire questions and responses can be found in Appendix 2.

In an attempt to achieve a cultural, gender and age diversity, the voices represented are from a reasonably wide demographic, but have been limited, through the necessity of researcher accessibility and because of cultural differences, to a Euro/American, English-speaking demographic. Non-English-speaking European, Asian, Indian, African, South American and Middle Eastern audiences perform differently in the playhouse than their Western English-speaking cousins. To discuss their sometimes more demonstrative or more inhibited performances is outside the scope of this research. It is also important to acknowledge that in the geographic demography that I discuss in this book, similar to cultural differences in acting styles,[8] there are cultural differences in audience performance. This would be an interesting study in itself, but again is beyond the purview of this book. I do, however, often note the city of residence of the audience member and sometimes include comments that have a geographic cultural discourse. The age range of the interviewees, post-show discussion and questionnaire participants was from 18 to 84. The gender ratio was approximately two females to one male, reflecting current female/male ratios attending Broadway theatres in the 2013/14 seasons.[9]

Many theatre texts have pigeon-holed the audience, and audience development statistics have often constructed them as a homogeneous, voice-less mass. It is hoped that this book provides a fresh reading of the audience from the perspective of the audience members themselves, the actors and, a group rarely acknowledged in any kind of theatre research, the ushers. The audience members' comments that are included in this book, and the hundreds more that I could not include for purposes of brevity, are often unique, perceptive, humorous, interesting, sincere and provocative. Some are deeply personal, and some are brimming with enthusiasm: "I just love the atmosphere. Without theatre I feel I would be cutting off a limb" (Agnes 2014, PI). They are all, in some form, a celebration of what Fischer-Lichte (2008) calls the "enchantment" of theatre as seen, perhaps for the first time, from the point of view of the audience members themselves.

Mainstream Theatre

The research has been limited to a discussion of audiences attending mainstream professional theatre events in Western English-speaking countries to privilege and document what Bennett considers an "almost entirely neglected […] significant segment of the market" (2005: 407): mainstream theatre.[10] Much scholarly debate continues to concentrate on audiences at fringe theatres. Yet, as Peter Davison argues, fringe theatres "seem considerably more removed from the dreams and actualities of life of most of the population than is mainstream theatre" (1982: 133).

Defining the borders of mainstream theatre in terms of inclusions and exclusions is difficult. While it is relatively easy to distinguish mainstream theatre from its fringe theatre counterpart,[11] the margins among commercial, popular and mainstream theatre are nebulous. The trajectory of mainstream theatre often traverses the grounds of the popular and commercial. The majority of the theatre-going population attends mainstream theatre which attracts a more heterogeneous audience and is where you are most likely to find what Nicholas Ridout calls the "non-professional theatre-goer" (2006: 15).

For the purposes of this research, mainstream theatres included Broadway and West End plays and musicals in New York and London, and some Off-Broadway and Off-West End mainstream playhouses. In Sydney, Toronto, Chicago and Glasgow, I conducted my research at state theatre companies, large performing-arts centres, commercial theatres and subscription theatres that were predominantly attended by the general public. I acknowledge that an audience at a mainstream drama will give a different performance, and also arrive with different expectations of how to perform than if they were attending a musical; I therefore generally try to identify genres of productions. Mainstream theatre is where I turn to discover the ordinary audience member's voice. What is often called conventional or traditional theatre is where most of the main stream of individuals goes to see a play or musical.

Book Structure

Many of the aspects I discuss in each chapter are informed by the interview content. The open-ended questions yielded a rich pool of responses on a range of topics. An analysis of the responses revealed dominant discourses or recurring attitudes that then informed my argument. For example, many audience members, when asked to describe the atmosphere of theatre, discussed their experience of sitting in a theatre auditorium and their proximity to the stage with such clarity that their insights influenced my decision to include a central discourse on theatre space in Chapter Five, "Audience as Community." Similarly, any reference to co-creation proffered by audience members in the interviews focussed on reciprocity and "leading and following." These aspects of co-creation then formed the basis of my exploration of co-creation in Chapter Seven. In one sense, the research included in this book is not necessarily audience-based, but audience-led.

The book is divided into two parts. Part I concentrates on the audience as a performer, the audience performance and the history of audience performance. Part II discusses evolving and emergent audience roles in the twenty-first-century playhouses. Chapter One, "Audience as Performer," details the praxis that constructs the audience as performer using the actor's lexicon. Theodor Lipps's understanding of empathy and its associated phenomenon, emotional contagion, provides the paradigm through which I explore the audience's gestural, vocal and paralingual repertoire of actions performed during the theatrical event. It is not only an audience's prescribed embodied behaviours that characterise audience performance: aspects such as performing to an audience, playing a role, wearing a costume and preparation are important signifiers. Actor, audience and usher comments paint a picture of this inversion of the performer/audience correlative. This chapter also explores elements that restrain expressive audience performance, particularly theatre etiquette.

Audience performance is not only culturally but historically informed. The next two chapters document the history of audience performance in Western mainstream theatre that occurred in conventional indoor venues. Rather than give a comprehensive overview beginning with Greek theatre – a book in itself – I start at a time when audiences last gave demonstrative performances, the beginning of the nineteenth century. Baz Kershaw, Neil Blackadder, Richard Butsch and Dennis Kennedy, among others, have already mapped changes in audience roles. My purpose in exploring audience behaviour as performance is to privilege and re-think the roles audiences play in the theatre and document their performances. Rather than concentrating on critical reviews of audiences from newspapers and popular magazines, I use accounts written by eye-witnesses of audience performances: the actors, other audience members and theatre managers.

Chapter Two is entitled "Stage Etiquette" for the simple reason that it was the audiences of the period from around 1800 to the 1880s that ruled the auditoriums *and* the stage and would often dictate rules of behaviour to the actors. During this period, audiences gave some of their most dynamic performances in the history of Western theatre. The theatre auditorium was clearly demarcated into the pit, the gallery and the boxes. Audience ensembles who frequented each section gave distinctive and often humorous performances. Audience performance changed radically in the second half of the nineteenth century. Although many aspects can account for this change, Chapter Three, "Theatre Etiquette," concentrates on how the changes in auditorium lighting and the implementation of rules of theatre etiquette subdued demonstrative audience performance. I begin in the 1880s as this was the decade that electric lighting was first introduced into theatres making it much more practical to darken auditoriums. This was the period where theatre professionals began to dictate the rules of etiquette to the audience. Ever resourceful audience ensembles, such as the fashionables, found new ways, however, to perform in the theatre. From the end of the Second World War until the turn of the millennium there is little to report on audience performance.

Chapter Four, "Audience as Critic," considers how the role of the audience as critic, suppressed for over a century, is re-surfacing in the contemporary theatre. Two vehicles for audience criticism give the audience new opportunities for critical contribution: the post-show discussion and the use of technology devices for audience feedback. Drawing on Bertolt Brecht's construction of aesthetic criticism, I discuss how playing the role of critic can bring much eudaimonic, that is, long-term pleasure. This chapter includes the largest compilation of the very insightful comments about the content of productions made by audiences as critics. The chapter concludes with a case study of Steppenwolf Theatre in Chicago that holds particularly innovative audience-centred post-show discussions.

Chapter Five, "Audience as Community," considers how the physical design of the theatre, the comfort of the seating and the audience members' proximity to the stage and each other can either encourage or inhibit community formation. Audiences also form a community when they perform together and when they talk with each other. In this chapter, Goffman's concepts of frontstage and backstage behaviours are used to argue that what were previously considered backstage practices confined to the family television room, are now practised frontstage in the theatre auditorium. Recent studies show that the "new" and younger theatre audiences are attending the theatre to find community. I conclude the chapter with a case study of Signature Theatre Company in New York, exploring the way that Signature have re-designed their theatre space to create a stronger sense of community.

Constructing the audience as a consumer is predominantly considered in theatre studies to be counter-productive to the aesthetics of cultural experience. In Chapter Six, "Audience as Consumer," I argue that while the contemporary audience's demonstrative performance in the auditorium is limited, opportunities for playing the role of audience consumer are manifold. Yet little research in theatre studies has considered the very celebratory activities of the audience consumer. This chapter gives due homage to one of the most notorious and colourful contemporary audience consumers: the tourist. Abraham Maslow's hierarchy of needs pyramid is a useful tool for exploring how esteem is built through the purchasing of theatre merchandise, theatre packages and the theatrical experience itself. The case study explores a public space where audiences rehearse their self-conscious performance as consumers in preparation for their theatrical experience: the red stairs of New York's Times Square.

The final chapter, "Audience as Co-creator," considers how the actors and the audience perform in the electric air of the theatre in the synergy of co-creation. Sartre's concepts of co-authorship underpin my explanations of what is called by audience members and actors alike "feeding each other" (Owen-Taylor 2014, PI) in the circular reciprocity of co-creation. Rather than try to understand or measure[12] the more cerebral approach to co-creation taken in audience research, I simply document the much more palpable *performance* of co-creation in theatre through my own observations and descriptions given by the actors and audience members I interviewed. This chapter includes the most comprehensive inventory of audience performances in contemporary playhouses given in the book. I turn to White's theories of invitations in the case study to explore how the "groundlings" audiences and the actors at Shakespeare's Globe in London co-create a unique twenty-first-century theatrical experience.

Contemporary audiences – as active critics, consumers, co-creators and members of an entitled community – are demanding much more from the theatrical event than what was previously on offer; more than the event, they want the theatrical experience. The audience has taken on a more performative role in Western mainstream theatrical events in the twenty-first century both within the playhouse and without. In the conclusion, "New Possibilities," I discuss what it means to "be" an audience member in the twenty-first century. Audience performance that is acculturated from various practices of screen viewing and technology devices used in the audience and foyers work to cast the audience in the role of critic much more than is acknowledged. New audience ensembles are entering theatres and are creating quite a stir. The tourist voice may be unfairly denigrated in theatre studies, but it is loud, influential and is keeping much of the theatre industry alive. The compelling voice and multiple talents of the mainstream audience performer contribute to the aesthetics of theatrical production. The role of the audience as critic and co-creator in mainstream theatre continues to expand and influence the way the theatrical event is constructed. These changes herald a new age for the audience as performer. Let us take a peek behind the curtain and see what this performance looks like.

Notes

1 Schechner's concept of "restored behaviour" is similar to, but also different from, Goffman's social performance. I discuss some aspects of restored behaviour in Chapter One and in my Chapter Seven case study.
2 All of the listed approaches fall under the rubric of Audience Reception studies, which, as its title suggests, considers an audience's response to the theatrical event. As McConachie points out, "receive," "response" and "reaction" derive from behaviourism (2008: 3) and suggest a more passive, one-way, sender–receiver directional mode. The active/passive debate in Audience Reception studies fortunately seems to have reached some form of stasis. I believe that consideration of the audience as a co-creator has had some part in signalling its closure. Audience performance is clearly active.
3 Another audience ensemble could also be considered a "professional" audience – the claque. I allude to the claque at times as they too perform in the theatre, but in a more rehearsed, prescribed and generic way.
4 I had hesitations in using the term "ordinary." It is a value-laden term in itself and is problematic as such. I have considered using "usual" or "general" but since Freshwater and others cited seem to have broken some ground with this epithet I have employed it, but with some reluctance.
5 This number is based on the current (2014) average run of a Broadway show, which is eight months with seven performances a week.
6 With the exception of the Glasgow parents of a friend I had met just once before.
7 For particular examples see Janelle Reinelt et al. (2014), Matthew Reason (2010) and Martin Barker (2003).
8 For a discussion of cultural differences in acting styles see Heim (2013).
9 During the 2013–14 Broadway season 68 per cent of the audience members were female and 32 per cent male (Hauser 2014). In my interviews 62 per cent were female and 38 per cent male. There are no comparative studies from West End audiences available.
10 Bennett's more recent writing on audiences in journal articles and book chapters has given some attention to mainstream audiences, but on the whole theatre studies neglects research into significant mainstream performances which could benefit from its vast methods of analysis. Due, perhaps, to its initial and seemingly continued framing as the antithesis of the mainstream (Schechner 2013: 4), performance studies also has yet to apply the rich plethora of analysis, theory and introspection that has developed in performance research to an exploration of mainstream performances.
11 Immersive theatre is a particular exception as I have sometimes heard it referred to as mainstream. I asked several regular theatre attendees that I interviewed about *Sleep No More* in New York, perhaps one of the best-known immersive productions, and only a few had heard of it. Those few that had attended were all under 30. For this reason, and for the purposes of making some distinction, I have placed it outside of the mainstream.
12 Although several praiseworthy attempts to measure the cognitive process of co-creation have been undertaken in audience scholarship, I believe that, like meaning-making, it is extremely difficult to quantify.

References

Barker, Martin (2003) "Crash, Theatre Audiences, and the Idea of 'Liveness'", *Studies in Theatre and Performance*, vol. 23, no. 1.

Bennett, Susan (1997) *Theatre Audiences: A Theory of Production and Reception*, 2nd edn, New York: Routledge.

——(2005) "Theatre/Tourism," *Theatre Journal,* vol. 57, no. 3: 407–28.

Bishop, Claire (2012) *Artificial Hells: Participatory Art and the Politics of Spectatorship*, London and New York: Verso.

Blau, Herbert (1990) *The Audience*, Baltimore: Johns Hopkins UP.

Bogart, Anne (2006) "The Role of the Audience." *TCG National Conference 2006*, 9 June. Transcript.

Boileau, Kevin (2000) *Genuine Reciprocity and Group Authenticity: Foucault's Developments or Sartre's Social Ontology*, Maryland: University Press of America.

Bourdieu, Pierre (1979) *Distinction: A Social Critique of the Judgement of Taste*, trans. Richard Nice, London: Routledge.

Carlson, Marvin (2004) *Performance: A Critical Introduction*, 2nd edn, Routledge: New York and London.

Conner, Lynne (2013) *Audience Engagement and the Role of Arts Talk in the Digital Era*, New York: Palgrave Macmillan.

Davison, Peter (1982) *Contemporary Drama and the Popular Dramatic Tradition in England*, London and Basingstoke: Macmillan.

Dolan, Jill (2005) *Utopia in Performance: Finding Hope at the Theatre*, Ann Arbor: Michigan UP.

Fischer-Lichte, Erika (2008) *The Transformative Power of Performance: A New Aesthetics*, Milton Park: Routledge.

Freshwater, Helen (2009) *Theatre & Audience*, Houndmills: Palgrave Macmillan.

Glow, Hilary, Katya Johanson and Jennifer Radbourne (eds.) (2013) *The Audience Experience: A Critical Analysis of Audiences in the Performing Arts*, Bristol: Intellect.

Goffman, Erving (1959) *The Presentation of Self in Everyday Life*, New York: Random House.

Grehan, Helena (2009) *Performance, Ethics and Spectatorship in a Global Age*, New York: Palgrave Macmillan.

Hauser, Karen (2014) *The Demographics of the Broadway Audience*, New York: The Broadway League.

Heim, Caroline (2012) "Humour and Charm in a Story of Race, Headwear and Healing," *The Australian* 16 July.

——(2013) "Found in Translation: Debating the Abstract Elements of Cultures Through Actor Training Styles," *Theatre, Dance and Performance Training*, vol. 4, no. 3: 353–67.

Husserl, Edmund (1962) *Ideas*, London: Allen and Unwin.

Kennedy, Dennis (2009) *The Spectator and the Spectacle: Audiences in Modernity and Postmodernity*, Cambridge: Cambridge UP.

McConachie, Bruce (2008) *Engaging Audiences: A Cognitive Approach to Spectating at the Theatre*, New York: Palgrave Macmillan.

Oddey, Alison and Christine White (2009) *Modes of Spectating*, Bristol: Intellect.

Pavis, Patrice (1980) *Dictionnaire du Theatre: Termes et Concepts de L'analyse Theatrale*, Paris: Editions Sociales.

Rancière, Jacques (2009) *The Emancipated Spectator*, trans. Gregory Elliott. London and New York: Verso.

Reason, Matthew (2010) "Asking the Audience: Audience Research and the Experience of Theatre," *About Performance*, 10 (2010): 15–34.

Reason, Matthew and Dee Reynolds (eds.) (2012) *Kinesthetic Empathy in Creative and Cultural Practices*, Bristol: Intellect.

Reinelt, Janelle, (P.I.), David Edgar, Chris Megson, Dan Rebellato, Julie Wilkinson and Jane Woddis (2014) *Critical Mass: Theatre Spectatorship and Value Attribution*, The British Theatre Consortium. Final report.

Ridout, Nicholas (2006) *Stage Fright, Animals and Other Theatrical Problems*, Cambridge: Cambridge UP.

Sartre, Jean-Paul (2010) *Being and Nothingness: An Essay on Phenomenological Ontology*, trans. Hazel E. Barnes, Abingdon: Routledge.

Schechner, Richard (1988) *Performance Theory*, 2nd edn, New York: Routledge.

——(2013) *Performance Studies: An Introduction*, 3rd edn, Abingdon: Routledge.

White, Gareth (2013) *Audience Participation in the Theater: Aesthetics of the Invitation*, New York: Palgrave Macmillan.

Woodruff, Paul (2008) *The Necessity of Theater: The Art of Watching and Being Watched*, New York: Oxford.

PART I
Audience Performance

1

AUDIENCE AS PERFORMER

They were really, really good.

(Rachel 2013, Audience member, PI)

They're catching everything.

(Steven Hauck 2013, Actor, PI)

They are trying to be funny.

(Maree 2014, Audience member, PI)

They're comatose. They're dead.

(Paul Schoeffler 2013, Actor, PI)

They just knocked me sideways.

(Lindsay 2014, Audience member, PI)

They are laughing in the wrong places.

(Janet Fullerlove 2014, Actor, PI)

In the theatre, individuals come together as strangers from diverse backgrounds to form two troupes: actors and audience members. This concept stems from Grotowski's imperative that in his theatre laboratory the producer has two ensembles to direct, the actors and the spectators (1980: 157). Meeting across the footlights, the two troupes watch, listen to, perform for and appraise each other. They are co-dependent. The actors "feed off the audience" (Hauck 2013, PI); the audience sometimes "get very full" (Judith 2014, PI). That theatre audience members "perform" as well as watch others perform onstage at first seems a stretch of the imagination. Some audience members consider it absurd: "[A]t talkbacks, actors always talk about what the audience does. I don't understand, we are just sitting here" (Heim 2013). Others find that their "best audience experience is when people are laughing or clapping and seem excited by it; when the audience are engaged and alive" (Francesca 2014, PI). In theatre studies there is a plethora of research about actors' performance but little consideration of the gregarious and capricious performance of the audience.

What constructs the theatre audience as performer and what constitutes their performance? Similar to the onstage actors the audience members perform for an audience – other audience members and actors – they play a role and they wear a costume. Drawing from a limited repertoire of actions, the contemporary audience plays their role of audience during the actors' performance. According to Blau's requisites, the audience only actualise as a troupe of performers in the presence of their co-troupe, the actors. In my interviews, when asked what it means to "be an audience" the most frequent response was "the interaction between the players and the audience" (Fiona 2014, PI).[1] In the encounter between the two troupes, the audience's kinetic, paralingual and verbal expressions combine to produce a rich, multiform performance that not only creates new meanings for the live event but can change, enrich and inform the experience of the event for audience members and actors alike. This chapter explores the aspects of the event that construct the audience as performer and describes the responses that make up the audience performance and the subsequent restraints placed on demonstrative expression in the contemporary theatre. I start with a discussion of empathy as it is a crucial part of audience symbiosis. Audience members respond to performances because of their empathic connection with what transpires onstage.

From Empathy to Performance

Empathy in theatre studies usually refers to the audience members identifying with the feeling states of the onstage character and the actor themselves. In actor training studies empathy considers the actor relating to a character or another actor.[2] Drawing analogies with actor-to-actor empathy, I am interested in the under-explored area of empathy among audience members.[3] "Empathy" is a volatile term that, similar to "audience," bears many different definitions depending on its cognitive, behaviourist, psychological, philosophical or phenomenological reading. It is a term translated into English from the German *Einfühlung* – meaning "feeling into" – in 1909 by Edward Titchener (21). In its most elementary sense empathy describes the process by which one person is affected by another's emotional state. In 1920, Theodor Lipps was one of the first theorists to discuss the empathy of the audience member for what he called the aesthetic object: the acrobat or the dancer onstage (1965). His observations initiated a discussion of empathy in an aesthetic and performance context that has been articulated, re-articulated and dis-articulated by a tradition of theatre theorists and practitioners.[4]

In his early writings, Lipps distinguished between aesthetic empathy and natural empathy. Most discussion of Lipps's work has concentrated on aesthetic empathy or has conflated the two distinct forms. Aesthetic empathy is the "feeling into" the aesthetic artwork, or the acrobat onstage; in theatre this is empathy for the character onstage. *Natureinfühlung*, natural empathy, occurs in everyday life when we "glimpse a laughing face [and] cannot grasp the laughing face without the evocation of the same kind of inner activity" (1965: 409). Lipps asserts that this kind of inner activity is highly pleasurable and induces a "feeling of freedom and unconstricted ease in the activity" (1965: 407). Positive natural empathy is synonymous with pleasure. Negative empathy, discussed later in the chapter, is its antithesis. Lipps goes on to argue that "empathising is experiencing" (1965: 411) not just knowing.

As the concept of empathy has evolved over time, numerous types of empathy have been proposed. Most fall under the rubrics of "cognitive" or "affective" empathy. Affective empathy, which "involves the capacity to enter into or join the experiences and feelings of another person" (Hojat et al. 2002: 1563), is the most consonant with Lipps's natural empathy. The experiences of the other touch my emotions to the point that there is a drive to respond with a similar and appropriate emotion or behaviour.[5] This drive is a need to – what is called in psychoanalysis – "equalise," to match or adjust to the expressions or emotional responses of another. Empathy is shown when individuals respond to each other. To see how this is played out in the theatre, let us return to our two performing troupes of actors and audience members.

The actors, who are often initially strangers, meet at the first read-through of the play. Right from the first reading and over the course of the rehearsal period actors empathise with each other; that is, the individual actors – consciously or otherwise – relate and adjust to the emotional states of others, an essential process in creating a collaborative environment for coordinated activity to occur. They become a cast. Similarly, strangers enter the theatre auditorium and – consciously or otherwise – during the course of the theatrical event, adjust their emotional and behavioural repertoire of actions to produce a fertile climate for social interactions and colla- boration. They become an audience. The cast and the audience do not form homogeneous masses, but rather emerge as colourful troupes of performers made up of very different individual personalities.

In the entity called "audience" an interesting phenomenon occurs: the individual audience members "catch" each other's emotions and mimic each other's responses to the onstage performance. Backstage, actors often comment that the audience are "catching everything." Audience members do not only catch what the actors throw them – and throw it back in a laugh or a sigh – they catch each other's emotions and behaviours through empathising or feeling with them. This intriguing mimicry is known as emotional contagion; a process during which "as a consequence of mimicry and feedback, people tend, from moment to moment, to 'catch' other's emotions" (Hatfield et al. 2009: 24). Interestingly, many psychologists and counsellors appropriate an acting idiom "moment to moment" to describe the spontaneous and performative nature of this experience.[6] Once caught, audience members perform these emotions by "automatically mimick[ing] and synchronis[ing] facial expressions, vocalisations, postures and movements" (Hatfield et al. 2009: 20). A laugh will ripple through an auditorium as audience members catch the contagion. An individual will start applauding and soon the slapping of hands creates a pervasive soundscape.

As described by actor Nicholas Bell, at these times the audience are living "in the moment" (2013, PI) of the fictional world of the play. Audience members are sensitive to this contagion. Mary, a teacher from Toronto, states that "when people laugh it's infectious" (2013, PI). Audience members catch or are infected by the contagion of laughter, crying and even applause. Emotional contagion is an empathic response.

It is often through emotional contagion that the individual audience member becomes part of the audience collective. Just as Joseph Chaikin has argued, the actors in an ensemble share a language and are receptive to one another's rhythms (Blumenthal 1984: 57), so too the audience members respond to each other's rhythms. This is empathy in action. The empathic, intersubjective and synchronised response to the other in the shared world of the auditorium becomes the lived experience of the audience performance. Empathy is an integral part of the audience's expressive, shared performance.

The Audience's Audience

A little-discussed dynamic that occurs during performances is the actors' empathy for the audience. Sensitive to the rhythms of the audience ensemble, they too enter into and "feed off" the audience members' emotions and behaviours. Actors have a lucid understanding of what an audience "does": the audience's performance. At interval, during or after the show, actors backstage frequently comment on audience performance. As demonstrated above, these comments often replicate audience discussion of actors' performance. The familiar buzzing of comments that illuminates a large foyer of maybe hundreds of audience members during interval is mirrored in the cramped, glittering dressing rooms of actors. This delightful yet unconscious reproduction is rarely considered. Actors' backstage comments can give latent insights into what characterises an audience's performance; the actors are the audience's audience.

For Goffman, "the individual offers [her]his performance and puts on [her]his show 'for the benefit of other people'" (1959: 28). For the audience, Goffman's "other people" are the actors who regularly discuss, scrutinise and critique audience performance. If actors were given the opportunity to write reviews of audiences it would be fascinating reading. In the safe, liminal space of the dressing rooms actors share their most caustic or complimentary thoughts on audiences with other actors, to the innocent walls or to their own empathic mirrored reflection. Backstage conversation is dominated by comments on audience performance: "They didn't laugh at my line! They always laugh. What's wrong with this audience?", "Did you hear the sighs of utter disgust toward me during that scene?" and "Did you see that guy in the third row walk out? I don't think he came back" (Heim 2006). These comments reflect how vital audience performance is to actors and how it affects them. It helps shape, invigorate, deflate, impede and support their own performance. Steven Hauck, who has worked on and off-Broadway in plays for 23 years, sees the audience as the "third actor" and argues that when an audience is performing well, you feel like you are being lifted on this wave of energy. You are riding their energy. The energy you expend feels less because there is this momentum that is carrying you forward. Whereas on a night when it's not, you feel like you are picking up a ten pound weight and moving it.

(Hauck 2013, PI)

In a form of emotional contagion the actors catch what Hauck calls the energy of the audience and use this momentum to carry their performance forward.

Performance is defined by Goffman as "all the activity [of the performer] that has some influence on the observers" (1959: 32). The actors' very success is dependent on a strong audience performance and is often called by actors "giving good audience" (Sullivan 2013, PI). Actors often playfully challenge the audience to "come on, show me" (Schoeffler 2013, PI). A lively, corporeal audience performance is anticipated, courted and sometimes realised. In contemporary curtain calls there is a growing penchant for actors applauding the audience, and compliments in post-show discussions such as "you are an amazing audience" (Carney 2013) proliferate. There seems to be an intimation of subservience in this practice. Paul Schoeffler, who has been working on Broadway for 25 years, states that actors sometimes need "to earn the audience" (2013, PI). The actor/audience relationship is multifaceted and intimate. To discuss in detail its complexities is outside the scope of this study. It is sufficient to say that actors are emotionally affected by audiences and that both troupes are co-performers in the theatrical event. Jason Robards states what seems understood, if unspoken, by most actors: "An audience is really another performer in the play" (Mitgang 1983).

The audience has two additional audiences: other audience members and, a group that is rarely acknowledged, front-of-house staff, particularly the ushers. In the darkness of the contemporary theatre auditorium, audience members have few opportunities to watch each other during the onstage performance. Their lit performance space has been relegated to cramped foyers or sidewalks during intervals. Although for some audience members "interval is one of [their] favourite things" (Rosemarie 2013, PI), intervals are now being shortened and are facing extinction. Yet contemporary audience members make the most of their limited time in the limelight of intervals, and watching other audience members perform continues to be a favourite pastime.[7] Even during the darkened acts, audience members are acutely aware of each other's performances. David is a regional manager from New York. He and his partner "often sit at the side so we can see behind us or to the side. You can look out into the audience and see their response: it's great to see" (2013a, PI). Clay is a landscape artist from Chicago he "love[s] to people watch" at the theatre: "I watch people's faces, and you can tell if they're enjoying it or smiling, or feeling something different. Then at the interval I speak to people, find out what they thought about it" (2014, PI). The pleasure of observing the repertoire of actions that make up the audience performance is obvious in these examples.

In Broadway and West End theatre houses the ushers' role is frequently reduced to behaviour control. These "service specialists" (Goffman 1959: 153) help audiences negotiate their way in playhouses, give them call times and direct them in rules of theatre etiquette. In this their role is not dissimilar to that of the stage manager. They are, however, not only the arbitrators of theatre etiquette, crowd controllers and amenities experts; they are also keen observers of audience performance. Ushers are the audience's third audience. Having ushered in Sydney for 15 years, Kevin Fokes still "can't think of anything more enjoyable than watching audience reactions" (2013, PI). Marc Bonanni has worked front-of-house on 25 touring and Broadway shows for seven years. Every night he and his colleagues "compare notes on the audience. […] The fun part is watching the audience." Bonanni goes on to state: "Sometimes I think, oh my God, *Mamma Mia*, but then when I see the audience standing on their feet, having the time of their life, that's what makes it" (2013, PI). For Bonanni and others, the repeated viewings of actors' performances grow predictable during the season. The audience members perform differently each night. As Sydney actor Andrew Henry argues, "an audience reaction will never be the same twice, it will never repeat" (2013, PI).

Similar to actors, ushers can differentiate between a weak and a strong audience performance. Theatre manager David Conte has been working front-of-house on Broadway for 17 years. He has noted that an audience "can be particularly lively or particularly dead" (2014, PI). Interestingly, Sartre emphasises that there are days when the audience shows genius, and days when the audience are terrible (1976: 139). The specific night of the week determines the kind of audience performance; a Friday performance can be distinguished from a Wednesday matinee performance not only demographically, but also by the content of the audience performance. The audience members can give a louder performance on a Saturday night, listen more on a Thursday, talk more on a Wednesday matinee and laugh less on a Friday. Conte refers to Saturday night as "date night" and matinees as "blue haired ladies performances" (2014, PI). Ushers are particularly adept at reading the visceral signifiers of audience members. Usher Jodie Payne knows when an audience "are really fragile, angry, enjoying themselves, visibly upset or offended" (Payne 2013, PI).

The Audience's Role

Audiences play a role in the theatre; they take on a specific role in giving feedback to the actors onstage. This is not a conscious choice but it occurs because theatre is a live encounter between two troupes. The role of the audience that is discussed most often in theatre studies is audience as audience. Other roles discussed later in the book include audience as critic, community, consumer and co-creator. The patrons at a theatrical event play the role of audience prescribed from their preconceived and pre-learnt repertoire of actions. They have been trained in how to perform the role of audience through watching others perform as audience members, through practice, through a list of theatre etiquette rules and through acculturation from modes of watching entertainment on screens.[8] Contemporary audience members in mainstream theatres playing the role of audience have a limited repertoire of actions to perform: laughing when appropriate, occasional crying, applauding at the right time. Perhaps because of this, some theorists have seen the audience's role as having become homogeneous. Kennedy argues that contemporary audiences are confined to "predetermined and relatively compliant roles" (2009: 155). While some audience researchers explore how the audience as audience role has changed over time from patron to customer (Kershaw 2001: 141), active to passive (Butsch 2000: 3), few researchers consider that audiences as performers are multitalented and their role often changes from performance to performance.

Directors and actors are less myopic and have different conceptions of audiences than theorists; they cast their audiences in a variety of roles. Drawing on Grotowski's concepts, director Anne Bogart argues that it is essential that directors:

> Always cast [their] audience. Are they a peeping tom, or are they at a graduation ceremony? Are they a jury? The audience can feel when they are considered. [...] Because you have considered them, the audience feel like they have a place.
>
> *(2013, PI)*

Tim Crouch tries "to give the audience a character" but argues that in some of his productions "sometimes mis-casting occurs" (2013).

This casting of the audience by directors draws from the content of each play. Actors, however, respond to the audience members' spontaneous performance in the theatre:

> It's a block booking from the morgue.[9]
>
> *(Tony Sheldon 2013, PI)*

> All I see is a sea of blue heads.
>
> *(Bernard Liebhaber 2013, PI)*

> It is an intelligent audience.
>
> *(Janet Fullerlove 2014, PI)*

> The audience is like an oil painting.
>
> *(Sullivan 2013, PI)*

Willmar Sauter cites several studies indicating that "the spectator basically reacts to the personality of the actor" (2002: 126). My study of a vast array of actors' comments reflects that actors have a tacit understanding of, and react to, the personality of the different audiences they encounter each night as reflected in the statements above. The audience role can differ from performance to performance.

The Audience's Costume

The audience performs for an audience, they play a role and they also wear a costume. Goffman includes the costume of a performer as part of the individual performer's "front," part of their "expressive equipment" (1959: 32). As discussed in the following history chapters, wearing costumes has always been an expressive part of the performance of theatre audiences and persists today. My conception of audience costume includes the general fashion that is worn to attend a theatrical event, the branded costuming that signifies allegiance to a particular production or theatre company plus quasi-theatrical costumes worn by particular audience ensembles. Aoife Monks argues that the actors' and audience's costumes play "an important part in fashion's requirements for display, [the theatre stage and auditorium] is designed for clothes to be received, admired and enjoyed" (2010: 36). Audience members are fascinated by the costumes others wear. Audience members I interviewed, particularly males, were often preoccupied "with how people are dressed" (Jim 2013, PI). When asked about changes in audience experience over time, interviewees characteristically cite audience fashion as the number one change (see Appendix 1). Gina, a retired office worker from Britain, emphasises that

> when you went to the theatre you used to get really, really dressed up and now people just go in jeans and tee-shirts. They really used to get dressed up in almost ball gowns years ago with all their jewellery – it was a big thing to go out to the theatre.
>
> *(2013, PI)*

Audience members predominantly lamented that contemporary audiences no longer wear decorative costumes to the theatre.

Branded costumes are often pre-purchased or even purchased at the production and donned during interval: t-shirts, caps, hoodies and onesies. Some audience members wear branded costumes to perform their loyalty to particular productions. The groupies of contemporary Broadway musicals are part of a fascinating subculture of audience performers that often wear branded costuming and see themselves as members of the cast. They have a large repertoire of actions that construct them as performers (discussed in Part II), but the most significant of their actions is the wearing of not only branded costuming but theatrical costumes. Augmenting their role as audience performer beyond that of single ticket buyers, some groupies wear the costumes of the onstage characters to the multiple performances they attend. In the last Broadway revival of *Les Miserables*, a groupie attended numerous performances dressed as Cosette, completing her act with an entrance at the stage door to visit her fellow cast members. Groupies also bring props and other paraphernalia into the performances extending the diegetic world of the play into the auditorium. Girls and guys-night-outers are other ensembles that wear themed costumes to the theatre (discussed in detail in Chapter Six). This kind of blurring of the sites for performance poses interesting questions about the use of theatrical space in the contemporary theatre. Role-playing in character costumes takes the concept of aesthetic empathy between the actor and the audience member to a completely different level that is akin to Lipps's perception of "oneness" experienced with the onstage characters (1979: 375). Performing, although unconsciously to an audience of actors and ushers, playing the role of audience, wearing a character costume and, to a lesser degree, dressing for the occasion of the theatre work to construct the audience members as performers.

The Audience's Preparation

Just as actors backstage are preparing to go onstage, audience members are preparing for the performance in their own backstage. The foyer, including the amenities, is the audience's backstage where they prepare for or enjoy a brief respite from their performance. It is here that

> costumes and other parts of the personal front may be adjusted and scrutinised for flaws. Here [the audience] can run through its performance, checking for offending expressions when no audience is present to be affronted by them; here [members] who are expressively inept can be schooled or dropped from the performance. Here, the performer can relax; [s]he can drop his[her] front, forgo speaking his[her] lines, and step out of character.
>
> *(Goffman 1959: 115)*

Carlson calls the audience backstage an audience support space where they "prepare themselves for their different 'roles'" (1989: 133).

Preparation is encapsulated in that effervescent word "anticipation," which so aptly describes the heightened state of the expectation audiences experience as they wait for the performance to commence or re-commence. For management accountant Ray, the excitement of preparing for the theatre event is "amped up by anticipation" (2014, PI). Anticipation reaches its peak in the moment before the performance begins. June, a retired secretary from Glasgow, describes how for her "there is a rustle, somehow, among the audience and you get that sense of expectancy and delight really: very often delight" (2014, PI). Audience members may read their programme or share what their know of the forthcoming production all in preparation for that moment when the lights dim in the auditorium and the illuminated stage becomes a microcosm of soon-to-be-realised imaginings.

Like many contemporary dramatic performances, the audience performance has two acts, which I call performance and discussion. Act one, the audience performance, takes place in the theatre auditorium during the onstage performance. Act two, the discussion, occurs after the performance (and is detailed in Part II of the book).

The Performance

Upon entering the theatre, the audience performance commences. The audience performer knows their *call time* and has already been *blocked* into where they are sitting when tickets were purchased. They *wait in the wings* until the chimes in the foyer, the audience's *backstage*, signal their *five-minute call*. Ushers direct them to their *beginners' positions* in the auditorium. Their performance area *goes to black* and they are given a *visual cue* from the stage to watch and listen. They wait patiently for their first *vocal cue* then deliver their *opening laugh*. From this point on they are performing *moment to moment*. Audience performers are highly skilled at *ad-libbing*. At interval they *find their light* and retire to their *backstage* space: enjoying refreshments, adjusting their make-up in the mirror, socialising, discussing the actors' performance and reading their programme. On returning to the auditorium, their performance continues. There may be a cathartic moment and they weep. Audience members often speak their thoughts out loud in a *soliloquy*. At the conclusion of the performance they follow the *stage directions* by applauding their onstage co-performers who *cue* them by *bowing*. They again *find their light* and either leave the theatre or stay in the auditorium for their *second act*: the discussion.

The auditorium performance is a diverse medley of sound and movement. If you were to score it, it would be a series of kinetic, paralingual and verbal contributions that make up the audience's repertoire of actions. This score is what I call an audience text (Heim 2012: 189–97). Bernard Beckerman argues that "Theatre involves the senses of an audience more completely than almost any other artistic form" (1970: 161), yet so little research has considered the audience's sensory responses as a performance in and of themselves.

Kinetic performance includes applauding, eating or drinking in the theatre, interactions with mobile phones, and various other actions such as walking – including the infamous "walk-out" – sitting, standing, opening/closing/dropping programmes, squirming, tapping feet, shaking heads, chewing, fidgeting, kissing, touching, rummaging in handbags, drumming fingers, taking photographs or videos. Fernando Poyatos documents a list of what he calls "paralingual alternates" (1982: 88) that are part of the onstage actor's repertoire of sounds. This paralanguage is shared by the audience members and includes laughing, crying, singing, snoring, coughing, sighing, snorting, sneezing, hiccoughing, groaning, chewing, gasping, yawning, humming, catcalling, cheering, booing and other utterances recognised by the Webster dictionary such as Ahem, Hm, Hep, Hist, Ho, Humpf, Pff, Psst, Tsk, Ugh and Uh-huh. Verbal utterances include talking back to the stage and talking or whispering amongst selves: the audience "dialogue." Some of these actions are contributions to the event and others interrupt the theatrical event.

As discussed below, most of the audience gestures and utterances, whether contributory or interruptive, are contagious. McConachie argues that emotional contagion is not as pervasive today as in the period of the lit auditoriums (2008: 97). While this is obviously the case with the mimicry of facial expressions and other visual cues, I would argue that just as those that are visually impaired have a more acute sensory consciousness, contemporary audience's sensory awareness of each other is heightened in the dark. Similar to their increased attentiveness, their awareness of each other's repertoire of emotional utterances and states is augmented in the anonymity of the shadows. Whether they act on this perception or restrain their response is another matter. Carson, a British security guard, enjoys the enigma of emotional contagion that is often performed in darkened auditoriums:

"You can never see it. You can never see the clap or the laughter: that is the trick of theatre, that feedback that continuously rumbles on" (2014a, PI).

Rather than describe all of the gestures and utterances that make up the audience performance, I concentrate on those that are performed most often in contemporary theatre and that have the most impact as either contributions or interruptions for actors, audience and ushers alike. Because of etiquette strictures, the contemporary audience has a limited ambit of gestures. This also informed my selection. The majority of the gestures and utterances outlined below have a dynamic history that will be further expanded in the next chapter. Other emergent performance contributions and interruptions, such as the use of technology in the auditorium, are explored in Part II.

Laughter

One of the most pleasurable of all audience contributions is laughter. In laughter audiences experience, in Lipps's terms, the pleasure of empathy where "a free and joyful inner activity of my being has been evoked" (1979: 409). Alice attends around five Broadway productions a year: "I think sometimes the audience can make it. They start laughing and you start laughing too" (2013, PI). Laughter from one audience member can break down audience inhibitions and cause ripples of laughter. Laughing is predominantly a collective act and audience members rarely laugh alone. This congenial act of mirth is the most potent example of emotional contagion. An individual audience member laughs; other audience members inevitably catch the contagion and respond in some way by joining in, tittering or expressing annoyance or discomfort. In one sense, the audience member who initiates the laugh becomes the performer and the respondents the audience. A huge guffaw can be performed by an audience member in the back row and the audience laughs at the audience. The laughter eventually becomes a collective performance that is highly contagious and upon which actors are dependent in comedies. Linda, a school teacher, attends around ten plays a year. She recounted attending a production of *Wingfields Inferno* in Toronto which she did not find overly amusing. There was, however, "someone behind [her group] that was in hysterics." Linda continued: "[T]hat got us laughing because she was enjoying herself. She was having the best time. We got the giggles" (2013, PI). This is a compelling example of emotional contagion and what Copeau calls "the ravishment of laughter" (cited in Auslander 1997: 16).

It is surprising how many audience members are fascinated by each other's laughter. Jenny, a student, and Lottie an accountant from London are "always really interested in why people laugh" (Jenny 2014, PI). They enjoy discussing the performance of laughter in the auditorium:

> The person besides you laughs and so you say "I have to laugh too." You feel there is an expectation.
>
> *(Jenny 2014, PI)*

I can hear what [the actor] is saying, but I do not know why [the audience member] found it funny.

(Lottie 2014, PI)

It might be also that is he showing off to the audience as well: like, "I understand this; I am on another level."

(Jenny 2014, PI)

In this case the audience member can be seen to replicate what actors often do when they are "playing for laughs."

Actors are taught to "ride the laugh" of the audience, and "laughed off the stage" is idiomatic for a bad performance. Audience laughter is an entity in itself. Audience members often laugh in different places in each performance, they laugh in the "wrong" place, they laugh inappropriately, they laugh too long, or they do not laugh enough. Roy, an engineer from London, is sensitised to the audience laughter and appropriates acting expressions to describe this performance: "There is always that little pause, but the timing from the audience is spot on" (2014, PI). Stephen Aaron may argue that laughing is an interruption to the onstage action (1986: 54), but laughter does not interrupt the performance, it contributes to it. As veteran actor of the Broadway stage, Sondra Lee describes, "When I am doing comedy I will throw it out, more like a wave. You lay the thing out and when it comes back – that's usually laughter – you know you have hit the mark.[10] It has to do with the approval of the moment" (2013, PI). The co-performance that occurs when actors ride the audience laugh is one of the most poignant examples of the reciprocity that occurs between stage and audience. Reciprocity, discussed further in Chapter Seven, is one of the central tenets of empathy. The most engaging aspect about audience laughter for actors and audiences is its spontaneity and unpredictability. Laughter is the most sociable and capricious of all the paralanguages that make up the audience performance.

Crying

The old adage "laugh and the world laughs with you, weep and you weep alone"[11] holds some truth in the theatre. Crying in the theatre is often an autonomous performance. When it occurs, crying is an important part of an audience member's performance for its cathartic purposes and for its contribution to the onstage performance. Although crying in the auditorium is not always heard by actors, the empathy of an audience is often felt, and actors, such as Richard White, instinctively know when "an audience is with us" (2013, PI). Even though audiences do not acknowledge the trickling of tears, they are keenly aware of the moistening of eyes and stifled sobbing in the auditorium. In post-show discussions, audience members often refer to each other's emotive performance: "I think everyone is still drying their eyes: very moving, very, very moving" (Heim 2009). Contemporary audience members in Western English-speaking playhouses restrain their act of crying in response to stage actions for multiple reasons including embarrassment, etiquette rules and cultural expectations. Judith is a teaching assistant in a primary school. Crying in the theatre is part of her regular performance: "I would love to see *War Horse* but I know that I will come out absolutely feeling full and [crying] buckets. I try and hold myself back to a certain extent" (2013, PI). Jodie Payne has ushered at Sydney Theatre Company for nine and a half years observing that "audiences stifle their sobs, or if they get really upset they will leave" (2013, PI). How different from the excessive audience weeping in the eighteenth century where audience members laid their handkerchiefs out on the balcony rail in preparation for their performance (McAuley 2000: 248). The pleasure of crying is well documented.[12] Lipps argued that "the more I am touched by the sorrow and defeat of another person, [...] I have this most joyful and universal feeling" (1965: 411). Crying is an important audience performative that is not only cathartic and pleasurable, but contributes much to the onstage performance. It is one way for actors to recognise when an audience is "with" them.

Applauding

The finale of the audience's auditorium performance is applause. Applause is the largest ensemble performance in the auditorium. The slapping of two hands together is a curious phenomenon. Apart from stamping feet on a wooden floor, a practice that still exists in theatres in Europe today, applause is the most efficient way of producing un-uttered voluntary sound using body parts. Standing and applauding increases its effectiveness as a vehicle to signal pleasure, enjoyment, excitement and approval in the theatre. As Carlson contends, "We may do actions unthinkingly, but when we think about them, this brings in a consciousness that gives them the quality of performance" (2004: 4). Applause, particularly when it is a standing ovation, is often a conscious performance. Applause at the conclusion of a contemporary performance is the last bastion of the audience critic. In the past, this percussive gesture spelt the success or demise of productions. It still holds some traction as a critical tool for audiences today. Applause credibility is, however, slowly diminishing with the rise of the now obligatory standing ovation practised after every performance on Broadway and almost all in the West End.[13] Working against the spontaneity of emotional contagion, the mandatory ovation has redefined the meaning of applause.

While this practice may indicate the erosion of applause's critical value, it concurrently serves a new purpose as a vehicle for audience empowerment. The compulsory standing ovation can be seen as a signifier of audience authority and enjoyment of the entire theatrical experience more than approbation of the onstage performance. As Brandl-Risi argues, the audience are, in fact, applauding the audience (2011: 14). The more strident the performance of applause, the more the audience are showing or proving to other audience members that they have enjoyed themselves, regardless of whether the enjoyment is feigned or genuine.

This raucous signifier of enjoyment is the most striking example of the *cabotinage* of audience performance, particularly evident when the standing ovation is contrived and audience members attempt to upstage each other. The feigned and over-acted applause of the standing ovation is reminiscent of the performance of the French claque. To borrow Goffman's term, the claque are the "fabricators" (1959: 77) of applause whose spurious behaviour in the auditorium gives a false sense of success for the performance. The claque are, however, hired professionals who are paid to play the role of enthusiastic audience member. The claque still exists today in many Broadway and West End theatres, not only represented by hired actors, similar to the claque of the late nineteenth century, but now represented by producers. Producers can be seen moving strategically from place to place in the audience at previews and opening nights starting the applause and laughter. Carol Channing's husband/manager's hollow clapping reverberated through theatre auditoriums for 40 years, initiating the applause at every performance she gave.

Kershaw argues that "the more the audience applaud, the less the theatre belong[s] to them" (2001: 151). Yet the standing ovation can also be read as a signifier of belonging. The act of the standing ovation is, perhaps, the audience's defiant cleaving to their last sacred space for performance, the last rite of performance that is solely their own, a kind of standing and holding their ground, even though in the dark. More pragmatically, the standing ovation can be seen to justify the audience's extravagant expenditure on inflated ticket prices. Tony Sheldon has acted in professional theatres internationally since he was nine. He argues that the compulsory standing ovation is consumer driven: "[I]t has become insidiously *de rigueur*. Everybody automatically stands up, regardless of what the play is. People are paying so much for their tickets that they want to feel that they have gotten their money's worth" (2013, PI). Usher David Conte feels that audience expression is an obligation: "[A]udiences, I guess, want to express themselves and feel obligated to express themselves" (2014, PI). Margaret goes to the theatre around ten times a year and refuses to stand during ovations at West End performances. Rather than feel obligated she contends that "if you stand up for everything, you are putting everything on a level aren't you?" (2014b, PI). In light of any of the perspectives I discussed, the contemporary standing ovation has become more about the audience than the onstage performance. Whether performed as justification or approbation, in sincerity or counterfeit, this scripted audience gesture is becoming more of a sovereign performance than a mannered response.

Listening

Since there is a plethora of information on watching, gazing and looking in the theatre,[14] I concentrate on the often overlooked act of listening. Theatre audiences obviously watch the onstage performance, but they also listen to it. "Audience" derives from the Latin *audentia* meaning "a hearing, listening." For many centuries the audience were referred to as "auditors" (Blau 1990: 101). The scholarship on listening is predominantly and understandably confined to the concert hall. Since the auditorium went to black, theatre actors no longer watch audiences,[15] but they listen. Hauck states that he always has "that third ear cocked to an audience. I am listening to them listening: silence, but a kind of a poised silence. You can always tell if an audience is listening" (2013, PI). Numerous anecdotes from actors discuss the importance of an audience "really listening."[16] As Rancière argues, there is no reason that we should "assimilate listening to passivity" (2009: 12). The poised silence of listening is a vital part of audience performance that contributes much to the theatrical event. Silence itself does not always indicate listening. It can be a sign of boredom, disapproval or disbelief. Actors, in their uncanny way, "without possibility of error, [can] estimate the meaning of a silence. [They] never confuse indifference with emotion" (Jouvet cited in Gilder et al. 1950: 9). Attentive listening is one of the highest accolades that an audience can give actors.

The act of listening is difficult to quantify. Attention reflected in a poised silence is, perhaps, the closest way to describe the ephemeral state of listening that is sensed rather than heard or seen. Yet, as illustrated above, actors always know when audience members are really listening and actively seek their attention. In rehearsals, actors are often told to listen to other actors; in performance, the audience are invited to listen to the actors. A playwright's script is filled with stage directions to the actors to "pause." Listening is the audience performers' pause. It contributes to the onstage event and is a crucial part of their performance. Audience members are also intuitively aware of the act of listening. While they tend to watch each other at interval, during the performance, as one audience member described, you "listen to, more than watch audience responses" (Alice 2013, PI). Maggie attends around ten productions a year in Glasgow. She argues that "even [in] a silent response, feeling does transmit itself in the theatre: which is one of the other reasons I love going to the theatre – the realness of the interaction – audible and inaudible" (2014, PI). This is Barthes's listening that speaks (1991: 259) to the actors. In the chorus of silence that can only occur in live theatre, actors listen to the audience listening.

The Shuffle and the Fidget

The antithesis of listening in the theatre is what is described by actors, ushers and audience members alike as shuffling or fidgeting. The shuffle and fidget can be performed autonomously or as an ensemble. This performance includes, but is not limited to: looking around, shifting in the seat, jiggling of the legs, coughing, playing with a hand-held object, sighing, crossing and uncrossing arms or legs, yawning, playing with hair and stretching the neck side-to-side. As an ensemble performance it is amusing to watch. The jiggling, stretching and crossing of limbs are often contagious. Hans Gadamer argues that "The whole being of [a] gesture lies in what it says" (1987: 79). The meaning of the above gestures, when performed in the theatre auditorium, is explicit. The shuffle and the fidget predominantly signal inattention. Usher Kevin Fokes (2013, PI) argues that

> you can see whether [an audience is] engaged or you can see if it hasn't really got them. And I guess that comes down to just being drawn to the stage or whether there is a lot of fidgeting and looking around.

Actors are acutely aware of this improvised inattention and often change their performance accordingly. Sydney actor Anne Tenney knows that when an audience is "shifting in their seats and coughing [...], then they're definitely restless and things need to change" (2013, PI). During a performance the shuffle and fidget can also signal disapproval of or discomfort about the production or aspects of the production. They can shuffle just because of uncomfortable seating. Audience members have very accurate readings of these improvisations. During a London production of *Warhorse*, Sue, a school nurse, described how she "saw everybody [in] the audience sort of shuffling in their chairs" (2014, PI) until they were enthralled by the imaginative world of the play.

Another part of this improvisation that is related to attention is the lean-forward or lean-back. I have often witnessed audience members lean back in their seats and cross their arms in the auditorium. This is frequently read from the stage as defiance, a challenge or inattention. Conversely, the audience lean-forward signals attention, anticipation and/or absorption. Bell argues that he can see this performance from the stage: "[Y]ou learn to pick up when an audience is back in its seat and when it's leaning forward and is really engaged. You can see it" (2013, PI). In their preoccupation with watching their own and others' performance, audience members often observe the lean forward or back and describe it in the following terms: "[T]he audience was on the edge of their seats all night and it was just quality Bleasdale. It was very, very good. I was on the edge of my seat too" (Maggie 2014, PI).

The idiom "sitting on the edge of your seat," derived from the game of musical chairs, is associated with playful excitement, suspenseful anticipation and even anxiety. The audience performer is fully alert and attentive. They sit on the edge of their seat ready for the music to start, anticipating and even signalling their involvement in the play. Ushers understand this embodiment of attention only too well and, as Conte tells us, often observe the audience "sit on the edge of their seats. Literally I can see when people are leaning forward or leaning in paying attention" (2014, PI). The shuffle and the fidget and the lean back signal inattention, while sitting on the edge of the seat and the lean forward clearly signal attention.

The Walk-out

The walk-out is by far the most confronting performative act of the audience. When accompanied with an angry comment to the stage, as in a 2008 performance of *Women of Troy* at Sydney Theatre Company, the audience performer upstages the actors: *man gets to his feet, yells at stage and exits house left.* This audience performance can be etched in the minds of the onlookers for years to come. Similar to the emotional contagion of audience laughter, the walk-out can initiate other walk-outs as doubt is cast in the minds of others. It is extremely disturbing and interruptive for actors. Steven Tandy has worked as an actor in Australian theatre for 43 years. He finds it

> very distracting when an audience member walks out. [...] You get upset
> when people who were in the front row in the first act are not there

anymore at the start of the second act. That hurts you. It's amazing how hurt you get.

The audience walk-out has a profound effect on actors and other audience members alike. Tandy goes on to state that he goes "through a lack of confidence" (2013, PI). An actor will often change their performance in response, regardless of the actual meaning of the walk-out. KT Sullivan (2013, PI) and Steven Tandy (2013, PI) sometimes change specific ways they deliver lines or communicate with the audience as a result.

Often the walk-out is innocuous. As Goffman argues:

> [T]he audience [that is, the onstage actors] may misunderstand the meaning that a cue was designed to convey, or may read an embarrassing meaning into gestures or events that were accidental, inadvertent, or incidental and not meant by the [audience] performer to carry any meaning whatsoever.
>
> *(1959: 59)*

Audience members walk out of productions for a variety of reasons: they need to use the amenities, they need to attend to an emergency, they need to answer their phone or pager, they wish to show their distaste for the play or they are personally affronted by the play or production. Some audience members walk out because of the bad performance given by their fellow audience members (Maree 2013, PI). Interestingly, unlike actors, audiences generally comprehend the intended meaning of the walk-out; they are aware of the difference between a trip to the restrooms and a personal affront.

Ushers at the 2013 production of Toíbín's *The Testament of Mary* on Broadway regularly witnessed walk-outs by audience members insulted by the play's discourse. Some audience members refused to stand for the obligatory standing ovation or even applaud at Fiona Shaw's curtain call. The walk-out is obviously an interruption to the theatrical event. Interruptions disengage audience members and sever the relationship between stage and audience; the empathic connection is broken. The audience's attention often turns inward. Not only do questions of social etiquette arise, but audience members are forced to question the validity of the walk-out by judging their own response to the play. The walk-out is an insult to actors and an affront to audience and ushers but continues to play an important role in retaining audience autonomy. Walking out and applause are the only remaining platforms for audiences to express their genuine critical response.

All of these emotive performances: laughter, crying, applause, listening, the shuffle and the fidget and the walk-out directly inform the performance in some way. On a very fundamental level, when the emotional contagion of laughter occurs, the actor's pause will necessarily be longer, and the duration of the theatre work is changed. On an experiential level if, as Sartre argues, an emotion "is a transformation of the world" (1948: 58) then the theatrical experience is changed for those that cry, laugh, or are offended by the play and walk out. Not only is the experience changed for audience members, actors and ushers but, as argued in Chapter Seven, the onstage performance can be changed. Through their emotional contagion and their performed empathy for the aesthetic artwork or characters, the audience work with the actors to co-create the onstage performance. This is one of the primary reasons that no theatre performance is ever the same and is also one key feature in what differentiates the role of the theatre audience from the role of the cinema audience. The audience role that is performed in the encounter between actors and audience members is unique to theatre.

Audience members are not, however, actors. Generally speaking they are not skilled professionals, they do not have acting techniques to draw from, they are not trained and do not rehearse. The actors have lines to perform; the audience have nothing scripted to present. The content of the theatrical event comes from the stage. The audience, consciously or otherwise, are, however, performers in their own right. I am not contending that the audience *is* a performer. Rather that there comes a time in the theatrical experience when the audience play *as* performer: it is a role they play.[17]

Restraints

Audience performances are still, however, often tightly restrained even in our twenty-first-century theatre. In the auditorium there is a battle that is waged between the natural, emotional instincts of the audience performer and her/his understanding of decorum. As Bogart describes it: "What the audience is doing is stopping themselves doing what the actors are doing. Literally, their muscles are posed to imitate but they are restraining, because in the theatre you are not supposed to do that" (2013, PI). In the contemporary theatre not only do audience members restrain themselves from mimesis, but also excessive weeping and belly laughing. Any immoderate expressive behaviour is regulated because you are "not supposed to do that." In Western contemporary theatre auditoriums there are two regulators that restrain expressive behaviour: negative empathy and the code of "good behaviour": theatre etiquette.

Lipps argues that negative empathy occurs when the empathic experience is "not realised because 'something in me' opposes it" (Stein 1989: 15). In the theatre auditorium this occurs when an audience member empathises with a character on stage, has a spontaneous desire to laugh or cry, but checks their own response and restrains their impulse out of consideration for their fellow audience members or consideration of the actors because, as some audience members emphasise, "the performers deserve more than that" (Patricia 2013, PI). They may feel that a demonstrative response would inconvenience others by drawing attention away from the stage or compromise hearing. The "something in me" that inhibits expressive behaviour can also be cultural conditioning, a fear of embarrassment if I laugh too loud or cry in public because I am not supposed to do that. Lipps also calls this restraining of outward activity in "regard to good manners" (1979: 375) a type of negative empathy. It is this form of restraint that is born not out of empathy for my fellow audience members or actors but from theatre etiquette that is one of the concerns of Part I of this book.

Restraints are dictated in the theatre for a reason. Theatre etiquette continues to play an important role in the contemporary theatre in ensuring the comfort and enjoyment of all patrons and in signifying audience members as civilised human beings. From a more philosophical perspective there are, however, restraints inherent in the human condition itself. As Sartre states, "There are indeed many precautions to imprison a man in what he is, as if we lived in perpetual fear that he might escape from it, that he might suddenly break away and elude his condition" (2010: 59). I argue that in contemporary theatre, there are many precautions embodied in theatre etiquette that unnaturally imprison the audience performer.

In an attempt to "educate" new theatre audiences on appropriate behaviour, most theatre companies and many theatre critics have taken it upon themselves to inform potential audiences of the rules of theatre etiquette.[18] The rise of the authority of the theatre critic as a contemporary arbiter of culture, an expert and an educator in audience behaviour is remarkable. In a sardonic reading of etiquette strictures in *The Times*, critic Benedict Nightingale implores audience members to

> Never whisper, let alone talk, during the performance. If you're hard of hearing, hire a loop rather than bother your companion for info about the plot. And don't hum along with songs, even if they're by Rodgers and Hammerstein.
>
> Try your hardest not to be tall, which means shunning headgear and primped-up hair. And if you can't help your height, ask for a seat on the aisle or somewhere where you won't interfere with people's sightlines.
>
> Don't bring picnics. In fact, don't eat anything, not even your fingernails, even if the play is, well, nail-biting. If you must buy an ice cream in the interval, make sure you finish it and dispose of the carton before the restart. The scraping at remnants sounds like scratching on a wall.
>
> *(2009)*

As with all satirical expositions, there is an underlying agenda in Nightingale's rules of etiquette. He very smartly ridicules the extremities of contemporary etiquette codes while at the same time clearly articulating the expected norm that considerate theatre-goers approve of as acceptable audience performance.

In our globalised and technologised twenty-first century that is approaching information-saturation, etiquette documents are ubiquitous. Contemporary documentation includes rules on theatre company websites, rules on blackboards, rules in letters, rules in newspapers, rules on radio. Live or recorded announcements about etiquette have now become ritualised as a standard, pre-performance discourse. Theatre companies search for novel ways of presenting their rules including everything from witty rhyming couplets spoken by characters in the plays to taped recordings of the crunching of candy wrappers. The mobile phone announcement has emerged as a performance in itself and, as such, serves the same purpose as the prologues of eras past which sought to quell obstreperous audience behaviour and focus the audience's attention on the world of the play.

Theatre etiquette rules can be seen as one of Michel De Certeau's "structures" which are "nets of discipline" (xiv) that the "ordinary man" (1984: 5) of contemporary society is ensnared in. The "do not" list of strictures overwhelms the "do" list which generally only includes breathing, laughing quietly, applauding at the end of a performance only, wearing deodorant and sitting up straight. It would appear from etiquette rules that theatre is a serious business for which silence and a mentally alert but physically paralysed state is required of the audience for their own enjoyment. As Paul Woodruff argues, "in modern theatre, transgression is almost unheard of, and with its decline a lot of fun has gone out of theatre" (2008: 117). Transgression of etiquette rules is frowned upon by some theatre professionals.

Audience members tend to take differing attitudes to these imposed regulations. Most are inclined to restrain their performance according to etiquette rules.[19] When asked what position they take on behaviour moderation, audience responses generally fall into three categories: those that consider it offensive not to observe the rules, those that consider it respectful to obey the rules and those that "don't like to be told: it's common sense and I find it degrading" (David 2013a, PI). A number of mainstream theatre companies are attempting to liberate audiences from some of these etiquette strictures; but only up to a point. Audience members are given mixed messages: some more participatory behaviours are invited, while others are constrained. During the pre-show period of *The Testament of Mary* audiences were initially invited onstage to wander around the set and take photographs. Once back in their seats they were then told: "Make sure your cell phones are silenced," "If the kids call, don't answer," "There will be no speaking for the next 90 minutes."

Theatre etiquette places serious restraints on audience performance. In response to the learnt behaviour of etiquette there is a certain "bureaucratisation of the spirit" that results in a homogeneous audience performance "every appointed time" (Goffman 1959: 56). Schechner argues that theatre etiquette is a "restored behaviour" (2013: 35). It is not a spontaneous performance, but one that is restricted or prescribed from "what I am told to do" (2013: 34). The contemporary mainstream audience member has only a limited repertoire of actions – laughing, crying and applauding – and these are expected to be either moderated or performed at appointed times. Linda explains that part of her performance is dictated by etiquette rules: "I restrain myself because of theatre etiquette: I cry quietly" (2013, PI).

The silencing of demonstrative audience performance is an issue taken up by Kershaw. He argues that mainstream theatres need "unruly" audience responses to break contemporary theatre's current malaise (2001: 145). It is interesting that these responses are now considered unruly when only 150 years ago audiences were the gods and goddesses of the theatre whose applause, laughter, stamping, weeping and comments thrown at the stage combined to create a formidable and vibrant performance. Audiences of some European theatres still retain this right to be unruly (Heim 2012). Kershaw and Howard Barker assert that more drastic measures are needed to re-empower the audience, and both propose a return to a form of audience riot and a revolt against theatre company etiquette. It is difficult to ascertain, however, whether contemporary theatre audiences desire to, in Sartrean terms, elude their condition. New roles for the audience are emerging in contemporary theatre offering opportunities for audiences to break free from etiquette restraints.

This book argues that throughout history audiences have played many additional character roles that lie outside of the traditional audience-as-audience role discussed in this chapter. In addition to the roles of critic, community, consumer and co-creator, audiences have also been cast as voyeurs, celebrants, participants and witnesses. Individual iterations of all of these roles have been occluded, celebrated, suppressed, cultivated, ridiculed and privileged at different times through theatre history. It is predominantly the social and cultural expectations of how one must behave in public at particular times in history that either casts the audience into these roles or smothers their expression. Some of these roles are being re-articulated in the contemporary theatre, casting the audience as vital performers in the theatrical experience. Before I discuss these in Part II, it is necessary to research the character background of the audience performer and trace their performance history. Through a diachronic analysis, it is hoped some understanding will be gained of how the audience's role, audience, costume and performance changed so dramatically over the past century and a half.

Notes

1 See Appendix 1.
2 For a discussion of audience-to-character empathy see Woodruff (2008: 165–87), Beckerman (1970: 149) and Brecht (1964). For audience-to-actor empathy see Fox (2001: 357–72). For audience-to-dancer empathy see Reason and Reynolds (2012). For audience-to-actor/character empathy see McConachie (2008: 71–76) and Krasner (2006: 255–77). For actor-to-actor or actor-to-character empathy see Stanislavski (1936).
3 The research already undertaken in the audience-to-audience dynamic by Bruce McConachie (2008) and more recently and comprehensively in dance reception by Matthew Reason and Dee Reynolds (2012) takes a more cognitive and behaviourist approach. I am concerned with the lived experience of the happening of the audience performance.
4 These include Max Herrmann (1930), John Martin (1933), Bernard Beckerman (1970), David Krasner (2006), Simon Shepherd (2006), Bruce McConachie (2008) and Gareth White (2013).
5 Lipps altered his position on whether the "inner activity" of empathy was realised in outward behavioural expression. See Krasner (2006: 267).
6 See Rogers (1980: 147) and Ramanathen and McGill (2008: 827–36).
7 Of the 62 people that completed my questionnaire, 75 per cent spent time watching other people's reactions when attending the theatre. Of this group, 60 per cent said they watch other people because they "enjoy watching" their behaviour or are "fascinated by" their behaviour (see Appendix 2).
8 In an interesting inversion, Philip Auslander discusses how at the inception of television, television audience viewing was acculturated from modes of viewing theatre (2008: 17–24).
9 In my interviews, actors implored me to assure the reader that they do not actually mean this, they are often "saying it out of frustration" (Schoeffler 2013, PI).
10 "Hitting one's mark" in theatre refers to an actor having moved to the correct blocked position (mark) on the stage. Its use is also extended in the actor's lexicon, as in this case,

to describe moments when an actor has delivered a line that has hit the mark with the audience. That is, there has been a connection between actor and audience, when both actor and audience realise this moment.

11 This maxim has its beginnings in an ancient Latin saying concluding with "weep and the world weeps with you." The current version, with the ending "weep and you weep alone" first appeared in 1883 in Ella Wheeler Wilcox's poem "Solitude."

12 For a comprehensive history of the pleasure of crying see Lutz (1999).

13 There has been a significant amount of research into applause and the standing ovation. For some interesting perspectives see Kershaw (2001: 133–53), Ridout (2006: 164, 165) and Brandl-Risi (2011: 12–18).

14 See particularly Woodruff (2008) and Fensham (2009).

15 This is comparative to the nineteenth-century lit auditoriums where actors could see the performance of all audience members. Some actors that I interviewed, however, stated that they could still see the contemporary audience's larger performatives even in the dark.

16 See Cohen (2013), Little and Cantor (1970) and Funke and Booth (1963).

17 Although focussing only on "performance" not "performer," Schechner discusses the difference between "is" performance and "as" performance (2013: 38).

18 While this list is by no means exhaustive, prominent theatre critics that publish theatre etiquette rules include Benedict Nightingale, Lyn Gardner, Ben Brantley, Tom Williams and Alison Crogan.

19 In the questionnaire, 62 per cent of the participants said that they often moderated their behaviour according to etiquette rules, 30 per cent said that they sometimes moderate their behaviour, and only 8 per cent said they never moderate their behaviour (see Appendix 2).

References

Aaron, Stephen (1986) *Stage Fright: Its Role in Acting*, Chicago: Chicago UP.

Auslander, Philip (1997) *From Acting to Performance: Essays in Modernism and Postmodernism*, London: Routledge.

——(2008) *Liveness: Performance in a Mediatised Culture*, 2nd edn, London and New York: Routledge.

Barthes, Roland (1991) *The Responsibility of Forms*, trans. Richard Howard, Berkeley and Los Angeles: California UP.

Beckerman, Bernard (1970) *Dynamics of Drama*, New York: Alfred A. Knopf.

Blau, Herbert (1990) *The Audience*, Baltimore: Johns Hopkins UP.

Blumenthal, Eileen (1984) *Joseph Chaikin: Exploring at the Boundaries of Theater*, Cambridge: Cambridge UP.

Brandl-Risi, Bettina (2011) "Getting Together and Falling Apart: Applauding Audiences," *Performance Research*, vol. 16, no. 2: 12–18.

Brecht, Bertolt (1964) *Brecht on Theatre: The Development of an Aesthetic*, ed. and trans. John Willett, New York: Hill and Wang.

Butsch, Richard (2000) *The Making of American Audiences*, Cambridge: Cambridge UP.

Carlson, Marvin (1989) *Places of Performance: The Semiotics of Theatre Architecture*, Ithaca: Cornell UP.

——(2004) *Performance: A Critical Introduction*, 2nd edn, New York and London: Routledge.

Carney, Reeve (2013) Actor's post-performance comments. *Spiderman: Turn off the Dark*, Foxwoods Theatre, New York City, 18 April. Transcript.

Cohen, Robert (2013) *Acting Power: The 21st Century Edition*, Abingdon: Taylor and Francis.

Crouch, Tim (2013) "In Conversation with Tim Crouch," facilitator Sandra Gattenhof, Queensland University of Technology.

De Certeau, Michel (1984) *The Practice of Everyday Life*, Berkeley and Los Angeles: California UP.

Fensham, Rachel (2009) *To Watch Theatre: Essays on Genre and Corporeality*, Bruxelles: Peter Lang.

Fox, Michael (2001) "'There's Our Catastrophe': Empathy, Sacrifice and the Staging of Suffering in Beckett's Theatre", *New Theatre Quarterly*, vol. 17, no. 4.

Funke, Lewis and John E. Booth (eds.) (1963) *Actors Talk About Acting*, New York: Avon.

Gadamer, Hans Georg (1987) *The Relevance of the Beautiful and other Essays*, ed. Robert Bernasconi, trans. Nicholas Walker, Cambridge: Cambridge UP.

Gilder, Rosamond, Hermine Rich Isaacs, Robert M. MacGregor and Edward Reed (eds.) (1950) *Theatre Arts Anthology*, New York: Theatre Arts Books.

Goffman, Erving (1959) *The Presentation of Self in Everyday Life*, New York: Random House.

Grotowski, Jerzy (1980) *Towards a Poor Theatre*, ed. Eugenio Barba, London: Methuen.

Hatfield, Elaine, Richard Rapson and Yen-Chi Le (2009) "Emotional Contagion and Empathy" in *Social Neuroscience of Empathy*, eds. Jean Decety and William Ickes, Cambridge: MIT Press.

Heim, Caroline (2006) *Anne of the Thousand Days* backstage comments, Visy Theatre, Brisbane Powerhouse, Brisbane, 8–17 June.

——(2009) *The Miracle Worker* post-show transcript, facilitator Caroline Heim, Visy Theatre, Brisbane Powerhouse, Brisbane, 18 June.

——(2012) "'Argue with Us!': Audience Co-creation through Post-Performance Discussions," *New Theatre Quarterly*, vol. 28, no. 2: 189–97.

——(2013) *Leave it to Jane* post-show transcript, facilitator Caroline Heim, Lion Theatre, New York City, 26 April.

Herrmann, Max (1930) "Das theatralische Raumerlebnis," *Bericht vom 4. Kongressfuer Aesthetik und Allgemeine Kunstwissenschaft*, Berlin.

Hojat, Mohammadreza, Joseph Gonnella, Thomas Nasca, Salvatore Mangione, Michael Vergare and Michael Magee (2002) "Physician Empathy: Definition, Components, Measurement, and Relationship to Gender Speciality," *American Journal of Psychiatry*, vol. 159, no. 9: 1563–69.

Kennedy, Dennis (2009) *The Spectator and the Spectacle: Audiences in Modernity and Postmodernity*, Cambridge: Cambridge UP.

Kershaw, Baz (2001) "Oh for Unruly Audiences! Or, Patterns of Participation in Twentieth Century Theatre," *Modern Drama*, vol. 42, no. 2: 133–54.

Krasner, David (2006) "Empathy and Theatre" in *Staging Philosophy: Intersections of Theater, Performance and Philosophy*, eds. David Krasner and David Saltz, Anne Arbor: Michigan UP.

Lipps, Theodor (1965) "Empathy and Aesthetic Pleasure" in *Aesthetic Theories: Studies in the Philosophy of Art*, ed. and trans. Karl Aschenbrenner, ed. Arnold Isenberg, Englewood Cliffs: Prentice-Hall.

——(1979) "Empathy, Inner Imitation and Sense Feeling" in *A Modern Book of Esthetics*, 5th edn, ed. Melvin Rader, trans. Max Schertel and Melvin Rader, New York: Holt, Rinehart and Winston.

Little, Stuart and Arthur Cantor (1970) *The Playmakers*, New York: Norton.

Lutz, Thomas (1999) *Crying: The Natural and Cultural History of Tears*, New York: Norton.

Martin, John (1933) *The Modern Dance*, New York: A. S. Barnes.

McAuley, Gay (2000) *Space in Performance: Making Meaning in the Theatre*, Ann Arbor: Michigan UP.

McConachie, Bruce (2008) *Engaging Audiences: A Cognitive Approach to Spectating at the Theatre*, New York: Palgrave Macmillan.

Mitgang, Herbert (1983) "When Actors Review the Audience," *The New York Times* 21 April.

Monks, Aoife (2010) *The Actor in Costume*, New York: Palgrave Macmillan.

Nightingale, Benedict (2009) "The Smell of the Greasepaint," *The Times* 19 June.

Poyatos, Fernando (1982) "Non-verbal Communication in the Theatre: The Playwright/Actor/Spectator Relationship in Ernest," ed. Hess-Luttich, *Multimedial Communications 2, Theatre Semiotics*: 75–94.

Ramanathen, Suresh and Ann L. McGill (2008) "Social Influences on Moment to Moment and Retrospective Evaluations of Experiences," *Journal of Law, Science and Technology*, vol. 9, no. 2.

Rancière, Jacques (2009) *The Emancipated Spectator*, trans. Gregory Elliott, London and New York: Verso.

Reason, Matthew and Dee Reynolds (eds.) (2012) *Kinesthetic Empathy in Creative and Cultural Practices*, Bristol: Intellect.

Ridout, Nicholas (2006) *Stage Fright, Animals and Other Theatrical Problems*, Cambridge: Cambridge UP.

Rogers, Carl (1980) *A Way of Being*, New York: Houghton Mifflin.

Sartre, Jean-Paul (1948) *The Emotions: Outline of a Theory*, New York: Philosophical Library.

——(1976) *Sartre on Theatre*, eds. Michel Contat and Michel Rybalka, trans. Frank Jellinek, New York: Pantheon.

——(2010) *Being and Nothingness: An Essay on Phenomenological Ontology*, trans. Hazel E. Barnes, Abingdon: Routledge.

Sauter, Willmar (2002) "Who Reacts When, How and Upon What: From Audience Surveys to the Theatrical Event," *Contemporary Theatre Review: An International Journal*, vol. 2, no. 3: 115–29.

Schechner, Richard (2013) *Performance Studies: An Introduction*, 3rd edn, Abingdon: Routledge.

Shepherd, Simon (2006) *Theatre, Body and Pleasure*, New York, Routledge.

Stanislavski, Constantin (1936) *An Actor Prepares*, trans. E. R. Hapgood, New York: Routledge.

Stein, Edith (1989) *On the Problem of Empathy*, trans. Waltraut Stein, Washington: ICS Publications.

Titchener, Edward (1909) *Lectures on the Experimental Psychology of Thought Processes*, New York: Macmillan.

White, Gareth (2013) *Audience Participation in the Theatre: Aesthetics of the Invitation*, New York: Palgrave Macmillan.

Woodruff, Paul (2008) *The Necessity of Theater: The Art of Watching and Being Watched*, New York: Oxford.

2

STAGE ETIQUETTE (1800–1880)

[The audience members] roar with laughter, twist and wriggle about like eels, and almost drop out of their stalls in fits.

(Montagu Williams, Police Magistrate, 1892: 249)

Theatre audiences have a rich, colourful history of expressive performance. Up until around the 1850s, English-speaking Western audiences gave their most histrionic performances. Often upstaging their co-performers onstage with their antics, they cavorted and sang their appreciation or displeasure of the onstage performance. The audience members were the critics of the drama. In this role they dictated what was, or was not, appropriate behaviour for the onstage actors. There was a tacit understanding between the actors and the audience of what I call in this chapter "stage etiquette."

Compared with this vivacious performance, audience performance for much of the twentieth century appears lifeless, dull and restrained. Why did audience performance change from heterogeneity to homogeneity? Several audience historians hypothesise why this performance altered so dramatically: sacralisation of the arts, changes in lighting and theatre architecture, the shift towards Realism in plays and acting styles, and the rise of a bourgeois audience and commodity culture.[1] Each of these arguments holds validity. I acknowledge that all of these changes – some more than others – significantly influenced audience performance. In this chapter and the next I refer to these changes when they directly affect audience performance. The rules of theatre etiquette in playhouses emerge in the latter half of the nineteenth century as stage directions for a new audience performance appreciably ameliorating audience behaviour. The changes from a lit auditorium to a darkened auditorium also significantly impacted their performance. Both of these changes directly affected, and continue to affect, audience performance.

Audience performance obviously changed gradually over time. For the purpose of assigning some sort of reference date, I have used the introduction of electric lighting into theatres in London and New York in the 1880s to demarcate the change from stage etiquette to the pervasion of auditorium etiquette, what is contemporaneously known as theatre etiquette. This is the period when the most noteworthy changes in audience performance occurred. To undertake a comprehensive history of audience performance is beyond the purview of this research. I have predominantly excluded accounts of audiences of Variety theatre, Vaudeville, Minstrel shows, Burlesque, Pantomime and Opera.[2] Audience demographics also differed between theatres, which consequently affected audience performance styles. Some theatres attracted the fashionable audience, while others preferred theatres where they could enact more emotive performances. The demographics of different theatres have been considered elsewhere.[3] Some of these extant audience histories include descriptions of audience performance and have been invaluable sources.[4] Most audience histories rely on accounts of audiences by critics in reviews, and some include descriptions found in autobiographies and journals written by actors and audience members.

To privilege the audience voice, I have included a predominance of comments made by audience members about their experiences of attending theatre and their comments on each other. In adopting the audience's perspective I am proffering what De Certeau describes as "an approach to culture [which] begins when the ordinary man becomes the narrator" (1984: 5). Interestingly, many of the descriptions of audience performance are of the audience's *mauvais ton*. Personal observations of the audience by their audience, the actors, are also included. I concentrate on New York and London audiences with some reference to regional theatres and performances.[5] While the chapter commences with a brief overview of pre-nineteenth-century demonstrative performances, I begin a more detailed account at a time when audiences delivered some of their most polished performances as critics, co-creators and community: the first half of the nineteenth century. Rather than focus on separate histories of the audience as critic, community, consumer and co-creator, a collection of the audiences' performances in these roles are highlighted throughout this chapter and the next.

Historical Considerations

In Plato's *Ion,* the rhapsode Ion has a conversation with Socrates regarding the mimetic effects of his performances:

SOCRATES: And are you aware that you produce similar effects on most of the spectators?
ION: Only too well; for I look down upon them from the stage, and behold the various emotions of pity, wonder, sternness, stamped upon their countenances when I am speaking: and I am obliged to give my very best attention to them.
(380 B.C.E)

Throughout the history of theatre, in full daylight and lit auditoriums, actors have beheld the countenances of pity, wonder and sternness of the audience from the stage and have given their "very best attention" to them. As we shall see, audiences have not always given their best attention to the actors. It was often divided attention, inattention, and often in the contemporary theatre, it is continuous partial inattention. Included here is a selected list of particularly notable audience performances over the centuries where audiences either divided their attention or gave their full attention to the stage.

At various points in history, the audience attention was divided between the performances onstage and their own performances. The performances of the aristocracy of Restoration Theatre audiences of London and the fashionable audiences at the turn of the *fin de siècle* in London and New York are noteworthy examples. During these periods audiences, as part of fashionable communities, played their social role with much relish. Comparing the latest fashions, gossiping about the latest scandal and greeting acquaintances were all part of their social performance. The gaze at each other and the gaze at the stage were central to their performance of seeing and being seen. During the Restoration period, for naval administrator Samuel Pepys and his wife, watching other audience members was sometimes more stimulating than watching the play itself. In several entries in his diary Pepys turns his attention to other distractions in the audience, usually women. On one occasion in 1616 he "sat before Mrs. Palmer, the King's mistress, and filled [his] eyes with her, which much pleased" him (2003). The gaze at other audience members, albeit in this case the objectified female, heightened the live experience of the theatre.

A practice that began in the seventeenth century and continued in theatres through to the late eighteenth century was audience onstage seating. Higher priced tickets would ensure a prominent position onstage for audience members to display their costumes, deliver witty remarks and enjoy the titillation of close proximity to the actors. In productions of *Romeo and Juliet* in the second half of the eighteenth century, actress Susannah Cibber could only gain entry to the tomb of the Capulets by thrusting her way through crowds of onstage audience performers (Lynch 1953: 202, 203). In some productions, up to 200 audience members would sit on the stage seriously impeding actors' entrances and exits, but also emerging as guest characters in the plays through their often audible dialogue, interactions and conspicuous costumes. In playing this onstage role, audiences were more than co-creators of the drama, they were co-performers.

There are some historical accounts of audiences giving their full attention to plays. Audiences of the processional or wagon plays of the medieval period were often awed into full attention in the presence of the Sacrament. Spectacle or terrifying characters would often win full attention. Although the groundlings of Elizabethan audiences were often criticised for their barbarous and "filthy" behaviour, Alfred Harbage argues that a visit to the theatre was such a special occasion that audience members wore their finest costumes and were often very attentive during the play, the only distracting sounds coming from nut-cracking. Audience performance in response to the plays was expressive, and written accounts from audience members of the period included descriptions of "horse-laughs," "deserved applause," "flearing" (sneering and jeering) and "shouting together in one voice." Pamphleteer Thomas

Nashe describes how "teares of ten thousand spectators" (cited in Harbage 1941: 115) were shed during Shakespeare's *Henry VI, Part I.*

The critical galleryites of the early twentieth century, discussed in the next chapter, were exceptionally attentive audiences. Similar to the galleryites, although not as attentive, the pit audiences of the eighteenth century were renowned for their critical responses. Numerous accounts of the time, including prologues from plays, emphasise how the pit audience members' demonstrative performance clearly cast them as judges of the drama. The Epilogue of David Garrick's 1741 play *The Lying Valet* includes a discourse on the audience's role as critics:

> The poet, willing to secure the pit,
> Gives out, his play has humour, taste, and wit:
> The cause comes on, and, while the judges try,
> Each groan and catcall gives the bard the lie.

> *(1925: 44)*

Playing the role of critic, audiences performed their approbation or disapproval of plays of this period through demonstrative behaviour such as groaning or catcalling. It is not, however, till we reach the second half of the twentieth century that audiences give their full, undivided attention to the stage. Their role in the theatre by this point has, however, dramatically changed. Their attentiveness is no longer motivated by autonomous aspirations to critique productions, it is dictated by rules of etiquette.

Stage Etiquette

Up until around the middle of the nineteenth century, audiences in many ways ruled the playhouses. Numerous accounts of audiences during the first half of this century cite events where audiences dictated rules to the actors by calling out during performances, nonattendance, and some more aggressive behaviour. Drawing from accounts of this period, a general rule book of stage etiquette prescribed by audience members would include the following:

> Actors must give curtain calls
> Understudies, particularly for star actors, are disallowed
> Do not throw things at the audience
> Scene changes must not be missed
> Actors must recite every word the playwright has written
> The length of the play must not be shortened
> Actors must remember their lines
> Actors must not refuse to perform before a near-empty house

When actors or stagehands did not adhere to these rules, audience response was often hostile. Actors could be pelted with objects, hissed, shouted or whistled off the stage, run out of town and even fired at by a pistol while on stage.[6] This latter incidence is, of course, an extreme example but was not an isolated occurrence. The enforcement of stage etiquette not only demonstrates audience authority, but also illustrates the importance of the performance of the audience as critics of the drama.

The inventory of props thrown by the audience at the stage is extensive: fruit, vegetables, nuts, eggs, cakes, pies, gingerbread, fried fish, paper bags of flour, bottles, cutlery, coins, bon-bons, pen knives and keys. An audience member celebrated "the egg as a vehicle for dramatic criticism" (cited in Levine 1994: 28). The latter list is not exhaustive and does not include missiles thrown at the stage during the audience riots of the nineteenth and early twentieth centuries,[7] which included a range of larger objects from a lump of wood to several theatre chairs ripped out of the gallery by the prize fighter Wilson during one of the events leading up to the Astor Place Riot of 1849 (Cliff 2007: xviii). Not all objects thrown at the stage were for reprehension. Audience members as critics asserted their right to approbate good performances. As discussed below, they not only performed healthy servings of applause to show their approval, but also threw flowers at the stage at the conclusion of worthy performances, particularly those by star actors. Occasionally costly jewellery and cheques of up to $3,000, a mammoth sum in that time, were nestled in the floral offerings.[8]

Audience members as critics considered it their right to hiss a bad performance or a missed scene change and revelled in the "glorious privilege of hissing" (cited in Grimsted 1968: 67). Hissing emerged as a performance in itself. Some audience members perfected the art of "hiss[ing] like a serpent" (Ford 1850: 90) or "hiss[ing] – like so many mad cats" (cited in Henneke 1956: 177). A shrill and unremitting whistle from the audience could also drown out an actor's voice. Often accompanied with hissing or whistling, audience critics would shout disparagements at the stage such as "go home to [your] Ma" (Grip 1843: 135) or, referring to an acting style, "the man's a fraud" (Trekelle 1939: 208).

The audience clearly recognised their roles as critics. An audience member of 1801 delineates the performance of a "pit critic":

> [I do not] imagine that the whole business of a pit critic [...] should consist of finding fault or hissing every modest player, who hesitates, or every scene-shifter, who stumbles in sliding board.
>
> *(cited in Henneke 1956: 178)*

The gentry of the boxes considered themselves "brother critics" ("Chatham Theatre" 1825: 119), and the gallery critics, as discussed below, were the most vocal of all the audience critics. Whenever the theatre management, actors or gentry, questioned the audience's role as critics, audience members fiercely defended their "rights" to perform their disapprobation or approval. Accounts stating that "the people have an *undoubted right* to see and applaud who they please, and we trust that this right will never be relinquished. No, never!" (cited in Buckley 1984: 303) and the "right to hiss an actor off the stage is an undisputed right of anyone who goes to a theatre of his own will" (*Boston Weekly* 1824: 145) proliferated newspaper articles, judicial reports and magazines. The first half of the nineteenth century marks the period in which audiences were firmly established critics of the drama.

The Audience's Audience

On the other side of the footlights the audience's audience, the actors, anxiously awaited the verdict of the audience critics. Spying through "a peephole at the prompter's side of the stage, [...] the audience [was] watched by anyone anxious as to its character and behaviour" (Fyles 1899: 251). Backstage comments on audience performance were plentiful:

> What a jolly good audience!
>
> *(Kerr 1930: 86)*

> The audience are, upon the whole, cold.
>
> *(Kemble 1835: 132)*

Managers and actor/managers would also comment on audiences. In his diaries, Frederick Wilton, manager of the London Britannia Theatre, made a point of commenting on the audience performance in almost every diary entry. These comments included: good house, bad house, capital house, shy house, tremendous house, indifferent house, immense house, great house, decent house and wretched house (Wilton 1992). The audience had a different character every night.

The actors often took directions from audience members and bantered back and forth in friendly dialogue. One audience member describes an incident where the gentry in the boxes were not only in animated conversation with each other, but with the stage. As the heroine onstage was losing her battle against a villain, a dialogue ensued between a gentleman in the boxes and the heroine:

GENTLEMAN: 'It 'im in the eye, Sal!
HEROINE: *Shrieking* Lay dahn! I know 'ow to deal with 'im!

> *(cited in Walbrook 1926: 136)*

The actors were not antagonistic to audiences, they were co-performers. Co-creation was often described in terms of electricity as an "electric communication from the stage to the auditorium" (Scott 1899, Vol I: 144). As actor Percy Nash argued, it was not only the "electric current that charged the audience and held them enthralled" (1939: 260) from the stage, inversely, the "audience gives the inspiration and the electricity" (Scott 1899, Vol I: 116). As Jane Goodall argues, as early as 1814 it became a cliché for an actor's performance to be described as having an "electric effect" on audiences (2008: 82). For much of the nineteenth century "electricity" was used as a theatrical metaphor for the actor's enchantment and even seduction of audiences. As Scott's observation above illustrates, the highly charged electric air of the theatre was created through reciprocity between audience and actors. Paradoxically, it was the invention of electricity and the subsequent darkening of the auditoriums that placed constraints on the enactment of this co-creation late in the nineteenth century.

Character Roles

In these, for now, fully illuminated playhouses, we have a lucid picture of our two troupes of performers. As indicated above, audiences had a clear perception of their rights and also their identity as performers. Not only were they called "players" (cited in Davis and Emeljanow 2001: 217) in various newspaper and journal articles, they were also assigned particular character names: gods, pittites, goths, rowdies, greenhorns, dandies and b'hoys. Each of these character roles had their own distinctiveness. The gods of the gallery were known for their expressive, boisterous performance. Pittites resided in the pit and were considered by actors such as Henry Irving to be "the most critical part of the house" (cited in Tweedie 1904: 230). Goths were anarchical in nature and behaviour. Rowdies caused havoc. Greenhorns were unsophisticated but honest and genial. Dandies were preoccupied with appearances, and part of their performances was their "silly squealing" (*The Atheneum* 1825: 307). B'hoys, a subculture of the gods, ruled the theatres with their demonstrative and overwhelming performances. Some of the members of these groups worked collaboratively as an ensemble. Author Washington Irving describes a chorus emanating from the gallery ensemble in 1802 as "stamping, hissing, roaring, whistling […] growing in cadence"[9] (cited in Henneke 1956: 177).

The b'hoys were the most distinctive ensemble and contributed much to the drama. They had their own dialogue, "heigh-eigh" and "hi-hi," and were immortalised in the plays of the period particularly in the onstage character "Mose." Butsch argues that the b'hoys immediately recognised their own values and characteristics in this character. Over a dozen plays were staged in the late 1840s that included Mose in their *dramatis personae* (Butsch 2000: 48). Occasionally the auditorium was graced with the presence of a guest or star performer. Guest performers invariably upstaged the onstage performers. Attendance by George Washington, Martin Van Buren, Henry Clay, General Stonewall Jackson and Queen Victoria not only attracted larger than normal numbers of people to the theatre but also directed the gaze of the audience away from the stage. Guest audience performers were often given standing ovations or were "welcomed with continual cheers" (Leman 1886: 159). On one occasion a star auditorium performer, Henry Clay, and star onstage performer, Charles Macready, were given equal billing (cited in Grimsted 1968: 61).

Followers

Audiences had strong opinions about performance styles of the star actors of the period and they demonstrated their partialities. The b'hoys were devoted followers of Edwin Forrest and were often called Forrestites.[10] They preferred Forrest's more boisterous, flamboyant acting to other acting styles – namely the more intellectualised acting of Charles Macready in the 1840s, and the more studied approach of Edwin Booth in the 1860s. The b'hoys naturally identified with Forrest's performance style because it replicated their own. The dandies of America were strict Keanites and supported the British Edmund Kean during one of his more contested New York performances at the Park Theatre in 1825. In addition to those mentioned above, star actors usually had followers that supported them: Phelpsites, Kembleites, Macreadyites and Fechterites. Followers also supported lesser-known actors, and friendly rivalries between different audience ensembles were not uncommon. Veteran playgoer Peter Hanley discusses the Britannia audience in London in the 1840s and their allegiances to actors N. T. Hicks and H. Dudley:

> The audience may be divided into what may be termed Hicksites and Dudleyites; if Hicks was called before the curtain the audience would not be satisfied unless Dudley came also; so that neither of the actors could complain of the coldness of his admirers, for they were vociferously cheered nightly.
>
> *(1887: 41)*

Followers were exceptionally loyal to their preferred actors and would hiss or even throw missiles at rival actors.

Audience Performing Styles

From the b'hoys' loyalty to Forrest, it can be seen how the onstage and auditorium ensembles had comparative performing styles. Different audience members had "inside-out" or "outside-in" styles of performing. The colloquial idiom for an approach to acting that draws from emotional states within the actor is called an inside-out approach. The actor strives to realise and respond to the natural impulses inherent in the self. The actor that creates a character by working initially on the external appearance, movement and voice of a character is considered to have an outside-in approach to performing. The former of these approaches is predominantly associated with Stanislavski's methods, and the latter with a more traditional British approach.[11] Unlike almost any other time in theatre history, during the nineteenth century, the audiences sitting in different parts of the auditorium had different performance styles that were not dissimilar to the aforementioned approaches. The b'hoys, the gods, the pittites, the goths and the greenhorns that sat in the gallery and the pit can be seen to have had an inside-out approach to their performance. The gentry, and later in the century, the fashionables and *nouveau riche* who sat in the boxes, dress-circle and later the stalls and orchestras, can be seen to have had an outside-in approach to their performance. Similar to contemporary comparisons of American and British acting styles, comparing onstage acting styles with audience performance was a common practice in the nineteenth century.[12] Newspapers frequently compared the performances of audience performers in the boxes to those of the pit and gallery.

The pit and gallery audiences gave their emotions a rigorous public airing and responded to their natural impulses. They were, at times, accused of over-acting. Twynihoe Erle was a London scene painter. In his letters he described his performance as an audience member at the Britannia in the 1840s:

> We applaud far beyond the bounds of decorum, and laugh when there is anything unusually pathetic and affecting, till our eyes water so much that we can hardly see, and get at the same time such cricks in the back from paroxysms of spasmodic disturbance that we can barely sit up.
>
> *(1862: 16)*

Conversely, the box and dress-circle audiences were concerned with appearances rather than emotional engagement with the play. These were the audiences that came to see and be seen and were preoccupied with the latter. They often "forgot their habitual propriety as to indulge themselves in very audible conversation" (Wood 1855: 81). Fashion and socialising were of paramount importance to these rather gorgeous performers. Although their performance was often considered disruptive to actors and some audience members in other sections of the house, they had a significant contribution to make to the ambience of the *mise en scene*. The fashionables played an important role in adorning the theatres with glamour, style and beauty.

Audience Costume

For much of the nineteenth and early twentieth century, clothing worn to theatres was referred to as "audience costume." Audience costumes worn by the fashionables in the boxes

> served a distinct purpose – that of dressing the house. Box holders wore shining raiment. Evening dress was *de rigeur* for the men, and jewels glittered and flashed on the fair women who leaned back negligently in the upholstered chairs languidly waving fans or focussing opera glasses.
>
> *(Hornblow 1924: 7)*

This glowing portrait of the sparkle and charisma that exuded from the boxes is replicated in various descriptions of the audience in the popular press through much of the nineteenth century. Audience costume was vital in constructing the identity of the fashionables. The horseshoe arrangement of the boxes in the auditorium provided an excellent viewing platform for display.

The purpose of the fashionables' presence was often considered to be primarily decorative. At the Mackaye theatre, "Theatre parties of thirty or forty persons all in full dress, [were] seen every evening assisting to decorate the house" (*Spirit of the Times* 1880: 280). Actor/manager William Wood gave a vivid description of how the audience at his 1846 benefit performance in Philadelphia "gave a beautiful 'shading' to the amphitheatrical picture as it was seen from both the stage and boxes" (1855: 470). The descriptions of the auditorium in accounts of this period, particularly in the more fashionable theatres, frequently refer to the "beauty, fashion and intellect" that garlanded the house.

In order to gain multiple opportunities to display their garments, performers in the boxes would often arrive late or leave early, much to the chagrin of actors who were often critical of their behaviour:

> It is well known that in large cities [...] those who frequent the boxes [...] go there to show themselves [...] or they go for whatever reason the reader may please to imagine except to see and attend to what is going forward on the stage.
> *(Tasistro 1824: 65–66)*

The inattention of the box performers is well documented.[13] Their preoccupation with seeing and being seen was all part of their social performance. As performers, their audience was the fellow audience members in their circle, and this is where they directed their gaze. At times the fashionables' disregard for the stage was performed by sitting on the edge of the boxes with their backs to the stage (Wood 1855: 81; Trollope 1832: 124). There was no malice in these actions, the social performance and the costumes of their fellow box-performers were simply of much more interest to them than what transpired onstage.

Particular audience ensembles could be distinguished by their costumes. The dandies costumes were "stiff with starch" and "straightened" (*The Atheneum* 1825: 307). The b'hoys of the gallery wore felt top hats, red flannel shirts and high black boots (Butsch 2000: 47). The costumes of the fashionables' fellow audience members in the pit and gallery were a stark contrast. Garments were made of tweed, corduroy and woollen broadcloth and were often work-clothes. Little attention was paid to fashion, and items of clothing were abandoned for the sake of comfort. A gentleman in the boxes envied the "unrestrained liberty" of the pit audiences who "untrammeled by the chains of fashion [...] disdain the confinement of either coat, vest, stockings, and sometimes even shoes" ("Chatham Theatre" 1825: 119). Unfettered by the often stiff, restricting fabrics of garments worn by box performers, the pit and gallery performers were costumed in comfortable clothes, fully prepared to exert their lungs, slap their hands and stamp their feet in response to or in unison with their onstage co-performers.

The Audience Set and Lighting

To adequately display the costumes of the box performers, a backdrop was needed. This was taken into consideration in some theatres. The back of the boxes in the Bowery Theatre in New York were painted "of the apple-blossom colour, as being the most favourable to display the ladies to advantage" (cited in Grimsted 1968: 58). The crimsons, greens, purples and golds of the ornate theatres were likened to the drawing rooms of the fashionables. The auditoriums were their stage: "The most luxurious and beautiful places of amusement in the world" (cited in Henneke 1956: 107). Lighting the garments was also a concern. The warm glow of gas-lighting in the lit auditoriums was very flattering. Actor William Devereaux describes the experience of being an audience member at the Lyceum in London in euphoric terms:

> As you went up the red carpeted steps to the foyer you knew you had arrived – somewhere; some rare place. When you reached your seat you saw the frescoed line of the dress-circle with its clusters of candles, and the atmosphere began to affect you like the dim religious light of a cathedral.
>
> *(1939: 133)*

By the 1880s, the audience set extended into the foyers, which were often opulently decorated and, in New York, displayed large mirrors mounted on the walls and gold-framed paintings of star actors. Gazing into the mirrors, audience members played starring roles in their interval or pre-show performances. Inside the theatre, the auditorium *mise en scene* with its performers and star actors softly illuminated by gas-lit candles, thrown into a complimentary relief against the cream and gold picturesque sets, were primed for their performance.

Audience Performance

Verbal, paralingual and kinetic signifiers of stage censorship were just a small part of the repertoire of actions performed by theatre audiences of this period. Much of the audience performance detailed below was in response to and commensurate with the actors' onstage performance, casting the audience as co-creators of the drama. Audience performance was so compelling at times that one critic in 1844 found the "cavorting in the pit, gallery and boxes […] extremely interesting" and acknowledged a "new performer called Peg-leg [who] showed off in the gallery with great applause" (cited in Grimsted 1968: 61). Playgoers also found the performances of audiences "quite as entertaining as any part of the legitimate performance" (cited in Baer 1992: 174). To include every aspect of the audience's performance of the nineteenth century would be a huge task. Compared with the twentieth century, audiences had an extraordinarily large repertoire of actions, which they unselfconsciously performed to the joy, amusement or annoyance of each other and their co-performers onstage. I have, therefore, limited my ambit by including those performatives that are mentioned most frequently in accounts of the period. Hissing, throwing items onstage, sitting on the boxes and holding social conversation have already been discussed above. While many of these aforementioned practices were seen as disruptive, all of the following practices contributed much to the drama.

Laughter and Crying

Prolonged and excessive emotive performances were a regular occurrence in playhouses. In personal journals, audience members inevitably describe the laughter of this period in hyperbole. Roars of laughter, peals of laughter, convulsions of laughter, screams of laughter, shouts of laughter and shrieks of laughter resounded through the auditoriums. Erle describes one occasion where "Everybody laughed to such a degree that we all became quite limp and weak from the exertion" (1862: 83). This exhausting performance was often extended for periods of time. Seasoned playgoer William Northall describes the antics of an actor "keep[ing] an audience in roars of inextinguishable laughter for minutes in succession" (1851: 112). Laughter contributed to the sense of community. Audience member Henry Walbrook argued, "In the theatre [...] laughter makes for brotherliness [after a] scene that has sent wave on wave of merriment through a crowded audience, how pleasantly [...] everybody beams on everybody else!" Walbrook goes on to describe this moment in ecstatic terms as "the genial effervescence of such a moment" (1926: 41). This charming ode to laughter illustrates how laughter unified audiences.

Crying did not require such exertion yet was often described in terms of ensemble performance: "[A] wave of emotion swept over the house [...] men were furtively wiping their eyes, women were unashamedly 'having a good cry'" (Arthur 1939: 334). Watching other audience members cry was a pastime of assistant to the court Peter Hanley of London. In his *Jubilee of Playgoing* Hanley describes several incidences where he watched "many moved to tears" (1887: 67, 88). The empathy of audiences was often noted by actors and audience members alike (Tweedie 1904: 230; Hanley 1887: 77). Tears were not always concealed. Regular playgoer Marie Dickens noted that "the audiences at the Lyceum, night after night, dissolved into tears, no-one trying to dissemble either their feelings or their hand-kerchiefs" (1939: 80). Audience performance of tears and laughter was uninhibited, sincere and highly contagious.

Applause

Although applause was a standard tool of the audience critic, I have left discussing it in detail until now as it was such a pervasive practice and contributed much to the onstage performance. The clapping of hands was ubiquitous throughout performances. Audiences applauded after, and sometimes during, scenes that they empathised with or those that gave them pleasure: scenes full of pathos, well-delivered speeches, witty dialogue, humorous antics, songs, entrances of star actors, fights, impressive stage effects, costumes falling off actors, and actors ad-libbing with audience members. Their applause was often accompanied with laughter, crying and other kinetic and verbal responses outlined below. Lengthy performances of applause were not unusual. Thomas Ford, a supernumerary, observed audiences applaud a performance for five minutes in Boston (1850: 91).

Audience applause signified approbation, and the actors read it as such. At times it impeded the flow of the dialogue or the rhythm of the play,[14] but it was mostly courted and prized by actors. During one performance, British actor Henry Irving admonished the audience for their poor performance: "Gentlemen, I can't act if you can't applaud" (cited in Tweedie 1904: 230). Similar to riding the laugh of their audience, actors learnt to ride their applause. In a production in the 1870s of *As You Like It* in Baltimore, Miles Levick commenced a piece of dialogue prematurely, failing to ride the applause after his delivery of Shakespeare's "Seven Ages of Man" monologue. A very irate audience continued to applaud, stopping the show until Levick repeated the speech. The situation "became an absolute deadlock out of which there was only one way. The audience was master of the situation" (Barnes 1915: 54).

Actors could also discriminate a counterfeit performance of applause from a genuine one.[15] While most applause, similar to laughter, was described in hyperbole – storm of applause, round of applause, thunder of applause – actors could always identify hollow applause (Jefferson 1889: 461). Audience members were well aware of the effect applause had on their onstage co-performers. Ethel Tweedie, a travel writer from London, frequented and wrote about her theatre experiences. In her astute observations of the audience–actor dynamic she argued, "It is not surprising that hand-clapping should have an exhilarating effect, or that a volley of air vibrations should set the actor's blood a-tingling" (1904: 230). Applause was as much a part of the performance as laughter and crying; audience members often applauded throughout the onstage performance.

Lengthy applause at the conclusion of performances was only introduced at the inception of star curtain calls in London and New York in the 1820s leading to the introduction of company calls 20 years later. Audiences initially, however, found it unnerving to see characters spring to life and take their bows.[16] Even as late as 1904 Tweedie found it

> disconcerting […] to see an actor who has just died before in writhing agony, spring forward to bow at the end of some tragedy – to rise from the dead to smile – to see a man who has just moved us to tears and evoked our sympathy, stand gaily before us to laugh at our sentiment and cheerily mock at our enthusiasm? Could anything be more unartistic? A "call" often spoils a tragedy.
>
> *(1904: 181, 182)*

Similar to other practices, the curtain call soon became, however, a prerogative of the audience, who "called for the curtain" to be lifted at their pleasure. Emerging as another rule dictated by stage etiquette, Hanley observed that "when the curtain fell it was raised again in obedience to the call of the audience" (1887: 55). Applause during the performance was one of the most vital performatives of the audience. It fed, encouraged and sustained the actors, and its steady, percussive rhythm became the familiar backfill that underscored the audience text during performances.

Stamps, Cheers, Thumps, Roars, Catcalls and Waves

During the first half of the nineteenth century, some, if not all, of the above practices accompanied the performance of the applause of approbation. Audiences were incredibly resourceful. In addition to percussive claps, stamps and thumps, they used any and every kind of object they carried with them that could make a sound or be flung above their heads to vary their performance. Canes were thumped, and fans, handkerchiefs, shawls and hats were fluttered in the air. Verbal cries were sometimes an adjunct to the performance: audiences "vociferously cheered" (Hanley 1887: 41) or catcalled. Early in the century, three cheers were often given to the actors for outstanding performances. The "roar," which had its beginnings in the seating banks of Ancient Greek amphitheatres,[17] was another popular form of verbal expression. Certain theatres became associated with a particular kind of audience performance. Farces performed at the Adelphi Theatre in London were called "Adelphi Screamers."

Some of the most vivid descriptions of these exuberant performances came from those most opposed to them. Charles Dickens wrote entertaining descriptions in his disapprobation of these performances.[18] The most humorous descriptions of theatre audiences, however, were penned in 1832 by British travel writer Frances Trollope in her scathing discourse on the *Domestic Manners of the Americans*:

> The bearing and attitudes of the men [at the theatre] are perfectly indescribable; the heels thrown higher than the head, the entire rear of the person presented to the audience, the whole length supported on the benches, are among the varieties that these exquisite posture-masters exhibit. The noises, too, were perpetual, and of the most unpleasant kind; the applause is expressed by cries and thumping with the feet, instead of clapping.
>
> *(1832: 124)*

An important part of the "posture-masters" performances was the wave. The waving of garments or accessories came into vogue in audience performance around the middle of the nineteenth century. To express their pleasure, audience members waved any accessories they carried or wore over their heads. Dramatist Louis Parker recalled a performance by Henry Irving that was so overwhelming that he and other audience members "leapt onto the benches, [they] shouted, [they] waved handkerchiefs, caps, anything that could be waved" (1939: 104). The wave was predominantly performed consecutively with the standing ovation. The standing ovation of this period was commonly referred to in the popular press as the audience rising out of their seats *en masse* and often occurred, along with other plaudits, during performances.

Dialogue and Singing

There were four different kinds of dialogue that were performed by the audience during productions: soliloquies, ad-libbing, stock lines and prompts. A fifth dialogue, the general social conversations held predominantly in the boxes discussed above, was often disruptive. Audience soliloquies were performed when audiences were emotionally moved by the production onstage. They could consist of just a few words or whole sentences. In one of Edwin Booth's famous performances of Iago at the Winter Garden theatre in New York in 1863, during the smothering scene, an audience broke the stillness of the audience with, "What, is he a-slaughtering on her?" (*Harper's* 1863: 133). Soliloquies such as this occurred when audience members spoke their thoughts aloud. Ad-libbing occurred when audiences mistook the actions onstage for reality.[19] This dialogue was often performed by greenhorns and was ubiquitous in productions that were toured regionally. Jefferson describes a production of *The Lady of Lyons* in Mississippi during which the audience talked freely amongst themselves and to the actors. One old lady pleaded with the characters that the lovers should be "allowed their own way," and a farmer warned the villain of the play not to interfere again "if he knew what was best for him" (1889: 56, 57).

There were a range of stock comments hurled at the stage during performances that were part of the audience's standard dialogue. These included, among numerous others at different periods: "throw him over!" (Grip 1843: 135), "speak up!" (Wilton 1992: 108) and "now we shan't be long" (Saintsbury 1939: 359). Because regular playgoers would often see their favourite plays up to 20 or more times, they were very familiar with the actors' lines. The b'hoys were particularly fond of Shakespeare and were so familiar with the dialogue that they would often prompt actors when they forgot their lines, expecting thanks for their efforts (Cliff 2007: 201). This is a poignant example of the kind of banter that occurred between the two troupes of performers. Prompts also directed actors to perform some sort of action. Actor Adeline Billington recalled an incident where her husband was prompted onstage to eat some brimstone and treacle: "Give Billington some," yelled the gallery "until the noise increased to an uproar." After the actor had followed the audience's direction, the audience shouted, "He's taken it; three cheers for Billington" (cited in Scott 1899, vol. I: 371). There are various examples from the period such as this of audiences directing the action onstage. On these occasions, the audience troupe became more than co-creators of the drama, they emerged as directors influencing the onstage action.

Singing, either with the onstage performers or in autonomous performances, was a regular occurrence. Northall recalled several occurrences where firemen in the audience "would join the performers in some popular chorus, a bit of volunteer aid which, so far from giving offence to actors and audience, was highly relished by both parties" (1851: 72). The gallery ensemble regularly joined in singing popular airs which were played by the orchestras in between the acts. Up until the 1830s New York audiences would burst into loud singing whenever "Yankee Doodle" or any other patriotic song was played by the orchestra, much to the consternation of Trollope (1832: 124). Singing could also be a disturbance. During a production of *The School for Scandal*, the gallery boys of London "were singing a *rousing chorus* & scarcely a single speech was heard" (cited in Davis and Emeljanow 2001: 83). Not all extra-theatrical singing was a disturbance. Choruses sung at intervals added much to the ambience of the evening's entertainment. The songs often added an extra layer of meaning to the production.

Whistles, Oaths and Groans

The b'hoys of the New York theatres and the gallery boys from London had the most extensive repertoire of actions of any of the audience ensembles. While they regularly performed by singing, stamping, cheering, thumping, roaring, catcalling and delivering dialogue, they had a few unique activities that could be seen as their performer's bag of tricks: whistling, declaring oaths and groaning. Hanley describes an incident in London when the gallery boys took great offence to a particular actor and began whistling their derision during important parts of his dialogue. Incensed, the actor called on the officer of the establishment to remove the disruptive "blackguards." This was met by a "perfect chorus of whistling" (1887: 43).

Groans were mostly offered from the gallery and sometimes from the pit. In response to *The Lord Harry* at the Princess's Theatre in 1886, groans were delivered repeatedly from the gallery. Oaths and groans were performed to show disapprobation, but were also uttered in response to shocking scenes – "My God!" (Corbett 1939: 190) – and were voiced to empathise with onstage actors. Actor Tommaso Salvini described a performance of *Hamlet* where the gallery "manifested their sympathy with Hamlet's psychological difficulties by the groans with which they accompanied [his] immortal soliloquy" (cited in Levine 1994: 27).

Audience performance of disapprobation could, at times, seriously offend and unnerve actors. On one occasion repetitious and unremitting disapprobation resulted in a tragic outcome. Wood described an incident in Philadelphia where an actor in his theatre, Richard Fullerton, was singled out and incessantly tormented by a group of audience members during his performances. Wood argued that because of this constant derision, Fullerton's "terror and agony on entering the stage was truly pitiable. At length his little courage gave way" (1855: 85). On the morning after a performance of *L'Abbé de l'Épée* in 1802, Fullerton's body was found floating near one of the wharves in the Delaware River. This sobering account illustrates how co-dependent the relationship between actors and audience members can be and exemplifies the destructive potentials of negative audience performance.

Eating, Chewing, Spitting and Smoking

The consumption of vast quantities of food and beverage was part of the pleasure of attending the theatre but also became part of the audience's performance. On arrival at the theatre, audience members would settle in for the evening's entertainment with often complete meals or comfort food, which was either brought from home or purchased at the theatre. Often-mentioned hearty foods from records of this period include ham sandwiches, beef and soup, cold pease pudding, oysters and fried fish. Delicacies and comfort foods included mince pies, custards, brandy-balls, toasted chestnuts, gingerbread, cakes and all kinds of fruit. Just as many of these foods were geographically specific, many were also theatre or theatre-section specific. Oranges and ginger beer were popular at the Bowery in New York, and cold pease pudding in the London boxes.[20]

The most populist, contentious and celebrated snack was the humble peanut. Peanut cracking, throwing, consumption and disposal not only added much to the general ambience of theatres but emerged as an integral part of the audience performance. Here was a prop that was very versatile. *The Mirror* refers to the "music of cracking peanuts" by the b'hoys in the auditoriums at the Bowery Theatre in 1834 (cited in Odell 1928: 683). The sound of peanuts cracking was constant and, similar to applause, accompanied much of the onstage dialogue. Peanuts also worked to re-enforce the egalitarian identity of the characters of the pit and gallery. The peanut was the working-class equivalent to the custards of the gentry. There was nothing delicate or refined about eating the peanut. Its loud crack and splinter were a suitable complement to the extroverted performing style of the pit and gallery members, particularly the b'hoys. The peanut's fame and name spread rapidly and was soon immortalised in the naming of the "peanut gallery."

More interesting than the gregarious performance of food consumption in the theatres was, however, the throwing of food missiles. Throwing food became a controversial and spirited auditorium performance. Food missiles were occasionally flung over the head, from one audience member to another, onto the heads of the pit members below, and at the stage. In the 1840s in the Britannia, one member of the gallery threw his empty pint of beer over his head and "as it flew through the air, the other people in the gallery" unperturbed "quietly raised their eyes and watched its flight" (Wilton 1992: 161). Peanuts were the most often thrown missiles, and numerous articles of the period cite pit performers' consternation at having a shower of shells rain down on them from the gallery. Any item of food brought into the auditorium for sustenance or comfort could also potentially end up being flung on the stage if warranted by a bad performance.

The practice of "mastication" was extended throughout performances in the form of chewing tobacco. Unwanted juices from the tobacco were expectorated either onto the floor of the theatre or into spittoons when provided. This was a practice confined to the United States, and British visitors were appalled by the "incessant" spitting. Trollope was shocked to observe a well-dressed young man "take from the pocket of his silk waistcoat a lump of tobacco, and daintily deposit it within his cheek" (1832: 123). The smoking of tobacco in the form of pipes and cigars was, at different times and in different theatres, sanctioned and prohibited in auditoriums. Whether talking, eating, chewing, spitting or smoking, the jaws of nineteenth-century audience members received as much of a workout as their clapping hands and stamping feet.

Pre- and Post-performance Discussions

In preparation for and as an addendum to their auditorium performance, audiences engaged in ensemble warm-ups and cool-downs outside of but in close proximity to the theatres. Long queues formed outside theatres before performances. Waiting in one of these queues to enter the pit of the Lyceum in 1874, audience members "were a sociable crowd and passed their time in song and story" (Parker 1939: 105). During these often long periods of waiting, audiences were often entertained by street performers. Poet and regular playgoer Jessie Pope wrote a poem and article eulogising the performance of the London audience that "adorn a queue, [...] a very attractive queue for all that – charming costumes, charming faces, and every eye bright with excited expectancy." The female audience members in the queue transformed the "narrow side-streets into veritable flower gardens" (1912: 397, 399). Costumed audience performers warmed up their vocal chords, ate chocolate and shared stories in anticipation of the forthcoming event.

After the event, discussion of the performance would continue on the sidewalk outside the theatres, in nearby restaurants and around local street vendors. Walbrook discusses a group of regular audience critics that huddled around one particular stall in Trafalgar Square after theatre performances where

> earnest midnight debates with attractive strangers [took place] round a very popular baked-potato stall [...] in which all sorts of arguments and opinions were driven home with the wave of an umbrella in one hand, or a hot floury well-peppered-and-salted potato in the other.
>
> *(1926: 62)*

All audience members were critics of the drama. Their critiques, begun before the curtain came down, continued long into the night.

Audience Text

To conclude, the audience text of the auditorium performer from 1800 till around 1880 was a combination of sound and movement that often shook the auditorium. Walbrook describes one such event at the Sadler Wells theatre: "How we cheered, and how the house trembled to the shrieks and whistles of the gallery" (1926: 187, 188). At times frenetic, other times measured, the constant tittering, slapping, warbling, fluttering, humming and stomping of delight or disapproval was a captivating performance in itself that, at times, rivalled that onstage. As Walt Whitman stated of the Bowery Theatre audience: "The whole crowded auditorium, and what seeth'd in it, and flush'd from its faces and eyes, [was] to me as much a part of the show as any" (1888: 92). Only in those moments when "the audience paid the tribute of silence" (Hubbard 1917: 55) to an outstanding performance onstage, was the movement stilled. Yet even stillness, the audience pause, was performed on the audience's terms. In many accounts, actors considered themselves "servants of the public."[21] Stage etiquette was dictated from the audience members to the actors. The audience were the critics of the drama whose approbation or disapprobation was not merely inscribed in words on pieces of paper, but performed. This period in theatre audience history in the Western English-speaking world is one in which audiences gave their most lively, expressive and capricious star performances. Every night was their own "benefit" show.

Notes

1 See Conner (2013), Kershaw (2001), Davis and Emeljanow (2001), McAuley (2000), Blackadder (2003, 2000), Levine (1994), Mackintosh (1993) and Meyerhold (1969). Interestingly, theatre space theorists, such as McAuley and Mackintosh, provide some of the most insightful information on audience performance.

2 Since some of the actors that I quote worked across several genres such as Melodrama and Variety, and some theatres I discuss also programmed mixed genres, there are times when I step outside of this purview.

3 See Davis and Emeljanow (2001), Butsch (2000: 44–52) and Mackintosh (1993: 36).

4 I am much indebted to the audience histories penned by the following authors: Jim Davis and Victor Emeljanow (2001), Richard Butsch (2000), Lawrence Levine (1994), David Grimsted (1968) and Ben Graf Henneke (1956).

5 Audience performance is often culturally specific. Certain audience actions were performed more often in, or were unique to, British or American audiences. I have attempted to identify these differences where possible, but at other times some generalisations are made for the purposes of brevity.

6 For selected incidences where audiences enforced these rules see Butsch (2000: 51–53, 314), Wood (1855: 134) and Levine (1994: 72, 180).

7 Much has been written about audience performance at theatre riots. For some particularly interesting descriptions of audience performance at the Old Price riots of 1809 see Baer (1992: 173).

8 For a comprehensive and very amusing description of this practice see Henneke (1956: 168–72).

9 Irving does not actually find this performance delightful at all but appealed to have more police control over such behaviour. Others writers, such as Walt Whitman, sometimes celebrated these colourful performances. See Grimsted (1968: 55).

10 The b'hoys played a large role in not only the Astor Place Riots of 1849 – originally initiated through a rivalry between Forrest and Macready – but also in smaller riots of the period.

11 For a detailed outline of these two approaches and their history see Heim (2013).

12 In New York, newspapers and journals often equated the bombastic, expressive performance style of Edwin Forrest with the "good hearty tears" of the b'hoys and the more refined and intellectual performance of Edwin Booth and Charles Macready with "sophisticated audiences." See Butsch (2000: 62).

13 See Davis and Emeljanow (2001: 223) and Trollope (1832: 124, 222).

14 Editors of newspapers and some actors took it upon themselves to educate audiences about the appropriate time to applaud, but mostly to no avail. See Grimsted (1968: 63).

15 Actors could often distinguish the counterfeit applause of the claque mentioned in Chapter One.

16 Some actor/managers also found it unsettling. See Wood (1855: 260).

17 Although we cannot be certain, the Greek audience *Thorubos* was thought to be a kind of a roar.

18 Although Dickens's observations of nineteenth-century audiences have long been considered authoritative on audience behaviour, in an enlightening argument, Davis and Emeljanow point out the obvious biases and agendas in Dickens's discourse (2001: 163).

19 Lawrence Levine cites several of these humorous ad-libs (1994: 30).

20 See Henneke (1956: 134–44) for a more comprehensive overview of eating in the theatre and Davis and Emeljanow (2001: 10, 43, 76, 82, 83, 107) for various accounts of eating in the theatre referred to in this section.

21 "Servant of the public" was British star actor Henry Irving's maxim.

References

Arthur, George (1939) "Irving as Corporal Brewster" in *We Saw Him Act: A Symposium on the Art of Sir Henry Irving*, ed. H. A. Saintsbury, London: Hurst and Blackett.

Baer, Marc (1992) *Theatre and Disorder in Late Georgian England*, Oxford: Clarendon.

Barnes, John (1915) *Forty Years on the Stage: Others (Principally) and Myself*, New York: E. P. Dutton and Company.

Blackadder, Neil (2000) "Modern Theatre Scandals and the Evolution of the Theatrical Event," *Theatre History Studies*, vol. 20: 123–41.

——(2003) *Performing Opposition: Modern Theatre and the Scandalised Audience*, Westport: Praeger.

Boston Weekly Magazine (1824) 27 November.

Buckley, Peter (1984) *To the Opera House*. Ph.D thesis. State University of New York at Stony Brook.

Butsch, Richard (2000) *The Making of American Audiences*, Cambridge: Cambridge UP.

"Chatham Theatre" (1825) *The American Antheneum*, vol. 1, no. 14. 28 July.

Cliff, Nigel (2007) *The Shakespeare Riots*, New York: Random House.

Conner, Lynne (2013) *Audience Engagement and the Role of Arts Talk in the Digital Era*, New York: Palgrave Macmillan.

Corbett, J. H. (1939) "Irving as Fabien and Louis Dei Franchi" in *We Saw Him Act: A Symposium on the Art of Sir Henry Irving*, ed. H. A. Saintsbury, London: Hurst and Blackett.

Davis, Jim and Victor Emeljanow (2001) *Reflecting the Audience: London Theatregoing, 1840–1880*, Hatfield: Hertfordshire UP.

De Certeau, Michel (1984) *The Practice of Everyday Life*, Berkeley and Los Angeles: California UP.

Devereaux, William (1939) "Irving as Louis XI" in *We Saw Him Act: A Symposium on the Art of Sir Henry Irving*, ed. H. A. Saintsbury, London: Hurst and Blackett.

Dickens, Marie (1939) "Irving as Philip" in *We Saw Him Act: A Symposium on the Art of Sir Henry Irving*, ed. H. A. Saintsbury, London: Hurst and Blackett.

Erle, Twynihoe William (1862) *Letters From a Theatrical Scene-Painter: Being Sketches of the Minor Theatres of London as They Were Twenty Years Ago*, M. Ward & Co.

Ford, Thomas (1850) *A Peep Behind the Curtain by a Supernumerary*, Boston: Redding and Company.

Fyles, Franklin (1899) *The Theatre and its People*, New York: Doubleday, Page and Co.

Garrick, David (1925) *Three Farces by David Garrick*, ed. Louise Brown Osborn, New Haven: Yale UP.

Goodall, Jane (2008) *Stage Presence*, Milton Park: Routledge.

Grimsted, David (1968) *Melodrama Unveiled: American Theater and Culture 1800–1850*, Berkeley: California UP.

Grip, Gabriel (1843) "Theatrical Statistics," *Spirit of the Times: A Chronicle of the Turf, Agriculture, Literature and the Stage* 20 May.

Hanley, Peter (1887) *A Jubilee of Playgoing*, London: Tinkler and Hillhouse.

Harbage, Alfred (1941) *Shakespeare's Audience*, New York: Columbia UP.

Harper's New Monthly Magazine (1863), vol. 28, no. 163.

Heim, Caroline (2013) "Found in Translation: Debating the Abstract Elements of Cultures Through Actor Training Styles", *Theatre, Dance and Performance Training*, vol. 4, no. 3: 353–67.

Henneke, Ben Graf (1956) *The Playgoer in America*. Ph.D thesis. University of Illinois.

Hornblow, Arthur (ed.) (1924) "Olla Podrida: The Proscenium Theatre Box," *Theatre Magazine*, vol. XXXIX, no. 279.

Hubbard, Elbert (1917) *In the Spotlight*, East Aurora: Roycrofters.

Jefferson, Joseph (1889) *The Autobiography of Joseph Jefferson*, New York: Century Co.

Kemble, Frances Anne (1835) *Journal*, Philadelphia: Carey Lee and Blanchard.

Kerr, Fred (1930) *Recollections of a Defective Memory*, London: T. Butterworth.

Kershaw, Baz (2001) "Oh for Unruly Audiences! Or, Patterns of Participation in Twentieth Century Theatre," *Modern Drama*, vol. 42, no. 2: 133–54.

Leman, Walter (1886) *Memories of an Old Actor*, San Fransisco: A. Roman Co.

Levine, Lawrence (1994) *Highbrow Lowbrow: The Emergence of Cultural Hierarchy in America*, Cambridge: Harvard UP.

Lynch, James (1953) *Box, Pit and Gallery: Stage and Society in Johnson's London*, New York: Russell and Russell.

Mackintosh, Iain (1993) *Architecture, Actor and Audience*, London: Routledge.

McAuley, Gay (2000) *Space in Performance: Making Meaning in the Theatre*, Ann Arbor: Michigan UP.

Meyerhold, Vsevolod Emilivich (1969) *Meyerhold on Theatre*, ed. and trans. Edward Braun, New York: Hill and Wang.

Nash, Percy (1939) "Irving as Mephistopheles" in *We Saw Him Act: A Symposium on the Art of Sir Henry Irving*, ed. H. A. Saintsbury, London: Hurst and Blackett.

Northall, William Knight (1851) *Before and Behind the Curtain*, New York: W. F. Burgess.

Odell, George (1928) *Annals of the New York Stage*, Volume III, New York: Columbia UP.

Parker, Louis (1939) "Irving as Philip" in *We Saw Him Act: A Symposium on the Art of Sir Henry Irving*, ed. H. A. Saintsbury, London: Hurst and Blackett.

Pepys, Samuel (2003) *Project Gutenberg's Diary of Samuel Pepys*, ed. Henry B. Wheatley, trans. Rev. Mynors Bright. Available from: http://www.gutenberg.org/files/4200/4200-h/4200-h.htm [24 May 2014].

Plato (380 B.C.E) *Ion*, trans. Benjamin Jowett. Available from: http://classics.mit.edu/Plato/ion.html [24 September 2014].

Pope, Jessie (1912) "'Thereby Hangs a Tail': The Queues of the London Theatres and Halls," *Pall Mall*, vol. 49: 397–402.

Saintsbury, H. A. (ed.) (1939) *We Saw Him Act: A Symposium on the Art of Sir Henry Irving*, London: Hurst and Blackett.

Scott, Clement (1899) *The Drama of Yesterday & Today*, vols. I and II, London: Macmillan and Co.

Spirit of the Times (1880) "Spirit of the Stage," 24 April.

Tasistro, Louis Fitzgerald (1824) *Random Shots and Southern Breezes Containing Critical Remarks on the Southern States and Southern Institutions, with Semi-serious Observations on Men and Manners*, New York: Harper & Brothers.

The Atheneum (1825) "The Drama: Park Theatre", 17 November.

Trekelle, Rita (1939) "Irving as Modus" in *We Saw Him Act: A Symposium on the Art of Sir Henry Irving*, ed. H. A. Saintsbury, London: Hurst and Blackett.

Trollope, Frances (1832) *Domestic Manners of the Americans*, ed. Donald Smalley, 1960, New York: Vintage.

Tweedie, Ethel (1904) *Behind the Footlights*, New York: The Musson Book Co.

Walbrook, H. M. (1926) *A Playgoer's Wanderings*, London: Leonard Parsons.

Whitman, Walt (1888) *November Boughs*, Philadelphia: David McKay.

Williams, Montagu (1892) *Round London: Down East and Up West*, London: Macmillan and Co.

Wilton, Frederick (1992) *The Britannia Diaries: 1863–1875*, ed. Jim Davis. London: The Society for Theatre Research.

Wood, William (1855) *Personal Recollections of the Stage: Embracing Notices of Actors, Authors, and Auditors During a Period of Forty Years*, Philadelphia: Henry Carey Baird.

3

THEATRE ETIQUETTE (1880–2000)

> They have paid their money and if they don't like the play they have a right to say so.
> (*Cheers*) You have no right to bully them. (*Cheers and more shouting*).
>
> (Carl Hentschel, Print Illustrator, cited in Scott 1899, Vol II: 298)

Electric lighting was first introduced in theatres in London and New York in the 1880s. The new technology made it possible and much more practical to darken the lit auditoriums. From the late nineteenth century to around 2000, our perspective of the audience was also darkened. During these hundred or so years, audience performance changed radically. This was not only because of the gradual lowering of the houselights on the audience; demonstrative audience performance was discouraged in theatre etiquette rules that were proselytised from all four corners of the playhouse. The decades before and after 1880 were transition times between stage etiquette and theatre etiquette. A description of the changes in auditorium lighting and the implementation of theatre etiquette and its effects on audience performance are interspersed throughout this chapter.

By the early twentieth century, audiences had been almost abandoned in theatre histories. Whether this is because many expressive performers did, in actuality, abandon live theatre for the cinema or the sports stadiums, or because their performance, compared to the nineteenth century, was so subdued that it was not worth documenting, is difficult to determine. Because audience performance was constricted[1] and subdued by lighting and etiquette constraints, from around 1880 until the Second World War, audience ensembles explored novel ways to perform. Audiences changed from being loud, extroverted and demonstrative performers to playing the role of audience consumer. They embraced this newfound identity and some of their performances were incredibly emotive and flamboyant. This was the golden age of the fashionables and their sublime costumes. Audiences also took on new character roles at this time. The most infamous of these was the matinee girl who was pandered to by managers, courted by actors, satirised by critics and immortalised in songs, novels and plays.

After introducing the effects of reduced lighting and theatre etiquette on audience performance, the character performances of the matinee girls and other fashionable audience ensembles are discussed. These performances are seen as the audience's encore, their "last stand" before their demonstrative performance is almost completely suppressed. The second half of the twentieth century was a particularly constricted time for theatre audiences. My documentation of audience performance during these dark ages is noticeably sparse as behaviour in the auditoriums was generally restricted to laughter and applause.

From the Limelight into the Shadows

Although it was not until after the First World War when some select theatre audiences gave their final farewell performances in a lit auditorium, theatre managements were experimenting with various dimmed lighting states as early as 1859. The absence of a lit space in which to perform and to see and be seen had one of the most significant impacts on audience performance. On a practical level, as the theatre auditoriums were one by one darkened during the late nineteenth and early twentieth centuries, accounts of audience performance by audience members and actors diminish significantly. Audiences could still be heard, but were no longer seen.

Gas lighting was introduced into theatres in the 1810s and limelight for spotlighting in the late 1830s. Limelight was not, however, in regular use until the 1850s. Henneke argues that although the technology existed to dim the auditorium as early as 1850, theatre managers were in no rush to diffuse the lights. It was still of paramount concern that the beauty of ladies in the audience was well lit by the warm glow of the gaslights. One account from this period states that at the rise of the curtain the lights in the auditorium were actually "raised" (Henneke 1956: 58). As late as 1858, audiences were still calling for more light to be thrown on audience members to "give the ladies the opportunity of showing their pretty faces, as well as their beautiful costumes" ("Letter from Acorn" 1858: 121).

Avid playgoer Ethel Tweedie contested that it was actor/manager Henry Irving in London "who first plunged the auditorium into darkness to heighten the stage effect" (1904: 223) in 1872 (Henneke 1956: 61). Interestingly, Irving was inimical to electric lighting, which he found to "glare" and "flatten" (Nash 1939: 398). He continued to use gaslight in all of his productions, preferring its more subtle shades. From existing documentation, it is thought that the Savoy Theatre in London in 1881 and the Lyceum in New York in 1884 were the first theatres to be lit by electricity (Booth 1991: 90; Henneke 1956: 63). The infiltration of electric lighting and the subsequent darkening of theatre auditoriums heralded the demise of expressive audience performance. The dimming of lights always signals change of some description. Over the next three decades theatre audience performers, subservient to this lighting cue, gradually turned their gaze from each other onto the stage and slipped under the blankets of darkness that enveloped them.

Theatre Etiquette

While the darkening of auditoriums restrained the kinetic performance of the audience ensemble, almost concurrently, another perhaps more oblique institution was being imposed in the auditorium that began to occlude the effusive paralingual and verbal expressions of the audiences: theatre etiquette. More than the covert cues in the lighting, it was the enforcement of rules of theatre etiquette that restrained demonstrative audience performance. Just as stage etiquette emerged as a contract between audience and actors in the first half of the nineteenth century, theatre etiquette contracts were being distributed to audiences in printed and spoken word by theatre professionals. Up until the last third of the nineteenth century, stage etiquette was dictated by the audience, the traditional critics of the drama. With the introduction of theatre etiquette, the balance of power in the theatre changed from the audience members to the theatre professionals. In his memoirs, theatre critic Clement Scott compares the stage etiquette that existed in the first half of the nineteenth century to the theatre etiquette that pervaded the theatres 60 years later. In the 1840s, the "public dictated to the manager, who was the servant, not the master of the audience, and came on to the stage, hat in hand, to accept a verdict of approbation or reproof." By the end of the century, the manager was "grandiloquently speechifying to the public, dictating terms, protesting against fair criticism, and airing views and theories to his patrons" (1899, Vol I: 12). The inversion of the audience from master to servant by the 1900s, now with *their* hats in their hands, is particularly poignant in Scott's discourse.[2] The theatre professionals of the stage and the theatre management[3] began to dictate rules of theatre etiquette that would constrain demonstrative audience performance, almost entirely, for the next hundred years.

This was not the first time that theatre etiquette rules had been drawn up, posted or decreed, but it was the first time that they had been successfully enforced. Regulations prescribing a certain code of audience conduct for viewing theatrical performances have existed since the inception of organised theatre productions in ancient Greece and Rome. Documentation of audience etiquette rules from the ancient and pre-modern world include dramatists' prologues, police ordinances, personal letters, journals, magazines, travel guides and etiquette books. The Roman dramatist Plautus regularly appealed to his audiences on behalf of the manager in the prologues to his comedies to keep children quiet, not chatter about everyday affairs and abstain from any soliciting during performances. There are several petitions in medieval plays for audiences to keep silent during performances. In *The Mystery of St Etienne*, St Peter appeals to the audience to "listen peacefully for a little while, without making so much noise" (cited in Harris 1992: 152). A prologue by John Trantham in the middle of the seventeenth century entreated audiences to decline from throwing objects at the stage (Gurr 1996: 260). In the mid-eighteenth century, French police were stationed inside theatres to control any audience misbehaviour. This interestingly coincided with the introduction of the word "etiquette" into French parlance.

Pre-nineteenth-century accounts of theatre etiquette strictures are, however, sparse. It was not until the mid-nineteenth century, with the proliferation of general etiquette manuals, that theatre etiquette became a highly contested topic in American and British magazines, journals, letters and etiquette books.[4] As Blackadder (2003: 13) and Davis and Emeljanow argue (2001: 154), demonstrative audience behaviour was subdued in the second half of the nineteenth century during the gentrification of the theatres. In etiquette manuals of the mid-nineteenth century, "Talking and laughing aloud [and] mistimed applauding" in the theatre was considered "exceedingly vulgar" and immoral (Lunettes 1858: 167). "Boisterous applause and loud laughter" were thought ungentlemanly and it was considered un-ladylike to "indulge in extravagant gesture, laugh boisterously, flirt a fan conspicuously, toy with an eye-glass or an opera-glass, indulge in lounging attitudes [or] whisper aside" (Frost: 1869: 105, 106).

Interestingly, Trollope's *Domestic Manners of the Americans* can be seen as a harbinger of the demise of demonstrative performance. On its publication in 1832, Americans were incensed at being ridiculed by their cross-Atlantic cousins and made great efforts to disprove Trollope's accusations. Various accounts discuss incidences where audience members turned on their fellow performers and admonished their behaviour. In the Park Theatre in 1833, a fashionable in the boxes turned his back on the stage and

> [t]his was no sooner observed than a low murmur rose amongst the insulted part of the audience, which presently burst forth in to loud cries of "Trollope!" "Trollope" "turn him out," "throw him over," &c, and continued for several minutes.
>
> *(cited in Henneke 1956: 117)*

The habit of calling out "Trollope" for any "unseemly" audience performance mentioned in Trollope's condescending book was practised up until the mid-nineteenth century.

Records of the successful implementation of etiquette strictures in the theatres can be found around the mid-nineteenth century. Dickens gave a lengthy account of the successful gentrification of the Sadler Wells theatre on its change of management in 1844. To "quell [the] uproar" of the performing audience, disturbers of the peace, including "children in arms," were expelled from the theatre. Rules forbidding the use of bad language were "[p]rinted in great placards, and posted up in various conspicuous parts of the Theatre." These rules were also distributed in small hand-bills to each member of the gallery (1969: 347). Over the next 50 years, rules admonishing expressive performance were enforced. In theatres, these were printed in playbills, on placards, hand-bills, notices on the backs of seats and outlined in lectures by theatre managers before performances.

By the *fin de siècle* new contracts of behaviour emerged, formally and definitively pronouncing the termination of expressive audience behaviour. In 1902, *The Philadelphia Inquirer* published an article detailing the initiatives undertaken by each theatre manager in Philadelphia to purge theatres of their most obstreperous members, the gallery audience. In a "scheme to restore perfect order," etiquette rules included: no more whistling, howling and yelling, stamping feet or singing or whistling along to popular airs. Plain-clothes policemen were stationed in the gallery and any "attempts to revive old practices [were] promptly landed on by a stern minion of the law and, chances are, held on a charge of misdemeanour." In some theatres, lights were flashed onto the gallery to expose offenders, and others implemented a one-warning policy after which "if the offender persists, he is grabbed and put out." Some of the gallery audience's performance was incredibly disruptive, often warranting expulsion of the perpetrator from the theatre. Jeers and insulting remarks were sometimes hurled at the onstage actors and "well-dressed people in the boxes and the orchestra circle" ("The Gallery Gods" 1902: 3).

Along with the disruptive performances, the expressive contributions of the gallery were also subdued. *The Times* decreed in 1909 that

> the time when hissing was regarded, by course natures, as a fair alternative for applause [...] has passed in this country [...] the body of playgoers will not tolerate it as it disturbs their comfort and destroys the decorum which they believe should be preserved in the theatre.
>
> *(cited in Levine 1994: 194)*

In London theatres it was considered "deuced bad form" to laugh in the theatre, "the perfection of good manners [was] to sneer and yawn" (Scott 1899, Vol II: 188). By 1914, theatre etiquette rules in the *Ladies' Home Journal* considered audible whisperings during the play an "annoyance [that] amounts almost to a personal affront" and cautioned readers that if "there is heard in the general quiet a rustling or crackling of paper in the row behind you, as well as more or less audible moving of arms, you know candy is being passed" (Phillips 1914: 66). Only 50 years earlier rustling and crackling would have been drowned out by the general din, and arms moved constantly throughout performances to perform applause or wave hats.

Interestingly, while large audience gestures were being admonished in the auditorium, similar ameliorations were occurring onstage. With the rise of Realism and more naturalistic acting, actors were discouraged from using large gestures onstage. Not only were actors perturbed by the new "'modern' lighting" they were also expected to "curtail [...] their old theatrical gestures" (Carson 2014). In the nineteenth century, actors such as Henry Irving, Ellen Terry and Edwin Forrest were known for their idiosyncratic walks, excessive tears or hand gestures. These more demonstrative performances were now restrained and replaced by more contained and understated approaches to acting.

Yet it was this period of transition between stage and theatre etiquette that witnessed the most division between actors and audience members. During much of the nineteenth century the two troupes of performers worked together as co-creators, now hostilities were growing between the stage and the audience. Hostilities were also escalating among audience members. A sharp division began to grow between those that wanted to perform "appropriately" and adhered to etiquette rules, and those that desired to continue their demonstrative performance. It took much effort to quell this latter group and to establish what was considered by theatre professionals and some audience members to be a proper code of conduct.

There are numerous explanations for the tightening of theatre etiquette strictures in the second half of the nineteenth century that ultimately silenced theatre audiences. Levine argues that it was the rule makers at the turn of the century, the "arbiters of culture" who "disciplined and trained their audiences" in matters of artistic taste and propriety who censored audience response (1994: 184). Yet many of these arbiters of culture, the theatre professionals, were distressed by the notable changes in audience performance instigated by etiquette strictures. At the turn of the century, actor James Welsh bemoaned the apathy of London audiences:

> Sometimes they are so dull we cannot get hold of them at all until the Second Act, and sometimes it is even the end of the Second Act before they are roused to enthusiasm. [They] are always difficult to rouse to any expression of enthusiasm.
>
> *(cited in Tweedie 1904: 109, 110)*

In 1883, a British critic blamed the audiences themselves for their inertness: "[A]n every-day theatrical audience is chiefly composed of a very dull set of people […] who object to being emotionally excited" (cited in Blackadder 2003: 14). While some arbiters of culture lamented the successful constraint of audience performance, others revelled in the quieter auditoriums.

Just as the rules of stage etiquette had been communicated to actors and managers from the auditorium, theatre etiquette was often dictated to the audience from the stage. Theatre professionals, particularly managers, gave lengthy discourses on theatre etiquette in pre- and post-performance speeches. In 1898, British actor Henry Miller incensed by "a ripple of inappropriate laughter from the audience that briefly interrupted his performance" berated the audience after his curtain call, likening their response to that of hyenas (Butsch 2000: 80). Interestingly, audience members themselves would often rebuke each other for their unruly performances.[5] In 1916, an audience member wrote a delightful treatise against men that "catapult into their seats without warning." To rectify this bad behaviour, the female author choreographed an elaborate set of stage directions to transport male audience performers from auditorium right to left: "[A]ll sitters could rise, belongings held firmly and compactly […]. Entrant meanwhile could turn himself sidewise and prepare to glide gently in, elbows close to sides" ("The Trampling Playgoer").

Audience members were sometimes so incensed about their newly thwarted authority they banded together to stand up for their rights. In one noteworthy case, a gentleman in the stalls, the president of the Playgoers' Club, Carl Hentschel, admonished a manager for singling out the performances of the gallery members in a lecture from the stage during a production at the London Princess's Theatre in 1899. Hentschel continued debating with the manager, arguing that the gallery members were "bôna-fide people [who] have a right to express their opinion." The debate concluded with the audience delivering the final piece of dialogue: "let future audiences decide" (cited in Scott 1899, Vol II: 298, 299). This was, however, an isolated incident, and in the century to follow the "future" audiences would no longer have the privilege of delivering the last line, or any lines.

One of the reasons that the execution of theatre etiquette was so successful, even though its enactment had failed in past centuries, was because its implementation was concurrent with the gradual dimming of the lights in the auditorium. The lights were dimming, rules of behaviour were inculcated, the chasm between stage and audience was widening, but you cannot keep a good audience down.

The Galleryites

Theatre etiquette rules and darkened auditoriums took time to be established and during this implementation period, ever versatile and resourceful audience performers found new ways to construct their identity. During this time, some noteworthy audience ensembles survived and several new ensembles emerged. Some of these ensembles were adept at playing within the rules of theatre etiquette, often courting the popular press to sanction or at least review their performances.

An ensemble reigned in the galleries whose performance as critics of the drama rivalled that of their predecessors the b'hoys: the galleryites. The galleryites were predominantly women and their performance contrasted significantly with the fashionables. The new gallery audiences were praised by theatre critics, actors and managers alike for their "mental curiosity" and for being "responsive, sincere and discerning." The galleryites gave a distinctive, almost scripted performance. *Harper's Weekly* argued that they were

> the most enthusiastic in their applause, the most prompt to laugh where the laugh comes in, the first to show signs of boredom when the play is tedious or the humour stupid, [...] responsiveness is one of the greatest virtues of the gallery habitué.
>
> *(Pollock 1914: 401)*

These goddesses of the gallery were considered the backbone of the theatre. Through their performances, the galleryites formed a gregarious interpretive community of critics that would, at times, influence the public reception of a play. Articles in *Theatre Magazine* in 1919 and 1920 credited the voice of the gallery audiences for the success or the failure of productions.[6] As one galleryite argued:

> It is we who applaud when the show is good and hiss when it ought to be taken off the boards. The box-office man knows us and so do the actors. Our fifty cent pieces are the real money. [...] The leading lady knows where her salary is coming from.
>
> *(cited in Butsch 2000: 128)*

The actors implicitly understood that the galleryites were their critics. This sometimes fraught relationship was occasionally enacted during performances in exchanges between gallery and stage. In a 1904 London production of *The Flute of Pan* after a chorus of booing from the gallery, the lead actress Olga Nethersole appealed to the gallery "with tears streaming down her face and lift[ed] her arms in mute appeal" ("Gallery Gods 'Boo'" 1904). This was to no avail, the booing continued. Gallery audiences not only invested in the drama but were a crucial part of the drama, actively contributing to the theatrical event by playing the role of critic.

The Fashionables

One of the most resilient ensembles to survive and adapt to their new restricted performing conditions was the fashionables. In response to the birth of the commodity culture of the late nineteenth and early twentieth century, the fashionables established a new role in the theatre: audience as consumer. Although their decorative role had already been established, the fashionables took more of a starring role in the theatres in this period than at any other time. Contemporary consumerism in the theatre has its beginnings at this time in the construction of identity through the purchasing of social status. Although it can be argued that the role of the audience as consumer can be traced back to the inception of Western theatre, the concept of consumerism as we perceive it today had its birth in the Industrial Revolution of the late nineteenth century and the early modernist advent of mass-consumer goods. The role of audience as consumer was not only performed but celebrated by the rising bourgeois class, the fashionables. In purchasing a ticket in the New York theatre orchestra or London stalls, the fashionables were not only purchasing a cultural product, this product confirmed their social status. Attendance at the theatre was an opportunity to display the products that signified their identity as fashionable. It was fashionable to wear the latest costumes from the stage. It was fashionable to be seen in the theatre. It was fashionable to arrive late and leave early. It was fashionable to talk during performances. And it was fashionable to sleep during the second act. The most significant of their display products was their costume.

The playhouses of the late nineteenth and early twentieth century, both stage and auditorium, were platforms for the display of the latest dress fashions. In London, theatre professionals, including playwrights such as George Bernard Shaw, catered specifically to the fashion-conscious female and male audiences by staging plays that contained a discourse on fashion. An article in a millinery magazine of the time stated that it was not uncommon in the theatre for audiences "to applaud a successful toilette as they would a pirouette or bit of eloquent by-play" (cited in Rappaport 2000: 185). This is a pertinent demonstration of the emergent role of audience as consumer. The audience is no longer applauding the acting, the writing or the content, but the consumer items onstage.

The theatrical event became a shop window at which the audience consumer could browse while referring to the latest catalogue: the theatre programme. Illustrations of the onstage costumes were included in programmes alongside advertisements for couturiers and millinery houses. Florence Alexander, the wife of actor/manager of the St James in London, argued that "people went to the St. James's *before* ordering a new gown" (cited in Kaplan and Stowell 1994: 9). Department stores such as Lord and Taylor in New York and Harrods and Selfridges in London displayed all the latest onstage fashions. Audience members identifying or empathising with particular characters onstage would purchase their costumes and then wear them to subsequent theatre performances. The perimeters of stage and auditorium blurred as audience members emerged as characters in costume performing in the audience.

Not only did audience costumes replicate those on stage, the *mise en scene* was also sometimes reproduced. While illustrious society couturiers were invited to design onstage costumes, interior decorators were occasionally appointed to build sets *and* refurbish auditoriums. At the recently renovated London Criterion Theatre in 1879, Kaplan and Stowell emphasise that the audience "were aware of settling into seats reupholstered by the same hands responsible for the comfort of their *onstage* doubles" (1994: 39). During this period the consumer-conscious fashionables, mimicking the onstage fashionables, reclaimed some of their limelight and audience autonomy. It is not surprising, therefore, that the fashionables were hostile to the darkening of theatre auditoriums. The lights were gradually being dimmed on their runway.

As discussed in Chapter Two, throughout the nineteenth century, critical reviews of plays in newspapers and magazines were saturated with descriptions of the audience costume and performance. In some reviews, the play, playwright and actors were rarely mentioned. This practice continued into the early twentieth century and critics indulged in flowing descriptions of audience costume and settings. In the audience at the Union Theatre of 1876, "Intellect, beauty and fashion were represented and the toilettes of the ladies were exceedingly elegant" (*Spirit of the Times* 1876: 193). In Boston in 1874, "The presence of ladies […] brightens the house, flicking it here and there with pretty tints" (*Spirit of the Times* 1874: 360). Descriptions of audience performance also proliferated. Arthur Pollock argued in 1914 that it was a regular practice for a "theatrical reporter" to describe the response of an audience. The reporter "likes to say the gallery roared or the gallery groaned or the gallery gave vent to ribald comments or disconcerting catcalls" (Pollock 1914: 401). This not only illustrates the authority of the audience as critics of the drama, but also suggests that the audience's repertoire of actions continued to be recognised as a performance. The fashionables did not pose a threat to the stage and its newly established power structures. This is one of the reasons that their performances were allowed to flourish.

The Matinee Girl, the Stage-Door Johnny and the Tired Business Man

New stock characters emerged that attempted to continue demonstrative performance in the auditorium. The matinee girl, the stage-door Johnny and the tired business man gave very distinctive performances. All of these troupes were sub-ensembles of the fashionables and their performances received mixed reviews from their critics. The matinee girl had a long run of her performances in Broadway and West End auditoriums, playing her role from 1885 up until the First World War. The matinee girl always had an onstage love interest – a matinee idol – that she venerated. The matinee girl paid homage to her idol by attentive glances, unrestrained tears and hero worship. In behaviour similar to the followers of the earlier nineteenth century, she would visit stage doors after performances to chat with her idol, stroke his costume or procure an autograph.[7] The matinee girl cast herself as the heroine of the play empathising with every emotion her hero endured. Matinee girls often took this role so seriously that they sent scented notes called "mash letters" or violets to their idols, arranging private trysts and meetings, and sometimes even propositions of marriage. *Munsey's Magazine* in 1898 discussed how one matinee girl "described the costume she would wear at the matinee" (Munsey 1898: 39) in one such note, so that her hero would recognise her in the audience.

The girls not only worshipped male idols, but also star actresses. They collected and shared pictures and postcards of their favourite idols. The postcards presented the actresses in luxurious costumes portraying contemporary constructions of femininity that, as Veronica Kelly argues, catered to the "female desire for self-fashioning" (2004: 111). In this growing age of consumerism, theatre merchandise was first introduced for the matinee and gallery girl. Although sold outside theatres, leather-bound "hero books" and postcard albums could be purchased for audience members to display postcards, reviews and programmes, and to record notes about their idols (Butsch 2000: 124, Kelly 2004: 109). In the first two decades of the twentieth century, themed theatre merchandise, from chocolate soldiers to purple silk stockings and hats, were distributed to female audience members in New York (Schweitzer 2009: 2, 88). In what could be considered an early theatrical merchandise stand, in 1913, a "New York Store" was set up in the New York theatre offering a range of gaudy glassware such as ice-cream dishes for purchase. Similar to other audience ensembles that had characterised identities – the b'hoys and the galleryites – the matinee girl and gallery girls were part of a community. The girls formed clubs sharing their common dedication to the theatre or to particular idols and circulated merchandise. They often organised charity performances to raise money for causes such as earthquake victims and those living in settlement houses.

The matinee girl had several names – "Matinee Millies," "Matinee Marthas" and "Matinee Madames" – and her own dialogue that she performed sometimes during performances: "Isn't he just darling?"; "I think he's the most handsomest man I ever saw"; "It must be grand to be an actress" (Carroll 1972: 15, 16). *Munsey's Magazine* dramatises an incident after a matinee performance of *Bonnie Prince Charlie* where "a young woman burst into her club […] 'Oh, girls,' she cried, 'I've cried three handkerchiefs limp, perfectly limp!'" (1898: 35). As can be seen from this example, similar to the Mose character of the b'hoys, the matinee girl became a character in her own right, with scripted dialogue that was memorialised in plays, novels and songs of the period.

The stage-door Johnnies were the male equivalent of the matinee girl. Although they formed a smaller group, they were distinguished by their costume. The London Johnnies could be identified by "wearing the same Malmaison carnations in [their] buttonholes" (Williams 1892: 249), and the New York Johnnies by their shining silk hats, their bouquets and fur coats. According to a New York stage-door attendant "Dad" Packard who received generous tips from the Johnnies for delivering notes to actresses, the original Johnnies were "college boys, clerks and a sprinklin' of middle-aged duffers" ("Stage-door Johnny" 1922). Like the matinee girls, the Johnnies were also depicted in plays and musical comedies such as *Sally, Irene and Mary.* By 1922 new breeds of wealthier Johnnies in limousines replaced the sidewalk Johnnies.

Unlike the matinee girl and stage-door Johnnies, the tired business man only played a minor role in the playhouse in this period. It was significant enough, however, to warrant comment. The tired business man was satirised in newspapers as being "dull and vacuous" ("Topics of the Times" 1917) and condemned for his lack of discernment; he went to the theatre purely to be entertained. Many of his predecessors in the nineteenth century also only went to be entertained, so it is noteworthy that this character is singled out. The tired business man epitomised the disinterested fashionable that was easily distracted. Pollock cited one account where one of these characters "the jaded, the bored, the blasé" asked an usher what the name of the play was and, on finding out it was *Hamlet,* enquired as to the author (1914: 401). The tired business man often only attended the theatre to humour his "date." The date also had an idiosyncratic performance: she kept up a constant dialogue of chatter throughout the play. During these performances, the tired business man played a supporting role. This distinctive character enjoyed a much longer run in the audience than the matinee girl. By the 1950s in Britain, he was accompanied by "the tired domestic woman" (Trewin 1954: 225).

Guest Performers

In theatres where the auditorium lights remained ablaze, guest audience performers could still be spotted in the boxes. Visits by royalty or other celebrities became even larger events in the auditorium during this period. Audiences would give standing ovations for celebrities and even applaud them on the sidewalk outside the theatres. The fashionables did not like "to find their meditations" on the royal's box or some celebrity "interrupted by a riffle of applause." In London when royalty were present, "the singing of the anthem [God Save the Queen] was the real feature of the evening" (Scott 1899, vol. I: 252). Tweedie detailed the performance of King Edward VII "and his beautiful Queen: […] They laugh and chat between the acts, and no one applauds more enthusiastically. […] They use their opera glasses freely [and] nod to their friends" (1904: 262). The attendance of guest performers in the auditorium was a conscious reminder, to the actors and the audience members, of the magnetic presence and theatrical centrality of the audience in the playhouse.

When ordinary civilians became guest performers, which occurred during the First World War, almost entire audiences took starring roles as guest performers. At different times from 1914 to 1918 up to three-quarters of the audience members of mainstream theatres were costumed in khaki. As Gordon Williams argues, the

"Tommies" in the audience "were part of the entertainment for the fashionable matinee audiences." The servicemen were not only demonstrative performers but often made "direct comments, to the huge delight of the rest of the house" to the stage (2003: 4). In 1914, a guest performer in khaki responding to a line delivered by an actor ascended the stage and commenced singing with his onstage co-performer (Williams 2003: 49). All of these audience ensembles – the galleryites, the fashionables and the guest performers – although constrained by theatre etiquette rules, found ways to overcome or even use the etiquette rules to their advantage.

Props: The Hat

One of the fashionables' most effective vehicles of protest against etiquette strictures, and an indispensable accessory, was the hat. Similar to the peanut in the last chapter, the hat deserves special consideration as an important signifier and constructor of audience authority[8] and identity. The hat was used as a display item and as a prop. Numerous cartoons satirised the fashionables' hats, and the hat was lauded in plays of the period, such as *Tilda's New Hat*, and songs in musical comedies, rising to fame in the hit song "Hats" popularised in the 1909 production of *Our Miss Gibbs*. The hat, by this point in audience history, has been one of the most contested and celebrated audience accessories and props. Its notoriety and prolongation far exceeded that of other props such as the fan, the handkerchief and the cane that had been just passing fads.

In the early nineteenth century, the hat was worn in the theatre to guard against the cold, missiles thrown down from the gallery above – such as peanut shells, orange peels or bits of apples – or as a protector from the wax that would occasionally drip from the candles in the chandeliers. Even after auditoriums were heated and the pelting from the galleries was discontinued, audience members continued to wear hats which obstructed views of the stage. "Down, Down, Hats Off!" was the opening line of audience members at the commencement of onstage performances right up until the 1850s (Henneke 1956: 124–26). One of the most common uses of the hat in theatres was waving. Hats were frequently waved in the air to cheer actors.

Hats increased in size at various points throughout the nineteenth century, but the glorious matinee hat upstaged all other antecedents in size, ornament, infamy and status. From the 1890s till the 1910s, large brimmed hats often two or three times as large as women's heads were worn to the theatres and kept on during performances (Schweitzer 2009: 48) much to the consternation of other audience members and actors alike. The hat was a marker of social status;[9] the more decorative or fashionable the hat, the more attention drawn to the audience performer. The gaze of the audience was distracted from the stage and directed towards the decorative hats festooned with feathers, sequins, ribbons and flowers. Matinee girls hoped to attract the gaze of their idol with attention-drawing head plumage.

Etiquette rules admonishing the wearing of hats in the auditorium were posted everywhere including on the backs of seats. Three states in America successfully passed "high hat" laws, prohibiting hat wearing during performances (Schweitzer

2009: 48). As discussed above, when a manager stood before an audience with his hat in hand, it was a sign of deference to the audience. By refusing to remove their hats, audience members retained some of their lost authority. In a stand of defiance in New York, playwright Channing Pollock observed, "There were men that took off their coats and kept on their hats for no better reason than they were supposed to do neither" (cited in Henneke 1956: 127). Hat performances for display, protest or valorisation were a cogent signifier of audience autonomy.

Since some theatres continued to keep their auditoriums lit, during the period between 1880 and the First World War, many of the discussed character ensembles enjoyed extended runs of their performances. The star audience characters of this period – the fashionables – asserted their authority through playing the role of the consumer. It was a role they relished and perfected. Despite nascent tensions between stage and audience, the fashionables found new ways to align their performance with that of their onstage co-performers such as wearing identical costumes. The matinee girls and stage-door Johnnies dreamed their way into the stories onstage and cast themselves as thwarted lovers and pining love-interests, often continuing their performances at stage doors and in playgoers' clubs. As long as they could be seen in the auditorium, their performances thrived. They were the product of the gaze. Changes in lighting and the continued enforcement of etiquette strictures after the First World War changed demonstrative audience performance considerably.

The Auditorium Fades to Black

All visual displays in the auditorium during onstage performances were abruptly terminated when the audience's performance space finally went to black. By the 1920s, darkness settled over all theatre auditoriums.[10] Audience members and theatre professionals had mixed feelings about the black auditoriums. Dante scholar William Warren Vernon and journalist Henry Walbrook were devoted playgoers. In his text *A Playgoers Wanderings*, Walbrook states that Vernon "much disliked the latter-day darkening of the theatre on the rising of the curtain and the consequent difficulty in reading a programme or even making a note on it, and indeed it is hard to see the advantage of the new custom" (1926: 127).

Opportunities for co-creation were also severely restricted by the darkening of the lights. Erwin Piscator argued in 1940 that he was ashamed when actors looked over the heads of the audience refusing to meet their eye. When, however, "the eye meets the audience [t]he whole stage seems to come alive [which] brings back a vital contact and a greater reality of the action" (cited in Lilley 2010: 47). This fertile opportunity for co-creation is not possible if the gaze of the onstage performer cannot see that of its audience co-performer.

The darkening of the theatres combined with the enforcement of theatre etiquette strictures anesthetised demonstrative audience performance. *The New York Times* announced in 1927 that "the galleries are restrained, sedate" ("Gallery Gods in Fur Coats"). A prophetic decree from *The Philadelphia Inquirer* of 1902 that "the species gallery god is doomed to become as scarce as the extinct dodo" was fully realised ("The Gallery Gods": 3). Unsettled, perhaps, by the comparatively uncanny stillness, in the 1920s in America there were a few eulogies to the vivacious audience performer and one meagre attempt to re-stage a command performance. Several newspaper articles memorialised the past expressive performances of audiences and two theatres opened in Hoboken in which audiences were encouraged to boo, hiss and cheer (Butsch 2000: 128). Orchestras had been expelled from the theatres in the early 1920s because they only entertained matinee girls and "country cousins" and encouraged people to sing along with them causing more disturbances in the auditoriums. By the end of that same decade, three critics who had been instrumental in excluding orchestras admitted they had made an error and appealed for their re-instatement (Henneke 1956: 149). Arthur Hornblow lamented that the auditoriums were no longer dressed by their occupants and complained that the boxes in the 1920s were now filled with "a motley, miscellaneous crowd that only makes the house look drab" (1924: 7).

These reminiscences were, however, overwhelmed by several attempts to abrogate any remnants of expressive performance that still lingered in many theatres. Critic Robert Benchley engaged in what can be seen as one of the most vitriolic attacks on audience performance in the 1920s. In several issues of *Life*, and encouraged by a letter sent to him by playwright Shaw,[11] he discussed what he termed an "anti-audience campaign" (1920: 1188). The antithesis of the nineteenth-century reviewers, Benchley reviewed what he considered to be the bad performances of audiences. He waged "warfare […] against the coughers, the crooners, the nine o'clock arrivals" and those that "laugh, whether the script calls for laughs or not" (1921: 18). In another article, he admonished audience members that "have expressed their feelings to the utmost by beating their palms together" and who, once they have "gorged themselves with encores […] look about them for approval" (1920: 1189). Benchley's remarks were extremely misogynist at times, singling out women audience performers for their laughter and dialogue.

Theatre etiquette rules were very prescriptive by this time and audience members were asked to follow detailed directions. The gentleman in a party of playgoers

> follows the ladies down the aisle. Unless he checks his coat and hat, he should take them off in the vestibule, or remove his hat before reaching his seat. He should place his hat under his chair, and his coat should be folded and laid across his knees or placed in the back of his seat. The ladies should remove their wraps as soon as they arrive at the play house, unless they wear capes, in which case, they may simply let them slip down behind them.
>
> *("Etiquette of the Theatre" 1918: 10)*

This is just the opening in this article of elaborate instructions which, to a twenty-first-century theatre-goer, reads more like a comedy of manners.

Actors were divided in their responses to the more constrained audiences. Some exploited their new-found authority and admonished the audience for what they deemed to be bad behaviour. In a Broadway performance of *Macbeth* in 1928, Florence Reed "paused in her lines to demand the ejection of two [...] disturbers" (Stanton 1929: 87). Other actors questioned the loss of relationship:

> Now that we are rid of the friendliness of the spectator which used to seem such a nuisance, we prove how dear it was to us, and how much we miss it, by the efforts we are making to regain it and by our constant preoccupation with it.
>
> *(Jouvet 1936: 7)*

It is noteworthy that the working-class audiences of the 1930s continued with their demonstrative performances. The Federal Theatre Project set up affordable theatre for members of the working class who felt too intimidated or too impoverished to attend Broadway plays.[12] Critic Richard Lockridge contrasted their performances to those that attended Broadway productions: "It is an engaging audience. Its face is not frozen. It is not sitting on its hands. When it hisses, it is not self-conscious and when it cheers, it means it" (cited in O'Connor 1985: 182).

Small pockets of revivals of expressive audience performance occasionally occurred. During the Second World War, reductions in ticket prices attracting younger and more diverse audiences encouraged a return of demonstrative audience performance including a short run of booing and audience dialogue,[13] which was swiftly curtailed by the critics (Rebellato 1999: 106). Vitriol towards audience performance was still prevalent in some critical reviews and occasionally from the stage. New etiquette rules were enforced to inhibit even small audience gestures. In 1952 Sybil Thorn-dike commented, "Sometimes I feel like spitting at the audience because of the noise made by unwrapping chocolates" (cited in Rebellato 1999: 108). Other actors such as Clifton Webb who felt that audience response was their "bread and butter" complained that audiences had lost the art of laughing: "New Yorkers are apt to confine themselves to genteel snickers" (1947: 233).

During the 1950s and 60s the rules of theatre etiquette were firmly inscribed in the audience's consciousness. In Britain in the 1950s lectures were given to educate the audience, specifically younger audiences, in rules of theatre etiquette. During the late 1950s George Devine, director of the English Stage Company at the Royal Court theatre, began a campaign, equally as polemical as Benchley's but more successful, to curb demonstrative audience behaviour and obliterate any vestige of the audience's authority as critics. Associate Director of the Royal Court Lindsay Anderson decreed in 1957 that every programme should have "Judge not" inscribed as a warning to audiences.[14] Interestingly, this period also witnessed the abrogation of the standing and singing of "God Save the Queen" in the auditorium, a performance that had been given by audiences in Britain since 1745.

Not all theatre professionals welcomed this change. Sartre comments in this period: "What has become standard is the silence during the scenes: no coughs, no handkerchiefs. Which means that people are paying attention. [...] I am not sure I welcome this attention because the audience is not at ease" (1976: 234). Even the coughing and snivelling was being policed. The audience's performance had been restricted, their stage darkened; they were, perhaps, not at ease. Sartre's comment about audience attention is significant. Reminiscent of Plato's comment about the actor Ion giving his "full attention" to the countenance of the audience, we find at this time in theatre history that attention has been inverted and the audience are now giving their full, undivided attention to the countenance of the actors. American theatre critic John Steinbeck observed, "It seems to me that London audiences go to the theatre with the intention of trying to enjoy the play. The people sit quietly, they listen, and sometimes they applaud" (1952: 5). The changes in audience performance are strikingly obvious in this account.

Here, we are in the dark ages of audience performance. The following is an account of the audible audience text that the audience were allowed to perform over the next few decades:

> Performance commences.
> *Some intermittent laughter.*
>
> ✱✱✱
>
> Performance concludes.
> *Polite applause.*

There are, of course, exceptions during this period of passivity. During the opening of John Osborne's *The World of Paul Slickey* at the Palace Theatre in 1959, booing commenced during the performance and continued until the end. Noel Coward and John Gielgud were among those booing. One of the cast members, Adrienne Corrie, performed a two-fingered gesture to the booing and catcalling gallery first-nighters. At the opening night of *Macbeth* at the Old Vic in 1980, audience laughter and boos were performed throughout the play and swelled to a climax at the curtain call. No doubt, there are other exceptions. These demonstrative performances were, however, predominantly isolated incidences.[15]

Roy, a cockney, has been attending the theatre for 77 years. When asked if he had seen audiences change over that time he stated that when he went to the theatre before the Second World War, "It was exciting to go because of all [the] interaction." After the war it was "more subdued [...] the Brits still have this sense of humour, and this thing, this etiquette" (2014, PI). Interestingly, Roy identified etiquette as part of the audience performance that became *de rigueur* after the war. Other audience members concur:

> We weren't brought up to be [noisy]. You sat in the theatre quietly and you didn't do anything that would draw any attention to you. We were very contained.
>
> *(Kay 2014, Sydney audience member, PI)*

> We never used to, in our day, have food and drink.
>
> *(Doreen 2014, London audience member, PI)*

> Older audiences are brought up to be disciplined and silent.
>
> *(Maggie 2013, Toronto audience member, PI)*

It was during this period that audiences were, as Blau argues, "backed into the dark of a spectatorial space and granted there a newly privileged and statutory anonymity" (1990: 356). If audiences were to break out of the stupor that had settled definitively over auditoriums – if, indeed, they even desired to perform again – the invitation needed to be extended from the stage. And it was.

Musical Audiences from the 1980s

It is not until we reach the explosion of the spectacle musicals in the 1980s that we begin to hear a few murmurings from audience members. Similar to their co-performers onstage, audiences of musicals have always had a larger repertoire of actions to perform than audiences at plays. Newspaper articles of the 1980s make cursory references to audience applause and laughter during the inception of the megamusicals in the London and New York theatres.[16] Some musicals tentatively invited the audience to play a more performative role, luring them out of the shadows into better lit spaces. Some characters crossed the footlights into the spectatorial space, teasing the audience to break out of their inertia. Some actors went so far as to play the role of the audience, applauding the audience at the curtain call. These were small, but significant steps.

Intervals remained, however, the primary sites for audience performance. Not only was the spectatorial space of the auditorium no longer a site for performance, in some West End and most Broadway theatres, audiences had been deprived of their backstage area – the foyers – and had to, and continue to, take refuge on the sidewalks. The sidewalk had also replaced the smoking room, and many sole audience members congregated there to breathe in the fresh air.

During the mid- to late 1980s, a girl played her ukulele during intervals outside productions such as *Phantom of the Opera, Les Miserables, 42nd St* and *Broadway Bound*. She had an eye for audience performance as she was an actor and was used to observing the audience from the peek hole behind the curtain onstage. In addition to the one-person smoker's performances on the sidewalk, the girl observed several others: critical reviews, business deals, lovers' embraces and quarrels and occasional singalongs. The singalongs were sometimes performed in unison with or in opposition to the girl, as audience members naturally came out of the theatres humming well-known tunes. The critical reviews were often heated. On some occasions items other than coins or notes were thrown inside the girl's ukulele case. Ticket stubs were sometimes left, usually accompanied by some sort of exasperated dialogue such as "worst musical I've ever seen," "see if you can make sense out of it" or "you can sing better then that lot in there" – which was a back-handed compliment because the girl clearly could not.

Consequently, the girl attended the second half of many productions on Broadway and observed audience performance in the auditorium, which she found uninteresting compared with their sidewalk performance. Most audiences continued to observe etiquette strictures and sat very still in their seats. Applause at the conclusion of performances was, however, enthusiastic. The girl was surprised to see the actors applauding the audience at the end of a performance of *Starlight Express*. The audience performance did not appear to be worthy of this honour. Occasionally laughter rose above the level of a titter, particularly when an incident happened onstage or in the audience that was not scripted. Audience costume was a combination of smart-casual and casual, except on opening nights where the audience sparkled as much as the onstage actors.

One night, a phenomenon occurred in the auditorium which startled and delighted the girl. The actors crossed the footlights and start meowing and purring at members of the audience. They sniffed at audience members, rubbed against them and sometimes crawled over them. They hissed at those that made noises unwrapping sweets and invited others up onstage to dance with them. During interval, audience members went up onstage to make contact with the characters. Some audience members were unaccustomed to performing, and others, not having performed in years, were a bit rusty. They giggled in embarrassment. Audience members that were new to the theatre eagerly participated.[17] The girl had never witnessed an auditorium audience do anything except laugh and applaud. She was tickled. This records my own experiences of audiences in New York in the 1980s.[18]

Some megamusicals such as *Cats* began to bridge the gulf that had developed between the stage and the audience and, consequently, the two troupes of performers. Audiences still continued their role as consumers, but in a new context in the purchasing of merchandise. So overwhelmed were audiences by the glitz and technology of the spectacle musicals that for a decade or so they could only sit in stunned silence, awed by the explosion of crashing chandeliers, roller-skating actors and the whirring of helicopters, where the set became the onstage star. There was no need for etiquette rules as any verbal audience performance was drowned out by high-amped soundtracks.

By the turn of the twenty-first century, audiences were beginning to awake from their initial surprise at the spectacle. Invitations from the stage were becoming more frequent and glimmers of light were seen in the auditorium. Audience roles were emerging, some reminiscent of nineteenth- and early twentieth-century performance. New audience ensembles began to form: critics, communities, consumers and co-creators. The introduction of a new technology in the theatre, electric lighting in the 1880s, had ushered in the demise of expressive audience performance. The introduction of new technologies in the auditorium in the turn of the millennium heralded novel ways for audiences to perform. The first decade of the twenty-first century was a time when the concept of audience performance was re-imagined.

Notes

1 Continuing on from the previous chapter, I have excluded accounts of audiences of Variety theatre, Vaudeville, Minstrel shows, Burlesque, Pantomime and Opera. In genres such as Pantomime, audience performance continued to be demonstrative.

2 The Old Price riots of 1809, where the audience rioted against raised ticket prices for three months, also concluded with an apology from the manager and a lowering of the ticket prices. Audience sovereignty such as this would not be successful in the late nineteenth century as supremacy began to shift from the audience to the stage.

3 It is important to note that many theatres continued the actor/manager system throughout the nineteenth century. "Speechifying" was, therefore, often undertaken by actors who were also managers, incensed by what they considered distracting audience behaviour during their own performances.

4 The *Quarterly Review* reviewed more than ten etiquette books between 1835 and 1837, all of which were reprinted over ten times (Hayward 1837: 396).

5 See H. R. G. (1911: 6) and Browne Matinee (1917: X7).

6 For several citations from these articles see Butsch (2000: 126–29).

7 The matinee girl's visits to stage doors and obsession with star performers caused a moral panic in this period. In this, the matinee girl was, perhaps, the original groupie, a predecessor of the 1960s female rock and pop fan in search of sexual liaisons with her favourite singer. For the matinee girl the encounters were, however, rarely realised.

8 In the Old Price riots of 1809, as a form of protest during one performance, audience members stood up at the commencement of the play and donned their hats, and sat down at the conclusion taking their hats back off their heads. See Baer (1992: 173).

9 The Merry Widow hat worn by actress Lily Elsie in the 1907 production of the operetta *The Merry Widow* was an overnight hit and became a marker of social status amongst the fashionables for the subsequent three years. The hat sometimes reached three feet or more in diameter and was festooned with feathers, roses and even stuffed birds.

10 It was not, and continues not to be, pitch darkness. Ambient light was thrown on the audience from the stage lighting, and the introduction of compulsory lit fire-exit signs later in the century also cast light into the auditorium.

11 Shaw sent Benchley a letter in 1920 inciting Benchley to "start a campaign against the interruption of plays by applause and laughter" (Benchley 1920: 1188).

12 In later decades, various theatres in London such as Theatre Royal Stratford East in the 1950s set up initiatives to make theatre accessible to those from a low socio-economic background.

13 Opening nights were, however, an exception. In Britain, booing, and the walk-out in America were still regularly practised in the 1950s (Trewin 1954: 217–22). Occasional dialogue was also heard from the galleries (Trewin 1954: 223).

14 For a full account of Devine's campaign and its consequences see Rebellato (1999: 109–13).

15 I am indebted to actor Ian Cullen for sharing these anecdotes with me.

16 See Owen (1979) and "British Musicals Beat Broadway" (1983).

17 These accounts are all taken from actual audience experiences of the 1980s production of *Cats*. Some were taken from my own experiences, others are recorded in Tepper (2013: 87–94). Some "new" audience members attending theatre for the first time were disappointed to find that all subsequent theatre productions did not include interactivity (Tepper 2013: 92).

18 I also street performed for two weeks in front of West End theatres in London, where I saw the second half of the London production of *Les Miserables*. Audience performance was very similar. Just as an aside, while I have seen the second half of *Phantom* six times, I have never seen it in its entirety.

References

Baer, Marc (1992) *Theatre and Disorder in Late Georgian England*, Oxford: Clarendon.
Benchley, Robert (1920) "Drama," *Life* 23 December.
——(1921) "Drama: Destroy the Audience!" *Life* 22 December.
Blackadder, Neil (2003) *Performing Opposition: Modern Theatre and the Scandalised Audience*, Westport: Praeger.

Blau, Herbert (1990) *The Audience*, Baltimore: Johns Hopkins UP.

Booth, Michael (1991) *Theatre in the Victorian Age*, Cambridge: Cambridge UP.

"British Musicals Beat Broadway" (1983) *The Globe and Mail* 6 December.

Browne Matinee, Graham (1917) "IN THE MAIL BAG.; Down with the Noisy Playgoer," *The New York Times*, 4 February.

Butsch, Richard (2000) *The Making of American Audiences*, Cambridge: Cambridge UP.

Carroll, David (1972) *The Matinee Idols*, New York: Arbor House.

Carson, John (2014) cited in email from Trevor Danby, 14 August.

Davis, Jim and Victor Emeljanow (2001) *Reflecting the Audience: London Theatregoing, 1840–1880*, Hatfield: Hertfordshire UP.

Dickens, Charles (1969) *The Uncollected Writings of Charles Dickens: Household Words 1850–1859*, ed. Harry Stone, London: Allen Lane.

"Etiquette of the Theatre" (1918) *The Half-century Magazine*, vol. 5, no. 4.

Frost, S. A. (1869) *Frost's Laws and By-Laws of American Society: A Condensed but Thorough Treatise on Etiquette and its Usages in America*, New York: Dick and Fitzgerald.

"Gallery Gods 'Boo' Mrs Craigie's Play; Olga Nethersole Hysterical, but Fails to Arouse Sympathy" (1904) *The New York Times* 13 November.

"Gallery Gods in Fur Coats" (1927) *The New York Times* 6 March.

Gurr, Andrew (1996) *Playgoing in Shakespeare's London*, 2nd edn, Cambridge: Cambridge UP.

Harris, John Wesley (1992) *Medieval Theatre in Context*, London: Routledge.

Hayward, Abraham (1837) "Codes of Manners and Etiquette," *Quarterly Review*, vol. 59: 396.

Henneke, Ben Graf (1956) *The Playgoer in America*. Ph.D thesis. University of Illinois.

Hornblow, Arthur (ed.) (1924) "Olla Podrida: The Proscenium Theatre Box," *Theatre Magazine*, vol. XXXIX, no. 279.

H. R. G. (1911) "To the Editor," *The New York Times* 1 September: 6.

Jouvet, Louis (1936) "Success: The Theatre's Only Problem" in *Theatre Arts Anthology* (1950), eds. Rosamond Gilder, Hermine Rich Isaacs, Robert M. MacGregor and Edward Reed, New York: Theatre Arts Books.

Kaplan, Joel and Sheila Stowell (1994) *Theatre and Fashion: Oscar Wilde to the Suffragettes*, Cambridge: Cambridge UP.

Kelly, Veronica (2004) "Beauty and the Market: Actress Postcards and their Senders in Early Twentieth Century Australia," *New Theatre Quarterly*, vol. 20, no. 78: 99–116.

"Letter from Acorn" (1858) *Spirit of the Times* 24 April.

Levine, Lawrence (1994) *Highbrow Lowbrow: The Emergence of Cultural Hierarchy in America*, Cambridge: Harvard UP.

Lilley, Heather (2010) "Vital Contact: Creating Interpretive Communities in a Moment of Reception," *About Performance*, vol. 10.

Lunettes, Henry (1858) *The American Gentleman's Guide to Politeness and Fashion*, New York: Derby and Jackson.

Munsey, Frank A. (ed.) (1898) "The Matinee Girl," *Munsey's Magazine,* vol. XVIII, New York.

Nash, Percy (1939) "Irving as Mephistopheles" in *We Saw him Act: A Symposium on the Art of Sir Henry Irving*, ed. H. A. Saintsbury, London: Hurst and Blackett.

O'Connor, John (1985) "The Federal Theatre Project's Search for an Audience" in *Theatre for Working Class Audiences in the United States, 1830–1980*, eds. McConachie, Bruce and Daniel Friedman, Greenwood: Westport.

Owen, Michael (1979) "A London Hit Arrives," *The New York Times* 23 September.

Phillips, Eleanor (1914) "Theatre Manners," *Ladies Home Journal*, vol. XXXI, no. 10.

Pollock, Arthur (1914) "What the Gallery Wants," *Harpers Weekly*, vol. 59.

Rappaport, Erika Diane (2000) *Shopping for Pleasure*, Princeton: Princeton UP.

Rebellato, Dan (1999) *1956 and All That: The Making of Modern British Drama*, London: Routledge.

Sartre, Jean-Paul (1976) *Sartre on Theatre*, eds. Michel Contat and Michel Rybalka, trans. Frank Jellinek, New York: Pantheon.

Schweitzer, Marlis (2009) *When Broadway was the Runway: Theatre, Fashion and the American Culture*, Philadelphia: Pennsylvania UP.

Scott, Clement (1899) *The Drama of Yesterday & Today*, vols. I and II, London: Macmillan and Co.

Spirit of the Times (1874) "Music and the Drama," 21 November.

Spirit of the Times (1876) "Music and the Drama," 1 April.

"Stage-door Johnny Figure of the Past" (1922) *The New York Times* 29 January.

Stanton, Sanford (1929) *Theatre Management*, New York and London: Appleton and Co.

Steinbeck, John (1952) "Your Audiences are Wonderful," *Sunday Times* 10 August.

Tepper, Jennifer (2013) *The Untold Stories of Broadway: Tales from the World's Most Famous Theatres*, vol. I, New York: Dress Circle Publishing.

"The Gallery Gods Must be Supressed" (1902) *The Philadelphia Inquirer* 5 October.

"The Trampling Playgoer" (1916) *The New York Times* 16 April.

"Topics of the Times" (1917) *The New York Times* 21 August.

Trewin, Wendy (1954) "A Woman's View," *Theatre Programme*, ed. J. C. Trewin, London: F. Muller.

Trollope, Frances (1832) *Domestic Manners of the Americans*, ed. Donald Smalley, 1960, New York: Vintage.

Tweedie, Ethel (1904) *Behind the Footlights*, New York: The Musson Book Co.

Walbrook, H. M. (1926) *A Playgoer's Wanderings*, London: Leonard Parsons.

Webb, Clifton (1947) "The Actor Looks at the Audience," *Harpers Bazaar*, vol. 81.

Williams, Gordon (2003) *British Theatre in the Great War: A Revaluation*, London: Continuum International Publishing.

Williams, Montagu (1892) *Round London: Down East and Up West*, London: Macmillan and Co.

PART II

Contemporary Audience Performance

INTRODUCTION TO PART II

I had been doing musicals like *Sunset Boulevard*, *Phantom of the Opera* and some plays and comedies. None of those encouraged audience interaction. That wasn't in the brief. Even *Les Miserables* was just telling a story. But *Mamma Mia* was really a phenomenon. Suddenly people were getting up and dancing up the front, down the aisles. They were everywhere: dancing, dancing, dancing and singing. Since then a lot of musicals try to encourage that. I think it is a fantastic, joyous thing; well I love it myself. We send thousands of people each week away into the night, happy, singing ... it is a great feeling.

(Grubb 2014, PI)

Having been taught "not to draw any attention" to themselves, because "you are not supposed to do that," audiences could not initiate any further engagement with an onstage performance themselves beyond those prescribed by theatre etiquette. Yet the audience was restless. Front of house staff were busy enforcing etiquette so permission for more demonstrative performance would not be granted from the auditorium. As with *Cats*, the invitation had to once again be relayed from the stage. Actors such as Janet Fullerlove are acutely aware of the role they play in granting permission for audiences to perform even a simple response such as a laugh:

There is this [issue] of giving the audiences permission. [...] We have to give the audience permission to laugh. Don't let them feel they have to strangle their laughter or strangle their response or keep it down. We need to give them permission to respond.

(2014, PI)

Soon after the turn of the new millennium, invitations to the audience to perform more demonstrably began to issue from the stage. Actor Robert Grubb has been working in theatre in Sydney for 36 years. In the opening quote he identifies his first "invitation" production as being *Mamma Mia* in 2001. Following *Mamma Mia*, other productions in mainstream theatres gradually began to include invitations such as *We Will Rock You* in 2002. It was not until 2005 with the opening of *Jersey Boys* and *The 25th Annual Putnam County Spelling Bee* that audience invitations from the stage began to really gain momentum. While this was most prevalent in musicals, by the time we reach the second decade of the twenty-first century, plays are also including invitations to the audience to play a more performative role in the theatrical experience.

Why this change occurred is difficult to determine,[1] just as it is difficult to understand precisely why the audience were told to curtail their expressive performances in the late nineteenth century. Needless to say, over the next decade and a half of the twenty-first century expressive audience performance *was* progressively sanctioned from the stage.

Part II of this book documents how this permission is granted and what kind of performance the audience are invited to give or co-perform with the onstage actors. Twenty-first-century audience performances in response to the invitation are often so spontaneous and exuberant that veteran actors are frequently "really surprised how people do embrace it" (Owen-Taylor 2014, PI). At times I move beyond the permission from the stage to discuss how ever resourceful and self-expressive twenty-first-century audience members have brought new behaviours into the playhouse that are acculturated from other modes of spectating and consuming. For most of the twentieth century, audiences have been playing a generic role in the theatre: audience as audience. In this twenty-first century, theatre audiences are being invited to play multiple roles – as critics, as communities, as consumers, as co-creators – and many are throwing their hands in the air in celebration.

Note

1 Aston and Harris (2013: 114–33) proffer some enlightening feminist perspectives on the liberation of female audiences in *Mamma Mia*.

References

Aston, Elaine and Geraldine Harris (2013) *A Good Night Out for the Girls: Popular Feminisms in Contemporary Theatre and Performance*, Houndmills: Palgrave Macmillan.

4

AUDIENCE AS CRITIC

We talk about everything really. I mean, first of all it is the story, the characters, the emotions, but then we will also discuss how the staging has affected our reception of all those impressions.

(Susan 2014, Audience member, PI)

It was only just over a century ago that everyone listened to the critical opinions of audience members. Audience authority was so potent that productions would remain open or face impending closure depending on the critical responses of audiences, not critics. This can still happen on Broadway, but it is the voice of one professional critic rather than the resounding cheering or declamatory condemnations of thousands of audience critics that has this authority. How small our world has become. Yet invitations are being proffered to twenty-first-century audiences providing new ways for them to perform their criticisms regaining, through this, some of their lost influence. This chapter considers how audiences play the role of critic and explores two emergent vehicles for audience critique: post-show discussions and digital reviews.

Bertolt Brecht was one of the first theatre professionals to attempt to cast the audience in the role of the critic of the aesthetic object: the play or musical.[1] Brecht considered the audience to be "one skilful in judging of the qualities and merits of literary or artistic works" (OED, "Critic")[2] and went so far as to suggest that "a critical attitude on the audience's part is a thoroughly artistic one" (1964: 140). Brecht credited the audience as having their own aesthetic, their critical responses were worth fostering and listening to. The audience has a vital role to perform as critics in the theatre. No one understands this better, or concedes to the "critical" role audiences play, than actors. London actor Helen Oakleigh actively seeks this criticism: "I go as close to the audience as possible; I try and listen in. The audience gives the most honest feedback. How can you improve without honest feedback? The audience are critics in their own right" (2014, PI).

Earlier I discussed two remaining activities that audiences perform as critics during the theatrical event: applause and the walk-out. In theatres where the standing ovation has not become *de rigueur*, the intensity of applause at the conclusion of productions often signals the audiences' critical response to performances. During the curtain call the actors face the audience stripped of their role, and the audience, playing the role of critic, meter out their applause. An interesting inversion of authority can occur at this point. When the actors bow to the audience they are not only saying thank you, but in many ways are acknowledging the audience's role as performers and critics.

When audience members walk out of a performance in response to aspects of the production, they are fully embodying the role of critic. Though there is often no dialogue accompanying their exit, the standing and the purposeful striding or even embarrassed scuttling out of the theatre speaks volumes. From the moment audience members applaud or walk out of a performance, they perform the role of critic: "One who pronounces judgement on any thing or person" (OED, "Critic"). It is a significant and spontaneous critical response. The walk-out and applause occur during what I described as the audience's act one. Let us turn to what Diane Paulus calls act two: the discussion.[3]

The Discussion

Habitually, in the moment after the applause, the audience discussion begins:

CAROL: What did you think love?
IAN: I liked it. *(Pause)* How 'bout you?
As they leave
CAROL: Terrible.
IAN: *(Laughing)* What?
CAROL: I feel like I've just been dragged through a tornado.
IAN: But they were so good. She was amazing. The look on her face when he said, "shut up": mustard.

Critical comments may be shared by audience members covering a diverse range of topics (see Appendix 1). In addition to the general discussions of actors, costumes, staging, sets and music, audience members can share insightful critiques of the casting, the interpretation and the structure of the productions. Rosemarie, a personal assistant, attends around eight plays a year in Sydney. Casting is an important part of her discussion:

> I often say "I wouldn't have put them in that." [One actress] in *Cat on a Hot Tin Roof* was really good, but she was just not beautiful enough and it was really distracting. She wasn't sexy enough.

(2013, PI)

Joan, a commercial truck driver from New York, goes so far as to share how she would interpret characters:

> I might talk about how the lead actress should be a little more lively, she shouldn't be a mannequin. I explain how I would play a character a little bit tougher, or a little bit nicer or a little bit more romantic.
>
> *(2014, PI)*

Lindsay works in management and communications in London. She and her partner will debate "did the actor interpret it that way or did the director tell the actor to do it that way?" (2014, PI)

Wayne is an ex-serviceman from Toronto. He has seen *Phantom of the Opera* multiple times and often talks about the production with his family after the performance:

> My daughter was new to it, so the two girls were chit chatting about how it develops, the format of it, how it flowed. There are beautiful transitions in the scenery, and it's seamless.
>
> *(2014, PI)*

Maggie is a student from Glasgow. Her discussions cover a broad and thoughtful range of subjects:

> [I]n general we would talk about the truth that the play was – the truth that came out in the performance – about the quality of the script; about the humour and why it was funny; about the pathos and why it was sad; about the bathos and why it was funny and sad; about the insights and the thoughts that we would never have thought had we not been to that play … and other things as well.
>
> *(2014, PI)*

Audience members, I have found, can be astute critics and their discussions are not limited to the formats and content of newspaper reviews. In their critical commentary, the audience can be seen as what Harry Berger (1989) refers to as the armchair critic.

Rising from their theatre armchairs, the critical commentary continues as the audience members walk down the aisles to the foyer. Some stop at the exits to share their opinions with ushers. Ushers are privy to a large amount of honest, uncensored, critical feedback from audience members. As one usher at the Broadway production of *Spiderman* stated, "They come out and tell me all about it, and they tell the truth" (*Spiderman* usher 2013, PI). As is common practice at the Queensland Theatre Company, the Front of House duty managers send a report[4] to the company outlining audience feedback from ushers who speak to people as they leave the theatre, particularly if they leave early. Comments included: "This production was excellent"; "A total disaster"; "Had enough"; "That gave me a headache"; and "The worst play I have ever seen" (Klepp 2008). Some artistic directors listen to the critical responses of their ushers. Sydney Theatre Company head usher Payne states, "I can speak to Andrew [Upton] and Cate [Blanchett], give them feedback, and say what I think" (2013, PI). It is heartening to know that some theatre professionals listen to the voice of the audience critic and the usher critic.

As they wend their way out of the theatrical world of imaginings in the auditorium, audience members are often filled with thoughts, ideas, opinions and inspirations that seek expression. Once outside the theatre, Rosemarie finds she cannot go home straight away: "We go out afterwards because we are so hyped up" (2013, PI). The authentic reviews of productions occur behind closed doors in surreptitious conversations in cafés and bars, on the way home or at home. These discussions have been called various things: "the memorial experience" (Beckerman 1970: 131), "the cool-down" (Schechner 2013: 246) and "the countersignature" (Reason 2010: 27). "Countersignature" is, perhaps, the most apt description as it "authorises" the audience members. The discussions are an integral part of the theatrical experience. In the *gemütlich* environment of a softly lit coffee shop or the babel of an animated bar, audience members often critique, share and even argue about the production. Others may prefer to ruminate on their own. Pam regularly attends Sydney productions with a play-going group. The members have agreed to a group rule to put their thoughts in their pockets and keep their criticisms to themselves (2013, PI). It often takes verbal or silent evaluation for the production to be fully concretised. Margaret goes to the theatre regularly, and she and her partner enjoy talking about the production:

> We sometimes talk about it for several days. We might talk about it immediately afterwards and then, perhaps, the next day I will say "Oh I was just thinking about that; I know where that was coming from!" We try and analyse it a bit and criticise in our own way.
>
> *(2014b, PI)*

It was surprising and a little disconcerting how apologetic audience members were when they shared their responses to productions with me. Some, unused to sharing their often insightful criticism outside their family or friend circles, were taken aback that I was interested in their responses, but were eager to share.

In playing the role of critic in these pockets of conversations, the meaning of the production is changed, shaped and/or invigorated for those participating in the discussion. Maggie seeks some kind of formal forum to re-interpret the work with others:

> I sometimes speak to other people in the audience but most often in the bus going home because quite often [...] there are people waiting at the bus stop and the bus becomes bit of an informal forum. I think this is what is, perhaps, missing in theatre. There could be a time afterwards where people can talk.
>
> *(2014, PI)*

The experience of the production can be not only changed but extended when the participants in the discussion are a large group of audience critics.

The Post-show Discussion

Most contemporary theatre companies hold some sort of pre- or post-show discussion at least once in their season. Pre-performance discussions are normally expert-driven events where the audience is given a background to, or taught how to read the production and are often part of theatre education programs.[5] Since audiences do not play a performative role in these events, I concentrate on post-show discussions.

Each country, and inevitably each theatre company, employs different terms to describe the post-show discussion. In the United States discussions are most commonly known as talkbacks or post-shows. In the UK they are called platforms and post-show discussions. In Australia they are known as Q&As. Some progressive titles have emerged that are more of an invitation rather than a prescription: Afterwords, Join the Conversation, Speak-up and Argue with Us.

The Actor's Playhouse in New York first introduced audience discussions in 1959. The National Theatre in London launched a form of post-show discussion called platforms in 1963, and the Manhattan Theatre Club (MTC) held post-shows after each performance commencing in 1973. I first took part in a post-show in 1987 while performing Off-Broadway in Barker's *Women Beware Women*. As a young actor I found them stimulating and also daunting. This sparked my initial interest in post-shows and I have experienced first-hand how they have evolved. Post-show discussions are a relatively new phenomenon in the Western English-speaking world and have only become a staple audience event in the twenty-first century.[6]

New York experienced a resurgence of interest in audience discussions in 2002. Costly display advertisements in *The New York Times* publicised "Post-show Talk-backs" as a draw-card for the productions. Independent Broadway theatres such as the Booth, the Helen Hayes and the Lyceum held regular Tuesday or Wednesday night talkbacks. Interest spread rapidly to Off-Broadway. In the Bleecker Theatre, the Century Center and the Westside Theatre, talkbacks were mediated by playwrights, activists and even nuns. Although London Theatres such as the National continued their tradition of platforms, there was no apparent surge of interest in post-show discussions in other independent or West End theatres that could match the significant rise in popularity of the talkback in New York.

The Broadway League demographic questionnaire for the 2010–11 season included, for the first time, a question on post-show discussions along with their standard questions. Not only does the scheduling of post-shows influence ticket sales, but they are the most well-attended of all audience events. Over two-thirds of my questionnaire respondents indicated that they enjoy attending post-shows (see Appendix 2). The evolution of the post-show discussion parallels the emergence of audiences as performers. Although audience critiques now occur after rather than during the performance, in this twenty-first century the lights are once again being raised on the audience during post-show discussions.

Post-shows in Western English-speaking theatres tend to follow two formats: the question-and-answer model and the expert-driven model. Q&As can be seen more as an additional onstage performance or encore. The actors share stories, often re-enacting the event with physical gestures and comments to each other. The audience watches and laughs appropriately. Actors have mixed feelings about Q&As. Many understand its performative function. Similar to having to "talk to the audience in the autograph line, you have to continue the performance to some level" (Sheldon 2013, PI). For many it is a tedious activity. Lee "just hate[s] them: it has something to do with pandering" (2013, PI). Schoeffler finds them pretentious (2013, PI). White is justifiably insulted when people ask, "What do you do for a living?" (2013, PI). Conversely, Andrew Henry, a young Sydney actor, "love[s] them" and finds post-shows "endearing." He "like[s] creating a discussion with an audience" (2013, PI). Anne Tenney has been part of the Sydney theatre scene for 21 years and learns a lot from the audience during Q&As. Interestingly, Tenney argues that while she relates to the audience as a collective, as "audience," during the performance, during Q&As "they are individuals" so "you're hearing things that you're not necessarily feeling when you're actually performing" and the questions are "very, very interesting" (2013, PI). Audiences also have contrary opinions of post-shows. Although a large percentage enjoy them,[7] "like seeing how things are put together" and "knowing who the people are behind the story" (Edie 2014, PI), some "don't want to hear anyone else" in the post-show audience and would "rather just hear the expert talk" (Rosemarie 2013, PI).

In expert-driven post-shows a lecture is usually given followed by questions asked by the audience. Experts can be a theatre professional closely associated with the play such as the director, the dramaturge or the playwright or a specialist in areas covered by the play's subject matter. It is paradoxical that many post-show discussions are called "talkbacks" when the most recognised format of the discussion is actually a question-and-answer session with experts or theatre professionals. After a lecture the audience asks the questions and the theatre professionals give the answers, not the inverse. Lynne Conner argues that if a post-show is mediated by

> an expert of some kind […] [who] lectures rather than listens and does not work to create opportunities for productive talk or authentic conversation, then we are sending the message that we aren't truly interested in the audiences' response. We do so at our own peril.
>
> *(2013: 159)*

While both of these well-worn discussion models allow the audience to question the actors or expert, there is little opportunity for audience members to play the role of critic by sharing their spontaneous opinions on the performance.

Fortunately there are new post-show models that have been developed and used in mainstream theatres over the past decade that give audiences permission to share their thoughts, feelings and perspectives on productions. In 1993 Liz Lerman developed a unique feedback model for audience members to respond constructively to the staging of new works-in-progress at post-shows called the Critical Response

Process. The model is mediated by a facilitator not an expert. One of its primary aims is to foster a safe environment for audience critics (responders) to share their opinions on the work they have just witnessed by employing what Lerman calls "neutral phrasing" (Borstel and Lerman 2003: 48) to frame their comments and questions. In the last decade this process has been adapted and has been very successful in eliciting audience responses in mainstream theatres in the United States.

Lynne Conner's Arts Talk post-show model is, perhaps, the most considered and well-developed paradigm to elicit genuine audience-centred criticism. Conner asserts that because audiences have not been given any what she calls "paratexts" that facilitate how to understand and interpret arts events, they have "little or no experience with participating in productive talk [and] often go into a talk session with the expectation that the facilitator will tell them what to do" (2013: 124). Good facilitation is vital in Conner's ten key values and strategies for productive post-show talks (2013: 125–135). The post-shows become "a space for discovery, reflection and meaning-making" rather than "a mere transaction of information" (2013: 103). In these new models,[8] mediated by sensitive facilitators, it is the audience members rather than the theatre professionals that play a starring role as critics.

One of the first companies to introduce post-shows in New York, MTC, now conduct post-show introductions designed to privilege audience comments. In the initial stage, audience members are invited to respond to the play. Once the actors walk on stage, the discussion dispels into a standard question-and-answer session. This is an effective format as it satisfies those that desire to contribute and share their thoughts and those that prefer to listen to theatre professionals. After an MTC performance of Greenberg's *The Assembled Parties* in 2013, talkback facilitator David Shookhoff commenced the post-show with an invitation:

> We are interested in talking about what you saw and what you thought. […]
> I'd like to begin by asking you to reflect back on the past two hours, and if
> you would, think and share with us a moment that was particularly resonant
> for you: that is vivid for some reason, powerful, engaging, intriguing, aligned,
> by an exchange perhaps, a specific moment. Who's got something?
>
> *(2013)*

This New York audience immediately jumped at the invitation and fired moments at Shookhoff:

> The speech by Jessica.
> When I learnt that Scott died of AIDS.
> The line "You don't understand anything!"
>
> *(Heim 2013a)*

These moments can also be seen as Jill Dolan's utopian performatives: "small but profound moments" in the production when the audience is lifted into a utopic, hopeful vision of the world (2005: 5). Post-shows where the audience is invited to share their responses, as in the examples above, tend to serve three purposes: they give audience members a chance to "de-brief",[9] share community and play the role of critic. As one participant said after a discussion:

> There was an added richness from hearing other people's perspectives and views. It felt as if the audience became "friends" as we shared some deeper questions about life arising from the play. It was not a superficial or waffling conversation but an honest sharing.
>
> *(2010,* Shadowlands, *Brisbane, Post-show discussion)*

One of the most creative moments in post-shows is when audiences become an interpretive community. Eileen attends post-shows because she "like[s] to hear what other people think, what their analysis was and what they thought they had seen versus what [her] impressions were" (2013, PI). Audience members not only work collaboratively to negotiate meanings, but also to express strong opinions. Similar to the conversations held between companions listed above, the examples below demonstrate how varied the audience text of the post-show can be:

> I'd be interested to know what the rest of the audience thought about the degree of the physicalisation in the acting. It seemed to me that if the lid had been clamped down on the gesture and such the intensity of the play would have been stronger.
>
> *(2010,* Shadowlands, *Brisbane, Post-show discussion)*

> It was so dramatic how everything fell apart. The set collapse was spectacular. But the house collapse was really about the crisis which happened to Sheelah.
>
> *(2013,* Head of Passes *Chicago, Post-show discussion)*

> I think the gaze was the central character [in the play]. The relentless gaze that objectifies: under those conditions we can't know ourselves.
>
> *(2011,* No Exit *Sydney, Post-show discussion)*

> Now I understand why I hate my mother.
>
> *(2007,* Mrs Klein *Brisbane, Post-show discussion)*

> The writing was beautiful, her performance was transcending.
>
> *(2013,* The Assembled Parties *New York, Post-show discussion)*

> I'm a deaf person and it reminded me of when I was growing up. It's frustrating. You get bad tempered and you throw tantrums.
>
> *(2009,* Miracle Worker *Brisbane, Post-show discussion)*

> I found the music very tuneful and melodic. The music in productions today is very droll.
>
> *(2013,* Leave it to Jane *New York, Post-show discussion)*

I liked the bed. Either as a bed or as another object in the centre of the stage because I think it continually symbolised one of Henry's crucial problems: his problem of maintaining the male line, his obsession with it.

> (2006, Anne of the Thousand Days Brisbane, Post-show discussion)

I really loved the chemistry created by the small space. Back in Germany the actors always have this barrier between the audience and the actors.

> (2014, The Comedy of Errors London, Post-show discussion)

I have to admit, I don't like the cover [of the programme] very much. I don't like the "sex plus marriage equals bloodshed." I feel a bit hit over the head.

> (2006, Anne of the Thousand Days Brisbane, Post-show discussion)

The experience of productions can be altered as audiences collaborate to create a rich, varied audience text that adds much to the production for all those present. As one audience member shared, the post-show "enhanced and embedded the performance. I was enlightened by the interpretations of others" (*Shadowlands* 2010). In many ways post-show audience members become Rancière's emancipated communities: "a community of narrators and translators" (2009: 22) and, I would add, critics.

Contemporary audiences, unused to engaging in dialogue in post-shows, are often initially reticent to share their critiques in a community environment. Shookhoff above has discovered a novel way to free the audience voice. In my own facilitator introductions I invite audiences to "play the role of critic" by sharing a comment that they made to a friend as the lights came up at interval or after the show (Heim 2012: 192). Giving permission is central to liberating the voice of the contemporary audience critic. Once their role has been defined and the invitation has been offered, the post-shows can become lively, audience-centred discussions shared by a community of insightful audience critics.

The Pleasure of Performing Critic

In past chapters I have discussed the pleasure of empathy, the pleasure of crying and the pleasure of watching. There is also much pleasure in playing the role of critic. Brecht argued that we are living in a scientific age in which dialectics are a source of enjoyment because they "heighten both our capacity for life and our pleasure in it" (1964: 277). Sharing moments, critiquing the production and negotiating meanings with fellow audience members work to heighten and stimulate the theatrical experience. Both Aristotle and Plato argued that every activity contains a certain pleasure that is hedonistic or eudaimonic. Hedonistic pleasure is associated with short-term enjoyment and self-gratification. Eudaimonic pleasure brings long-term fulfilment gained from activities that harmonise with the audience members' values (Wirth et al. 2012: 408, 409). In *Poetics*, Aristotle argues that "to learn gives the liveliest pleasure, not only to philosophers but to men in general" (2008). *Theoria*, intellectual contemplation, was considered by Aristotle to be the highest form of eudaimonic pleasure. Conner (2013: 36) and Ubersfeld (1982: 132) argue that pleasure in the theatre is gained in the process of working towards meanings through understanding. The following is an excerpt from a post-show held after McCraney's *Head of Passes* at Steppenwolf where audience members worked towards meanings in an attempt to understand more fully one aspect of the play:

> I think she died.
> Walking into the white light.
> (*Surprised*) Oh, she dies?
> Well, if she was spitting up blood already, that's to the end. You are close to the end.
> The angel was escorting her away.
> But I don't think it matters if she dies at that moment. I think the implication is that she's headed towards death, and towards the release she has been seeking.
> I concur.

(Heim 2013b)

Audience members asked questions of each other, negotiated and searched for meanings and reached some sort of understanding. In addition, there were revelations along the way such as the audience comment "Oh, she dies?", which worked to alter the meaning of the theatrical experience for some of those present.

Brecht argues, "You can't possibly confine criticism to the intellect. Feelings also play a part in the process" (1965: 89). Emotive responses often dominate post-shows. Criticisms in post-shows are frequently preceded by a feeling: "I was very touched when … "; "I was most surprised when … "; "I found it extremely moving when … "; "I got really annoyed when … "; "I felt trapped when … "; "My feelings and emotions were all up there, caught up in it when … "; "I felt totally drained". In these examples (taken from post-show transcripts from productions in New York, Chicago, Sydney and Brisbane between 2006 and 2013), the audience critics are expressing their aesthetic empathy for characters or moments in the production, and in this activity there is much pleasure (Lipps 1965).

Critiquing the production through a post-show discussion contributes to the audience's eudaimonic pleasure. This is the "critical attitude" that Brecht argues is "deeply enjoyable" (1964: 146). Playing the role of critic gives audience members the opportunity to extend the pleasure of the event and concretise the theatrical experience. Pleasure increases significantly when meaning-making is social (Conner 2013: 4). When playing the role of critic in a post-show discussion, the pleasure is shared with an emancipated community. This community is not dissimilar to the galleryites of the early twentieth century who won the admiration of theatre professionals for their mental curiosity and sincere and discerning commentaries during performances. Since their platform has changed, perhaps this century the audience critics will not have the lights turned out on their post-show performance. Throughout the ages, the audience have found much enjoyment in playing the role of critic.

The Role of the Audience Critic in Previews

There are some select performances in contemporary productions when theatre professionals do, however, still take note of the audience's auditorium performance. Audiences often have a critical role to play in shaping productions before they open. Directors and producers sit in the audience during previews to "feel" how an audience is responding to a play or musical, especially when the production is a new work or when there has been a large monetary investment in the production, which is the case for most contemporary professional productions. Producer of the Broadway musical *Motown* Kevin McCollum spends most of his time listening to the critical responses of audiences:

> I go to the show every night. Out of the 56 previews [of *Motown*], I saw 51. I constantly changed the show every night during previews, working with the team. This week, the show has opened, we are changing the opening. I'm changing the show because I'm responding to the audience all the time.
>
> *(2013, PI)*

McCollum is listening intensely to audience members' spontaneous critical reactions: applause, laughter, poised silence. He is also watching their engaged or disengaged performance: the lean forward or back in the seat, the shuffle and fidget. Sometimes scripts are significantly changed, or at least adapted, depending on the audience's response. Dial testing,[10] which has long been used in the media, is now being trialled in theatres to gauge audiences' emotive and instant responses to productions destined for Broadway. Audiences teach actors much about their performances by their critical responses: "[I]n previews you can learn a lot from audiences, so you can know, 'oh yes this moment and this moment.' You really have a working relationship with the audience" (Henry 2013, PI). Previews are unique events where audience critics, although often unaware of their critical role, help to shape the production through their performances.

In focus groups, audiences see an upcoming production that is in preview or is being trialled out-of-town and then are broken into small groups and asked for critical responses to the production and, sometimes, suggestions for improvements. Traditionally Broadway out-of-town trials were held in Boston, New Haven, Philadelphia, Atlantic City and Baltimore. Now they can be held in any regional towns, and some productions with prospects of moving to the West End or Broadway are trialled as far afield Australia. Out-of-town trials of West End productions, though not as routine, can occur in Chichester, Manchester or Plymouth.

In the theatre industry, focus groups have a fraught reputation. Some traditionalists feel that "it's very scary [...] to have audiences tell you how to make a show" (Taymor cited in Healy 2011). Others, such as producer Ken Davenport, rarely stage a production without holding a focus group. In 2011, producers of *Spiderman: Turn off the Dark* turned to audience focus groups after over 60 previews and a very thorough panning of the show by the media critics. Interestingly, after the producers responded to the feedback from the focus groups, the musical went on to set new Broadway records for opening-week gross box-office sales.

The idiom "telling the truth" and "honest feedback," which has almost become an oxymoron, are recurring terms used to describe audiences' verbal responses to productions. Actors' and ushers' comments recorded above frequently included these phrases. New York director Lynne Meadow emphasises that "you can't fool an audience, they either get it or they don't" (2013, PI). McCollum insists that "the audience tells the truth if you listen, if you don't let your ego get in the way" (2013, PI). It is hoped that in the anonymity of focus groups, helpful feedback that is not agenda-driven or biased for some purpose is shared by audience critics. Increasingly, audience members playing the role of critic in preview settings are contributing to the aesthetic artwork: the production.

Digitising Critical Responses

One of the most significant changes to the twenty-first-century theatre audience experience is the extensive use of modern technology. The audience's interaction with new technologies inside and outside the auditorium – before, during and after the play or musical – has considerably altered their performance. One often over-looked benefit of the digitised small and large screens is that they have opened up new and innovative opportunities for audiences to play the role of critic. The world of digital devices is rapidly evolving and it would be impossible to include all of the new technologies that are accessed by audiences. I concentrate, therefore, on current new media that offers audiences avenues through which they can perform the role of critic: hand-held devices and websites offering online reviews and comments.

It is remarkable that in the twenty-first century individuals have become so familiar and comfortable with hand-held digital devices. An accessory similar to a handbag or wallet, the mobile phone in particular is considered an extension of a persona, a lifeline to reach others and a vehicle for making personal opinions public. The mobile phone is also seen as an extension of the brain and often an extension of the hand (Kavoori and Arceneaux 2006: 31).

Let us pause to consider what this small device is capable of in the theatre auditorium. At the touch of a screen we have communication with significant others and friends as well as access to the internet to answer any questions about the production. The mobile is often used as a device to pre-order your drinks and snacks for interval, a notebook to write down phrases or impressions of the production, a flashlight to read the pro-gramme or wave in the air, a clock to determine when you need to take your seats, and a camera to document the performance and your attendance at the performance. The versatility of this compact luminous wonder can be extraordinary.

The portability of the mobile makes it a prime medium for critical commu-nication in the theatre auditorium. In many ways, the mobile is the contemporary equivalent of the hat of the nineteenth and early twentieth centuries. Like the hat in some ways, the mobile is a versatile accessory that can construct identity, draw attention and is often waved in the air replicating rock-concert enactments. It is also regarded as a public nuisance and receives just as much disapprobation in the press and online as did the hat in newspapers. It is intriguing that one small hand-held device causes so much disruption in the contemporary theatre for audience, actors and ushers alike.

It is almost redundant to discuss the interruption of the mobile phone in the theatre auditorium. Every audience member and actor has a perspective on the use of technology in the theatre and a story to tell:

> I totally disagree with technology in the theatre; people should respect the performers on the stage.
>
> *(David 2014a, Audience member, PI)*

> We had a phone go off last night. It's a distraction, we don't have any control over it. You kind of hate the fact they've done that to you.
>
> *(Henry 2013, Actor, PI)*

> Well I have to admit if people are doing that in a theatre or anywhere like that I just feel sorry for them − I think they are sad.
>
> *(Judith 2014, Audience member, PI)*

> I can't tell you how much I hate it. It divides their attention.
>
> *(White 2013, Actor, PI)*

The ringing mobile phone divides the attention of the audience by bringing the outside world into the theatrical experience, intruding into the magical world being created onstage. The outside world of personal lives and relationships and the inside world of the theatrical event both clamour for the attention of the audience. The shrill of a digital ring or tune is mightier than the actor's voice. While the onstage physical action is, perhaps, not broken, the actor's emotional connection with the character they are playing inevitably is. The fictitious world they have created can be shattered with a single bleat. Henry argues that when a mobile rings in the audience an actor is

> insane if you can pretend that it didn't happen. I think you have to acknowledge something has happened. That doesn't mean you stop or anything like that, but [you say] "Ok, let's just work harder […] Stay with me. This is why you are here, not because of that fucking thing."
>
> *(2013, PI)*

Audience members also have to work hard to block out this intrusion.

> You're sitting there waiting, and everyone has their little machines on. […] When it's dark, you can see the light. Well eventually, as everything quietens down, you just concentrate on the stage and the music.
>
> *(Wayne 2014, PI)*

Responding to the audience's preoccupation with their hand-held devices, some theatre companies attempt to work *with* rather than against the lure of technology. On 19 February 2012, as the auditorium lights went down for the opening scene of *Godspell* on Broadway, the back row of the Circle in the Square auditorium was illuminated by the glow of 30 cell phones poised and ready to tweet responses to the performance during the show. Although some regional theatres and concert and opera houses had already experimented with sanctioned tweeting during performances from around 2009, this was the first tweet seat performance on Broadway. Seven months later the Young Vic in London hosted its first tweet night where audience members were encouraged to tweet their own reviews of the play *The Three Sisters*, an assortment of which were posted online on the *Guardian* website. Two weeks later a *Guardian* Twitter Night took place during a performance of *Cat on a Hot Tin Roof* at the West Yorkshire Playhouse. Tweets such as "Amazingly detailed set, atmosphere equally enthralling. Result: complete immersion in Tennessee Williams' claustrophobic world #catreview" (Atulomah cited in Robinson 2012) were broadcast through the tweetsphere. Kershaw suggested that one way to return authority to audiences and encourage more demonstrative performance in the theatre was to "promote more selective inattention [and] locate it more in the auditorium" (2001: 150). Tweet seats certainly promote this.

While many audience members are tweeting their responses in the auditorium, some actors are tweeting backstage. Actors' tweets generally work as a glimpse into backstage life, and the Twitter hashtag #SIP (Saturday Intermission Pics) started in 2009 is used around the world for this purpose. Some actors' backstage tweets include comments on audience performance. During a Sydney production of *Hamlet*, actor Toby Schmidt tweeted his consternation at audience members' phones ringing during his first act (Alward 2013). Tweeting has taken a creative turn with an actor in the musical *Next to Normal* on Broadway in 2009 tweeting the entire musical from the point of view of the characters and The Royal Shakespeare Company tweeting an adaptation of *Romeo and Juliet* entitled *Such Tweet Sorrow* in 2010. While the tweetdaptation was twittering away, audiences could interact with the characters.

We are currently in the age of Twitter. In the hands of theatre company marketing departments, tweeting has become an effective advertising vehicle and has emerged as the most valuable tool for attracting young audiences. Roundabout Theatre Company tweets $10 ticket deals to its members aged 18 to 35, *Chicago the Musical* tweets contests, celebrations, twitpics and audience members' quotes. The *Addams Family* musical sent out tweets from the character Wednesday to try to reach a younger audience. Many musicals and plays in New York and the West End invite audiences to tweet questions to the theatre professionals to extend the pleasure of their experience. On the West End and at Shakespeare's Globe, slips of paper are handed to audience members as they exit with Twitter hashtags inviting audience members to "join the conversation." Twitter, in many ways, has become a new post-show discussion.

While creative uses of Twitter are expanding, the most significant audience opportunity introduced by the new technology is the chance for audience members to tweet their responses to plays during performances and to tweet their reviews of plays. The volume of audience reviews on Twitter[11] posted on the first night of previews portends that the mystery of opening night, in its current form, is in danger of becoming redundant. Savvy theatre companies on the West End and Broadway aware of this practice immediately favourite or retweet some of the more complimentary comments to their followers. A new world is emerging for the audience critic. Twitter reviews are a growing practice.[12] More than being just a marketing tool to adulate audiences, Twitter works to privilege audience perspectives, as does the online review.

Audience members are frequently invited to post their written responses or even image responses to productions on theatre company websites, Facebook sites and Instagram.[13] Foyers of theatres have touch screens where audiences can write their responses to plays, and entire audience reviews of plays are published in online newspapers. Armchair theatre critic bloggers have large followings all around the world, and many theatre companies have started their own "patron's blog." Some theatre companies interview audience members after performances and post the filmed interviews on their websites, while others invite audiences to film their own reviews in foyer booths that are then displayed on websites. Audience responses are now quoted on advertising material *alongside* or even instead of critics' responses: *The Book of Mormon* published audience responses to the musical in advertisements before the production opened.

Digital opportunities for audience members to share their critical responses to productions are ubiquitous. Audience members can text, tweet, type, post, pin, dial and blog their responses into the digital atmosphere any time, anywhere and to, almost, anyone. Technology is exploding at such a pace that it is outside the scope of this book to accurately document every digital opportunity for the audience critic. Any attempt at documentation would be obsolete in a short time. It is important to note, however, that the rapid evolution of new technologies assures a continuous influx of novel devices that have the potential to not only revolutionise the entire nature of critiquing productions, but invert the authority of the traditional theatre critic to the armchair critic.

For the purposes of this research, a more important question to consider is how has this digital technology changed the way audiences perform their role in the twenty-first century? These "little machines" grasped tightly in the hands of audience members hold so much allure and so privilege the text of the beholder that one of the most potent forms of advertising a production's merits or faults in these early decades of the new millennium has become word-of-text or word-of-tweet. Digital technologies have changed the way audiences perform their role in the theatre; since audiences have been precluded from verbalising or expressively performing their criticisms in the auditorium, some have taken their responses to the digital airwaves. In the auditorium, in the foyer, or after the event, luminous faces stare at rectangular boxes and feverishly tap their effusive or explosive aesthetic criticisms into the virtual auditorium.

After the post-war dark ages of audience performance, new media and audience-privileged post-shows provide platforms for the twenty-first-century audience's critical commentary to once again be heard. Their crisp, caustic, effusive and unfettered criticisms can be heard live in post-shows or on the digitised airwaves. New digital technologies have provided vehicles for audiences to take back some of their lost authority. It is, perhaps, no coincidence that the surge of interest in post-show discussions in New York coincided with the debut of the audience's digitised critical voice in the first few years of this new millennium.

Twenty-first-century audience aesthetic criticism is still in its nascent stage. One progressive theatre company that recognises and responds to this new age for the audience critic by providing a "public square" forum environment for audiences to play the role of critic is Steppenwolf Theatre Company in Chicago.

Case Study
Steppenwolf Theatre Company: Playing Critic in the Public Square

Since its inception in 1974, a primary initiative of Steppenwolf has been to promote critical debate. In 2005 the company began conducting focus groups to determine what kind of engagement audiences were seeking from their visits to Steppenwolf.[14] They discovered that their audiences were made up of individuals who were "lifelong learners" that "want to connect with Steppenwolf plays on both an emotional and intellectual level, and [...] want the plays to stimulate both introspection and debate" (Harlow et al. 2011: 10). In response to these findings, Steppenwolf have created forums for audiences to play the role of critic live and online.

In 2005, Steppenwolf held their first post-show discussion after a performance of Bruce Norris's *The Pain and the Itch* aware that audiences may need an opportunity to discuss the controversial content of the play. They were surprised at the audience appetite for discussing all elements, not just the contentious, and have consequently programmed post-shows after *every* performance of their productions since. Having observed, facilitated and documented post-shows in several cities, I am convinced that Steppenwolf's now well-refined and practised approach provides the most fertile and stimulating environment to elicit critical responses from audience members.

Steppenwolf invites audiences to join them in a post-show "public square" to continue the conversation that has begun onstage during the plays. Artistic director Martha Lavey has appropriated the public square metaphor to describe the purpose of Steppenwolf post-shows as "a place, a civic cultural space activated by the work on stage where we can negotiate meaning in an interpretive community" (2014, PI). Jenita regularly attends Steppenwolf post-shows for this purpose: "That's the point, so you can talk to people about what you saw and share interpretations" (2013, PI). Lavey sees the plays produced at Steppenwolf "as being a good exercise in citizenship" and extends the exercise and imperatives of citizenship into the discussions with audiences. One of Steppenwolf's "implied values" is empathy. Lavey's under-standing of empathy is "having the capacity to sit with other people's experiences and to negotiate meanings. [Empathy] is extended in conversations and through listening to other people" (2014, PI) in Steppenwolf public square post-shows.

Steppenwolf post-shows privilege audience members as critics by creating an optimal environment and encouraging audience interpretations. Their post-show model has been developed over the years, always maintaining the objective of valuing the audience voice. Steppenwolf discovered that a facilitator unassociated with the production or company invites more critical debate from the audience. Initially Steppenwolf theatre professionals moderated the discussions. For one performance a facilitator from the Chicago community was invited to moderate. They "found that without one of the Steppenwolf artists in the room the audience felt more likely to offer their own opinion and the conversation was a lot more open" (Carter 2013, PI). Steppenwolf facilitators are instructed to encourage the audience to self-direct and rarely give their own opinions by relaying questions back to the audience to resolve. They monitor their conversations with audiences to ensure that they are not expert-led. The facilitators complete a self-evaluation after each post-show. A successful discussion is considered to be one in which audience members initiate and continue conversations with each other (Lavey 2014, PI).

Since post-show discussions have been expert-led for so long, public square discussions such as these take time to flourish. Audiences need to be given permission to share their opinions in a safe, welcoming and revitalising environment where their interpretations are valued. I attended a post-show that occurred after a performance of Tarell McCraney's *Head of Passes* in May 2013 to join a troupe of Steppenwolf audience critics.

Steppenwolf Critics Live

The play has finished and there is a sense of expectancy in the group that remain in their seats. Some turn and share their thoughts and feelings with others in rows behind and in front. They seem to have met in this public square before. A facilitator steps into the space and addresses the crowd: "[T]his is a very emotional play. I am interested in hearing your reactions to it. Were there lines or moments you found yourself really connected to?" (Sikorski 2013). A man in the front row initiates the discussion: "They can't handle it. I can't handle it." He is visibly upset, overwhelmed. This "exteriorising" gives others the courage to share from the "private spheres of their life" (Bakhtin 1981: 133, 143). The questions begin:

> Would her life have been worse without her faith? Is it the answer, or a trip wire?
> I'm missing the reference with the four corner stones. What did they mean?
> But if you're an audience member who has some faith, then how do you
>   respond to this?
> What was the truth? That God did it?
> There must be answers![15]

The questions are not for the young woman. The exasperation of this last comment is met with a barrage of opinions from other audience critics. Questions and criticisms stumble over each other as meanings are considered, negotiated and some even discarded. The objective of this public gathering is not necessarily to attain a consensus. It embraces the imperatives of Mikhail Bakhtin's public squares of the "ancient world" where ideas, beliefs and opinions were "realised concretely […] made visible and given a face" (1981: 132).

At times the facilitator works to identify with the audience:

> This brings up a question for me just as an audience member. […] where we are talking frankly about religion and it's without cynicism. As audience members, how did that land with you? Being a person of faith or not. Did it make you feel more connected, or did it alienate you?
>
> *(Sikorski 2013)*

The interpretations that ensue after this question are enlightening. As if prompted by the audience's musings, the facilitator's last contribution to the discussion follows: "Ok, maybe this is a public place for us to generate discussion about what happens in life?" (Sikorski 2013). The facilitator takes a backward step at this point, handing the discussion over to this community of audience critics. At the conclusion of the discussion applause comes with the satisfaction of having experienced a social interchange where ideas, beliefs and opinions were not only shared, but given a face.

Interpretations shared by other audience critics changed my perceptions not only of some of the issues in the play, but gave me insights into others' perspectives on life issues in general. I was not alone in my impressions. Ellen and Don told me that on the drive home they will "talk about the play" with renewed insights. "The conversations with others" have given them "really rich material to talk about. They have increased [their] perspectives" allowing them "to see the play more fully" (Ellen 2013, PI).

Steppenwolf Critics Online

At Steppenwolf, critical discussion is extended online. Directly after a preview performance of the play, audience members' responses to the production are filmed in the Steppenwolf foyer. "Audience Response" videos form an integral part of Steppenwolf's online forum entitled Watch and Listen. This forum was developed to accommodate Steppenwolf's vibrant audience who have their "ears and eyes open" (Lavey 2014, PI) and thrive on critical debate. Watch and Listen includes a large variety of videos, photo galleries, articles and interviews recording various aspects of each production. The Audience Response clips are, however, the most frequently visited videos on the Watch and Listen page.

Lavey argues that "the expert is not necessarily regarded as the single barometer" of public opinion in our contemporary world, and spends much time deliberating who "people trust as a voice about a production or a performance that's a much more democratised experience" (2014, PI). Steppenwolf have discovered that audiences listen to audiences. The audience response videos were developed for the purpose of authorising the *audience's* "expert" opinions. Although initial videos were dominated by generic "this was great, come and see it" comments, Audience Response videos now include more critical opinions about the themes of the plays. These comments are all from one 2014 production:

> I was laughing my arse off.
> I was on the edge of my seat.
> What was done really well was this everyday reality with an undertone of menace.
> This is a play that asks you to do the weaving.
> It's borderline between tragedy and comedy. When does funny become tragedy? The entire play treads that line throughout.
>
> (*The Night Alive* 2014)

Audience comments are privileged over quotes from critical reviews, which appear only near the conclusion of the videos. As Steppenwolf have discovered, people trust the voice of their fellow audience critics.

The post-show discussions and Audience Response videos online are public square forums where not only are feelings exteriorised but opinions of audience members are made visible. Post-shows are a forum where the audience members become an ensemble of critics. The Steppenwolf ensemble of theatre artists includes 44 members. The Steppenwolf ensemble of audience critics may number in the hundreds of thousands. During the *Head of Passes* post-shows, the writer Tarell McCraney and director Tina Landau often sat silently at the back of the auditorium, listening to the audience's critical responses. A central tenet of Steppenwolf's mission is "to engage audiences in an exchange of ideas that makes us think harder, laugh longer, feel more" (Steppenwolf 2014). The Steppenwolf ensemble of artists are the audience's audience. They too are lifelong learners. Steppenwolf audience members' desire for *theoria* brings eudaimonic pleasure. Ellen, a teacher, has only missed two post-show discussions since she started subscribing to Steppenwolf ten years ago. She "loves" post-show discussions "almost to the point it's hard for [her] to go to a theatre where there isn't one" (2013, PI).

Steppenwolf public square forums are a fertile environment for citizens to interpret, share and negotiate meanings with a community of fellow critics. As Lavey argues, "people come to Steppenwolf for a sense of community" (cited in Harlow et al. 2011). The community conversation is "activated by the work on stage" (Lavey 2014, PI) and extends into the post-show discussions and then online. The online communities and conversations are more meaningful because the Steppenwolf audience members are no longer strangers. They have met before in the public square.

Notes

1 Brecht was, of course, very influenced by Piscator's imperatives of the audience retaining a critical distance from the performance text.

2 There are three definitions of a "critic" in the Oxford English Dictionary: the two that I have cited and a third, which is considered to be a combination of both.

3 Paulus argues that if you call a post-show discussion a post-show, audiences tend to have pre-conceived ideas about what a post-show means, which limits the potential for post-shows to become a forum for audience debate that is not additional to but an extension of the theatrical experience. See Paulus (2014).

4 Stage managers also write reports on audience performance.

5 It would be an oversight not to acknowledge the ubiquity of and significant audience interest in theatre education over the past two decades. Contemporary audiences have a yearning for knowledge and actively seek it (Carson 2004: 164).

6 Some of the most stimulating post-shows I have witnessed have been in Germany. Germany has a particularly rich tradition of post-show discussions called *Publikumsgespraeche* dating back to the 1920s which certainly not only privilege but are often directed by the audience voice. In the 1980s at the Volksbühne in Berlin, the audience discussions could be miniature performances. Authors such as Heiner Müeller would share their observations, and audiences responded by often querying the author, production and concepts. They often spent time discussing the play in relation to the world around them. The *Publikumsgespraeche* lasted for many hours and often concluded in the pub (Gröschel 2011). It can be seen from this example that post-show discussions are culturally prescribed. The tradition of *Publikumsgespraeche* continues today in theatre houses such as the Staatstheatre in Stuttgart (Heim 2012).

7 A comprehensive two-year study of audience-centred exchange conducted during arts events in Pittsburgh found that "[m]ost people need to talk in order to fully process their opinions" Conner (2013: 5, 6).

8 Other models exist that also privilege the audience voice. I developed a model in 2006 that I trialled with mainstream audiences in New York, Sydney and Brisbane (Heim 2012). Others used in community and youth theatre worth noting are the "community conversation" (Ellis 2005: 91–100), Laurie Brooks's talkbacks (2000: 58–60) and Lois Weaver and Peggy Shaw's porch model.

9 Comment taken from *Shadowlands* Survey (2010).

10 In a first for mainstream theatre in Portland in 2013, audiences recorded their responses by manipulating dials during the performance of the musical *Somewhere in Time* (Healy 2013).

11 The "#interval" tweet is most frequently used for this purpose.

12 A 2013 Ticketmaster survey found that nearly one in four people tweet about the production they are soon to see or after they have seen it, and this number rises to two in four in the 16–19-year-old demographic (Mermira 2013).

13 The above Ticketmaster survey found that around one in five theatre-goers are using social media to write reviews about what they have seen.

14 These focus groups were funded by a Wallace Foundation grant. The research was conducted in two rounds between 2005 and 2009.

15 Comments taken from *Head of Passes* post-show discussion 1 May 2013, Steppenwolf Theatre, Chicago.

References

Alward, Steven (2013) "A Quiet Attentive Audience – To Be or Not To Be?" *The Drum. Australian Broadcasting Corporation*. Available from: http://www.abc.net.au/news/2013-11-07/alward-hamlet/5075536 [17 December 2013].

Aristotle (2008) *Poetics*, trans. S. H. Butcher, The Project Gutenberg EBook of Poetics, by Aristotle. Available from: http://www.gutenberg.org/files/1974/1974-h/1974-h.htm [6 March 2014].

Bakhtin, Mikhail (1981) *Four Essays*, Austin: Texas UP.

Beckerman, Bernard (1970) *Dynamics of Drama*, New York: Alfred A. Knopf.

Berger, Harry (1989) *Imaginary Audition: Shakespeare on Stage and Page*, Berkley and Los Angeles: California UP.

Borstel, John and Liz Lerman (2003) *Liz Lerman's Critical Response Process*, Takoma Park: Liz Lerman Dance Exchange.

Brecht, Bertolt (1964) *Brecht on Theatre: The Development of an Aesthetic*, ed. and trans. John Willett, New York: Hill and Wang.

——(1965) *The Messingkauf Dialogues*, trans. John Willett, London: Eyre Methuen.

Brooks, Laurie (2000) "Put a Little Boal in Your Talkback," *American Theatre*, vol. 22, no. 10.

Carson, Christie (2004) "Turning Conventional Theatre Inside Out: Democratising the Audience Relationship" in *New Visions of Performance: The Impact of Digital Technologies*, eds. Gavin Carver and Colin Beardon, Meppel: Swets and Zeitlinger.

Conner, Lynne (2013) *Audience Engagement and the Role of Arts Talk in the Digital Era*, New York: Palgrave Macmillan.

Dolan, Jill (2005) *Utopia in Performance: Finding Hope at the Theatre*, Ann Arbor: Michigan UP.

Ellis, Anne (2005) "The Art of Community Conversation," *Theatre Topics*, vol. 10, no. 2.

Gröschel, Uwe (2011) "Re: Publikumsgespraeche," email, 12 December.

Harlow, Bob, Thomas Alfieri, Aaron Dalton and Anne Field (2011) "Building Deeper Relationships: How Steppenwolf Theatre Company is Turning Single-Ticket Buyers into Repeat Visitors," *Wallace Studies in Building Arts Audiences*, Bob Harlow Research and Consulting.

Healy, Patrick (2011) "Taymor Tries to Reclaim a Reputation," *The New York Times* 19 June.

——(2013) "Dialing up a Hit? Influence over Musical is in the Crowd's Hands," *The New York Times* 26 June.

Heim, Caroline (2012) "'Argue with Us!': Audience Co-creation through Post-Performance Discussions," *New Theatre Quarterly*, vol. 28, no. 2: 189–97.

——(2013a) *The Assembled Parties* post-show transcript, facilitator David Shookhoff, 20 April.

——(2013b) *Head of Passes* post-show transcript, facilitator Leanne Sikorski, Steppenwolf Theatre, Chicago, 1 May.

Kavoori, Anandam and Noah Arceneaux (2006) *The Cell Phone Reader: Essays in Social Transformation*, New York: Peter Lang.

Kershaw, Baz (2001) "Oh for Unruly Audiences! Or, Patterns of Participation in Twentieth Century Theatre," *Modern Drama*, vol. 42, no. 2: 133–54.

Klepp, Bronwyn (2008) "Re: Virginia Woolf Discussions," email, 28 November.

Lipps, Theodor (1965) "Empathy and Aesthetic Pleasure" in *Aesthetic Theories: Studies in the Philosophy of Art*, ed. and trans. Karl Aschenbrenner, ed. Arnold Isenberg, Englewood Cliffs: Prentice-Hall.

Mermira, Tina (2013) *State of Play: Theatre UK*. LiveAnalytics, Ticketmaster International.

OED "Critic." Available from: http://www.oed.com/search?searchType=dictionary&q= critic&_searchBtn=Search [5 December 2014].

Paulus, Diane (2014) "The Audience Experience," TedxBroadway 2014. Available from: http://www.tedxbroadway.com/video-gallery-tedxbroadway-2014/#!prettyPhoto/1/ [19 November 2014]

Rancière, Jacques (2009) *The Emancipated Spectator*, trans. Gregory Elliott, London and New York: Verso.

Reason, Matthew (2010) "Asking the Audience: Audience Research and the Experience of Theatre," *About Performance*, vol. 10.

Robinson, Adam (2012) "Cat on a Hot Tin Roof – Guardian Twitter Night," *same fan*. Available from: http://adamzed.tumblr.com/post/33770271396/cat-on-a-hot-tin-roof- guardian-twitter-night [17 December 2013].

Schechner, Richard (2013) *Performance Studies: An Introduction*, 3rd edn, Abingdon: Routledge.

Shadowlands Survey (2010) "Your Response." Available from: http://survey.qut.edu.au/site/ [12 October 2010].

Shookhoff, David (facilitator) (2013) *Assembled Parties* Post-show Discussion, 20 April.

Sikorski, Leanne (facilitator) (2013) *Head of Passes* Post-show Discussion, 1 May.

Steppenwolf (2014) *About Us*. Available from: http://www.steppenwolf.org/About-Us [19 November 2014].

The Night Alive (2014) Audience Response, 10 October. Available from http://www.steppen wolf.org/watchlisten/videos/detail.aspx?id=205 [10 November 2014].

Ubersfeld, Anne (1982) "The Pleasure of the Spectator," trans. Pierre Bouillaguet and Charles Jose, *Modern Drama*, vol. 25, no. 1: 127–38.

Wirth, W., M. Hofer and H. Schramm (2012) "Beyond Pleasure: Exploring the Eudaimonic Entertainment Experience," *Human Communication Research*, vol. 38: 406–28.

5

AUDIENCE AS COMMUNITY

There are many rooms in a theatre, the largest of which is called a "house." Before a performance begins, people in the other rooms – the *dressing rooms* and the *front of house room* – are preoccupied with the behaviour and volume of people that are soon to inhabit the house: the audience members. The people in the *front of house*, particularly the ushers, have the most personal contact with the audience members. They exchange pieces of paper, coins and booklets and direct them where to sit on chairs inside the house. At the same time, the people in the dressing rooms – the actors – are told that the *house is live* with people. Curious about their new neighbours, the actors listen to the audience dialogue or peek through the *fourth wall* of the house, determining whether it is a *full house* or a *small house*. The *houselights* are dimmed, the *stagelights* are raised, and the actors take turns walking into another room called a "stage." After this has gone on for some time, the *houselights* are raised and the people sitting on chairs often stand and may even *bring down the house* by slapping their hands together.

Bogart calls this phenomenon "being together in rooms" (2006). Sometime in between the dimming and raising of the houselights at interval, the audience not only become a collective but somehow subsume the name of the room they are in. They become the "house." Actors often ask the stage manager, "What is the house like tonight?" (Oakleigh 2014, PI). Backstage they will comment whether the house is good or the house is bad or quiet or listening or loud or dead. In these examples, the actors have substituted the word "house" for "audience."

People leave their diverse individual lives to enter into the community environment of a theatre. Actors acknowledge this generous act:

> To think that we would be worth seeing, for whatever reason. It's quite a tribute. Audiences come out of their living rooms, pay exorbitant money to park their cars, pay for the tickets, have a drink at interval and buy a programme.
>
> *(Tandy 2013, PI)*

Many actors share Tandy's sentiments. So curious are they, that they "like to have a peek at the audience" (Grubb 2014, PI) through the curtains, or watch the "house view" on screens backstage as the audience walk into the room adjacent to them.[1] Why is the audience room called a house, and how do the audience, in an extraordinary apotheosis, become a house? In this chapter, I suggest that when audience members enter into the communal space of a theatre – a house – in sharing and performing a common repertoire of actions, strangers become a quasi-community, they become a house. In the theatre, audiences "perform" community through their ensemble performances and through their socialising.

This chapter commences with a brief discussion of community, its interrelationship with the house in a theatre and the type of performances that work to create community. After a discussion of the impact that the physical space of a house has on an audience, I consider how twenty-first-century theatre audience performance is acculturated from communal performances given in another more familiar environment. An exploration of recent empirical research reveals that the "new" and younger theatre audience attends theatres to find community. The case study for this chapter discusses Signature Theatre Company in New York who have re-designed their theatre space to create a community environment.

Community Houses

Community is a volatile concept in theatre studies with theorists arguing for or against the concept of a theatre audience as a community.[2] Auslander contends that live theatre provokes our desire for community, but does not satisfy it (2008: 66). When compared with the social communities that were formed by audience ensembles such as the b'hoys and the matinee girls over a century ago, the contemporary theatre in its current iteration with its rules and darkened auditoriums no longer has these kinds of large social communities. There continue to exist, however, play-going groups that form small community ensembles.[3] Many researchers argue that audiences become a community through shared cognitive meaning-making. This is, however, difficult to support and is more obvious in a post-show discussion when audiences verbally negotiate and share meanings. I argue that individual audience members become a form of community through ensemble performances, dialogue in the theatre and through bringing "practised" behaviours into the theatre house.

In moments of emotional contagion, in ensemble performances of laughter, tears or applause, audiences can be seen to merge into a community. It is in that moment of "contagion – that unanimity which engenders a communion of the most dissimilar minds through a shared idea or a shared feeling" (Jouvet 1936: 11) that an audience become a community of performers. It is not only the performance of laughter, tears or applause that can create a sense community, equally the performance of annoyance or disgust can unite an audience. Susan, a teacher from London, described one experience when a mobile phone bleated for attention: "[Y]ou could feel that *frisson* of annoyance going through the audience that this inconsiderate person had just collapsed the illusion that was being created for us" (2014, PI). In this incident, the contagion of annoyance spread rapidly through the audience. Similarly, an audience will often join in communal applause when an audience member who is interrupting the onstage performance is thrown out of the theatre. In both these cases the audience form a community of mutual dissenters. Conversations may occur during intervals between strangers that are now co-conspirators, exonerating the actions of the ushers.

The community that is formed through ensemble performance is more of a communitas, a "'community of feeling' that is tied to neither blood nor locality" (Turner 1974: 201). Shirley goes to the theatre at least twelve times a year. When asked what it means for her to "be" an audience, she described how her sense of community changes after shared experiences:

> There is a difference in being part of a live audience. There's a different feeling at the end than there is at the beginning. When you first sit down you might smile to the person next to you, and then if you really enjoyed it, or if you've not enjoyed it, you make a comment about it [to them].
>
> *(2014, PI)*

Dialogue also works to form community. Before, during or after the performance snatches of conversation are shared between audience members: "you start talking to strangers about whether that was a good part" (Cheryl 2014, PI). In these moments of shared performance and dialogue the audience become a specific kind of theatre community: a house.

The House

This chapter could well be called "Audience as House." "House," describing the physical auditorium where the audience sit, was extracted from the sixteenth-century "Playhowsse."[4] By the seventeenth century, "house" was habitually used to describe the body of people that sit in the house of a theatre (Pepys 1663: 8). In the eighteenth and nineteenth centuries, as introduced in Chapter Two, the audience members sitting in various parts of the house were identified by the section's name: "the pittites," "the gallery" and "the boxes." Even today the audience are sometimes called "the orchestra" or "the stalls."

As can be seen from the introduction to this chapter, the analogies to a house are frequent in both the actor and theatre staff lexicons: fourth wall, full-house, live house, houselights, bringing down the house, stopping the house and front-of-house. Actors frequently talk about "breaking the fourth wall" of their performance space, the stage, to connect with audiences.[5] Actors have differing but usually strong opinions about breaking the fourth wall and directly addressing or interacting with audience members in some way:

> I think it takes a certain kind of courage.
>
> *(Owen-Taylor 2014, PI)*

I used to get scared. But now it doesn't bother me.

(Schoeffler 2013, PI)

You would be insane if you were to say that there is a complete fourth wall and that nothing exists past that. Something really important exists past that.

(Henry 2013, PI)

Some feel that it is the audience's performance that breaks the wall between the two rooms of a theatre. New York actor Sondra Lee generally disapproves of audiences breaking the fourth wall of the house "except with wild applause and appreciation" (2013, PI). An audience, simply by their very presence, have the collective power to break the fourth wall at any time they choose. It is not only the actors who build walls. Sydney actor Mark Owen-Taylor describes how he can sometimes sense a "wall of hostility" (2014, PI) coming from the audience. When the fourth wall of the house is broken, audience members and actors not only glimpse into the contiguous room of their co-performers, but make connections that can create more of a sense of community in the theatre.

Socialising in the House

Communication with other audience members is central to forming community. Communities are built through relationships. Sartre argues, "An audience is primarily an assembly. That is to say, each member of an audience asks himself what he thinks of the play and at the same time what his neighbour is thinking" (1976: 67). In the contemporary theatre, some audience performers do not think, they *ask* what their neighbour is thinking. College basketball coach Ron finds talking with others

fun […], especially when we're in London. I'm trying to figure out what this play's all about. To the person next to me I sa[y] "is it really like this over here?" You use the play as another avenue of communication.

(2014, PI)

Cheryl is a hairdresser from just outside of London. She describes feeling a sense of community at the theatre when "you start talking to strangers as you're walking out 'that's good' and 'that was great fun,' you have a bit of interaction with each other" (2014, PI). Many audience members used the word "interaction" to describe the shared experience.

Theatre is more enjoyable when it is shared. The majority of theatre-goers attend the theatre either with someone else or with a group. Of the audience members I questioned (see Appendix 2), 86 per cent said they most often attend the theatre either with one special friend or family member or with a group: "It's a social evening, and I don't consider going out on my own a social evening" (Gina 2014, PI). When asked why they prefer to go with others, audience members replied either "to share the experience, to share memories, to share interests,"[6] or because it was a social occasion. Fiona, an IT project manager, considers theatre to be

> a social thing – it is an opportunity to meet up with friends and it is nice to also share that experience with someone – you might talk about it during the interval or at the end. It feels a bit odd to go and watch a show and come away and not have any dialogue with anyone about it.
>
> *(2014, PI)*

Sharing dialogue with others during interval and after the play is not only an opportunity for audience members to play critic – conversing with others also brings eudaimonic pleasure. Marjorie is a homemaker from Britain, and to her the community aspects of theatre are synonymous with pleasure: "It gives you pleasure to go to the live theatre; you go to enjoy each other's company as well as the actors and actresses" (2014, PI). Interestingly, Marjorie includes the actors in her community circle.

Although there is predominantly no reciprocal dialogue between actors and audience, the two performing troupes have a relationship that contributes to a community of sorts. Actor Henry calls this "a working relationship with the audience. Even though you're not always [directly] interacting with them, it is through the sounds they make and the moments they pipe up in that you know" they are there (2013, PI). Here, the audience's paralingual responses work as a kind of dialogue to form community, discussed further in the proceeding chapter. In this twenty-first century, new relationships between actors and audience members are often formed in the virtual world. Actors and audience members sometimes talk with each other online. British actor Helen Oakleigh enjoys the immediacy, privacy and anonymity that this form of community interaction offers: "You're able to engage with people immediately. You have a stage door but not in a public way – social media is where you are getting that interaction, and it is nice" (2014, PI). Online access to actors is a virtual stage door.

Currently, Twitter is fast becoming the most immediate form of communication between actors and audience members and is re-defining the actor/audience relationship. British actor Janet Fullerlove, who has been working in theatre for 25 years, enjoys this exchange:

> I often have people who have been in touch with me saying "I've seen Janet Fullerlove in *Macbeth* and it's wonderful." And I'll thank them and they'll tell me when they're coming to the show. So yes, there's definitely that exchange which you didn't get in any form before Twitter. It's a new way that the audience and the performers are connecting.
>
> *(2014, PI)*

Although this generally happens outside of the theatrical event, audiences that have made a personal connection with performers through tweeting naturally feel more of a kinship during the performance. Ushers also engage in relationships that work to build community. Theatre ushers sometimes build up substantial relationships with audience members through regular communication. At Sydney Theatre Company, Payne "see[s] a lot of the same faces. There is a relationship there. The relationships with the patrons over the years have been really good. They ask you what you think of the show, have chit chats" (2013, PI).

The social event of theatre is relational. For the audience, the relationship starts with those you accompany. It continues, in a more ephemeral way, during the production with the onstage actors. At some point during or after the play, it is extended to the person next to you when the "armrest becomes the site of cordial negotiation" (Dolan 2005: 27) or with other audience members at interval. It can then effervesce into relationships with ushers as audience members leave the theatre and new relationships form with actors in the virtual world.

Interior Decorating

Theatre space theorists stress the importance of creating a physical theatre environment that fosters intimate actor/audience relationships.[7] The design of the theatre can truncate the liminal space between stage and audience so that audiences feel they are "in the same room" (Bogart 2013, PI) as their onstage co-performers. Susan attends the theatre around six times a year and argues that the design of the theatre has a large impact on her experience of the production. In a theatre in the round she feels "in the midst of" the onstage action, like "a fly on the wall in the living room." Whereas in a theatre that has a proscenium arch stage she "feel[s] more of an observer, more at a critical distance" (2014, PI). Not all audience members feel comfortable with this intimacy. John, a music professor, "personally prefers a bit of distance between [himself] and the stage" (2014b, PI).

Theorists also argue that the physical space of a theatre can provide a productive or unproductive setting for audiences to form a community. One of theatre historian Franklin Hildy's three maxims for contemporary theatre architects is: "Black is not a colour that should ever be found in the audience space of a theatre." He emphasises that theatres need to be psychologically warm for audiences: "You never see black in the original colour scheme of a historic theatre because black can never be a warm colour" (2006–7). June would agree:

> I like the King's Theatre in Glasgow because it is very old fashioned: lots of red plush and gold paint, just like the theatres always used to be. It adds to the excitement and brings a richness which you don't get in more modern, bare kinds of theatres.
>
> *(2013, PI)*

Several studies have been undertaken attesting that decorative rooms, similar to the theatre houses built in the eighteenth and nineteenth centuries, create a more fertile environment for demonstrative audience response. Audiences sitting in dull, grey or black rooms cry and laugh less when exposed to stimuli (McAuley 2000: 59; Mackintosh 1993: 81). A warm, inviting, intimate environment is more likely to produce a climate that encourages community performance.

Since the 1980s, directors and producers have begun to pay more attention to the decoration and lighting of the house. Hal Prince insisted on redecorating the house of the Majestic Theatre in New York to replicate a Victorian opera house for *Phantom of the Opera* (Carlson 1989: 200). In Baz Luhrman's Sydney production of *Strictly Ballroom* (2014), the walls of the house were decorated with dancehall posters. Audiences entered the house through doors festooned with lights to sit in sparkling, colour-coded seats. Projections in the house in *Let it Be* (2013) in London inscribe the audience and the walls of the house with technicolour images similar to those used on the stage. In these and many related examples, the house is no longer a set that reproduces a familiar environment – such as the drawing rooms of the late nineteenth century – but it emerges as a theatrical set. It becomes a place for performance where "[t]he whole room becomes the stage and, at the same time, the place for the spectators" (Grotowski 1980: 157). The decorated auditoriums have a festive glow that is conducive to audience performance.

Some mainstream productions are beginning to keep the house lit for part and sometimes all of the performance.[8] This practice not only privileges audience perfor-mance, but signals to the individual audience member that they are not experiencing the event alone, but as a collective community. Unaccustomed to lit houses, con-temporary audiences can, however, feel self-conscious under the glow of houselights, and this can inhibit their performance. It takes time for the audience collective that have been left in the dark for almost 100 years to adjust to the bright glow of houselights. Lottie and Jenny often attend London productions together. They have conflicting perspectives on audience lighting during performances:

> You feel much more exposed when the lights come up. You almost feel like "a fly on the wall" when the lights are off.
>
> *(Jenny 2014, PI)*

> I feel the reverse. […] It is almost an oxymoron to say that you're exposed in the dark, but I did feel far more exposed [during the show] when the lights were off. It was really unsettling.
>
> *(Lottie 2014, PI)*

Some audience members, such as Anne from Toronto, prefer to watch the audi-ence: "I don't focus [on the play]. I tend to look at what's around me all the time" (2013a, PI). For those select few, such as Anne, who strain to watch other audience members' responses during performances, any lighting in the house is welcome.

Changes in theatre seating have not only occurred because we have the technology for modifications, they have also been re-designed for comfort and to accommodate growing individualism. The seats in many mainstream theatres have become pro-gressively more plush and sleep-inducing over the past two centuries. The worn, crude benches that audience members used to stand on to cheer in the first half of the nineteenth century have been replaced in many theatres with individual, luxurious, velveteen padded armchairs. In some theatres, such as The Hummingbird Centre in Toronto, drink receptacles are attached to each seat similar to those in cinema houses. A pocket to hold programmes and a reclining button are all that is needed to replicate the television room armchair.

The comfort of the seats in the house is surprisingly not much of a concern to many audience members if the production is engrossing. Peter Brook has long argued this point, and contemporary audience members concur. Susan attended a theatre production that had "uncomfortable old seats," and with her "knees jammed against the seat in front of [her], it was terribly uncomfortable." She argued, however, that "the production was so good it [took her] mind away from all of that" (2014, PI). In an interesting seating inversion, during Sydney Theatre Company's 2014 production of *Macbeth*, audience members were seated on the stage while the actors performed in the seating banks. Elaine, an administrator who attended the production, discussed her experience: "[T]he seats were cramped and uncomfortable, but for two hours I didn't move: I was absolutely mesmerised" (2014, PI). Conversely, luxurious contemporary seating can lull the audience into a more passive and unresponsive state. Plush seating can also work against the camaraderie of community. Rubbing shoulders with an audience member on a shared bench or in a snug seating bank, as disconcerting as this may sound to some, does compel audience members to share at least cursory comments with their neighbour. The close physical proximity is also more conducive to ensemble performance and emotional contagion.

This shared experience is close to Rancière's concept of "being apart together" (2009: 59). The audience are in close physical proximity, experiencing the same event, thinking of what their neighbour is thinking, occasionally engaging in dialogue. Community formation does not, however, have to include dialogue or even gestural acknowledgement of the shared experience. Many audience members prefer this silent togetherness. Even if there is no eye contact or spoken words, the mutuality of performing together as an audience ensemble is being apart together.

Actors know only too well that togetherness is a vital part of community formation. A dispersed audience is an anathema to actors. It is often only when audience members sit in close proximity that emotional contagion or community performance of any kind can occur. Actor Robert Grubb argues that audiences "respond much better together in a group." When *Strictly Ballroom* first opened in Sydney, audience members would "crowd in and try and get as close as they could because they wanted to be 'here.' Therefore you had this audience, as a group, working as one almost. The laughter became infectious" (2014, PI).

As Mackintosh argues, "the architecture of the house aids or thwarts the actor/audience relationship" (1993: 127). The design of the house, the colour scheme, the lighting and even the seating can encourage or can hinder community formation between the actors and between the audience members. Even if the audience are apart together, "living bodies onstage address bodies assembled in the same place. [...] Theatre is in and of itself communitarian" (Rancière 2009: 16). Being together in rooms, audiences have multiple opportunities to feel part of a community and perform as a community.

Share Houses

A communal space that shapes behaviours and primes audiences for their theatre interactions is the family television room. One of the most frequent complaints that theatre-goers and actors have about audiences is their impropriety. Much twenty-first-century audience performance has not been gleaned from theatre etiquette manuals, but has been cultivated in the television room:

> If the audience is treating the stage like a television screen "I need to go to the bathroom," "I want some more chips" energy is lacking and the entire performance suffers for it, everybody in the audience suffers for it.
>
> *(White 2013, Actor, New York, PI)*

> You look down and see lights [from mobile phones] and they are very distracting. That drives me nuts. People think that they are in their living rooms.
>
> *(Linda 2013, Audience member, Toronto, PI)*

> When they get to a theatre people don't realise its live, they think they are at home watching television.
>
> *(Young 2013, Actor, Glasgow, PI)*

There is a history between media watching and theatre. With the arrival of commercial television in the late 1940s, viewers treated the living room as if it were a theatre. They closed the curtains in their houses; they dressed for the occasion and sat in a seemingly sacred semi-circle watching the marvels of the box in silence (Auslander 2008: 15–17).

Contemporary television watching has changed dramatically since that time and includes many more kinetic, paralingual and verbal expressions than those performed in the late 1940s. Viewers have their laptops in front of them while texting, using Facebook, streaming videos, sharing food, watching the television screen and continuing an ongoing commentary on the programme they are watching with those around them or in the virtual world. Some use their phones or tablets to media mesh: to virtually engage with the programme they are watching. Others use their devices to media stack: engage in activities unrelated to the programme on television. Television viewing is a communal activity even if the community is virtual. It is not surprising that new audience members, accustomed to this form of receiving entertainment, bring these more gregarious modes of viewing into the playhouse.

Goffman's concepts of frontstage and backstage behaviours are of particular relevance here. The family television room is a backstage space. Goffman includes a comprehensive list of what he calls the backstage language:

[R]eciprocal first-naming, co-operative decision-making, profanity, open sexual remarks, elaborate griping, smoking, rough in-formal dress, "sloppy" sitting and standing posture, use of dialect or sub-standard speech, mumbling and shouting, playful aggressivity and "kidding," inconsiderateness for the other in minor but potentially symbolic acts, minor physical self-involvements such as humming, whistling, chewing, nibbling, belching, and flatulence. The frontstage behaviour language can be taken as the absence (and in some cases the opposite) of this.

(1959: 128)

I include this lengthy inventory to illustrate how many acceptable frontstage actions of nineteenth-century theatre audiences have, by the late 1950s when Goffman was writing this, become backstage actions.

The following is a list of some isolated and surprising television room backstage activities that are now performed in frontstage spaces: the houses of theatres. Activities include people taking their shoes off and putting their feet up, stroking and kissing children, stretching out arms across the back of seats, bobbing heads up and down in time to the music, painting their toenails, eating sushi in the front row of theatres and French-braiding hair. These are Lee Strasberg's "private moments" (1988: 144) normally only performed in living rooms that have been brought into the frontstage of a theatre auditorium. Or is it a frontstage anymore? As Goffman argues, "By invoking a backstage style, individuals can transform any region into a backstage" (1959: 128, 129). The contemporary mainstream theatre auditorium has more of the appearance of a backstage space. Twenty-first-century theatre audience members, habituated from viewing behaviours performed in the family television room, are spreading their arms, unwrapping their enjoyment and sharing the experience with their fellow performers.

New Houses

As Tom, a lawyer from the United States, emphasises, "theatre not only creates community, it needs community to form its audience" (2013, PI). Since the 1950s in the United States, the theatre subscription model worked to create communities of audiences loyal to particular companies.[9] Many of those I interviewed who "subscribed religiously" (Ron 2014, PI) to certain theatre companies expressed a sense of ownership of the productions. They attended subscriber events and frequently discussed not only productions but also programming and staffing with fellow subscribers.[10] Alexander attends around 36 Sydney theatre productions a year. While I was interviewing him during an interval at the Ensemble Theatre – a theatre he subscribes to – ushers, bartenders, management staff and other audience members stopped to talk or share quips as they passed by. Fond relationships had formed over the years in Alexander's subscription community not only with other audience members, but also with theatre professionals. Artistic director Martha Lavey has built relationships with many of her subscribers through her post-show discussions at Steppenwolf Theatre Company. She has been in "five-year conversations" (Carter 2013, PI) with some of her Steppenwolf audience critics. During the past decade subscriber communities in the United States have, however, been declining (Harlow et al. 2011: 5–8). Theatre companies such as Steppenwolf are looking to the communities of the future to form new relationships.

For many years, theatre companies have been attempting to lure younger audience communities into the theatre. Theatre producer John Karastamatis asserts that the younger audience is the "Holy Grail" (Murdoch 2012) that theatre companies seek. A recent study showed a substantial increase in theatre attendance of young people. An extensive 2013 Ticketmaster study in the UK of 1,456 theatre-goers revealed that 16–19-year-olds are more likely to go to the theatre than any other age group. Transactional statistics over four years showed that attendance had increased by 71 per cent amongst 16–25-year-olds since 2009 (Mermira 2013). In my own interviews when asked to describe any particular changes in audiences over the past two decades, one-third of the actors observed that audiences had become younger.

What is, perhaps, more significant, is that two other studies revealed that audiences, particularly young audiences, go to theatre to socialise and seek community. A Wallace Foundation random phone survey of 1,231 people aged 18 and above in the United States discovered that for 67.9 per cent of theatre audiences, socialising was the prime incentive for attendance (Ostrower 2008: 91). In a 2012 Australia-wide study, 823 young people aged between 13 and 30 were interviewed about their theatre experiences. Socialising and finding a sense of community were some of the prime motivating factors for theatre attendance:

> It's really nice to have that sense of community, you know, when you go and see an art form. I think that's what I really like about it. The community aspect of it.
>
> *(Adams et al. 2012: 50)*

> I enjoy the communion and the community that happens in theatre and, yeah, the way it reflects life, and it is beautiful and sometimes scary and, yeah …
>
> *(Adams et al. 2012: 58)*

Of further import from this study was the young people's discussion of the physical space of the theatre. Adams and colleagues stated:

> A significant finding of this research has been the importance of the venue as a social and communal space. Young people spoke of the location in terms of either feeling comfortable or "at home," somewhere one might meet "a community of friends" or, in contrast, feeling uncomfortable or unwelcome or threatened.[11]
>
> *(2012: 99)*

Feeling comfortable and welcomed is essential for these new houses. Audience members I interviewed (see Appendix 1) frequently stated that audiences had become louder: "The audiences are so much noisier now I find: the younger generation. They stand up and they whoop and shout. We didn't do that" (Doreen 2014, PI). A new, younger ensemble of players is entering theatres, many seeking community, and they bring with them their own repertoire of actions.

Another audience ensemble that is dominated by young people is the groupies. Most groupies are in their late teens to mid-twenties (Bonanni 2013, PI). In the 2013/14 Broadway season "fans," many of whom are groupies, accounted for over one-third of all ticket sales (Hauser 2014: 32). Many groupies see productions, particularly musicals, 40 or 50 times. One groupie has seen *Mamma Mia* in New York over 175 times, and an IT specialist has attended over 300 *Rock of Ages* performances. The groupies talk to each other and cast members online, compete with each other and even attend the cast's baseball games (Schoeffler 2013, PI). Similar to the followers of the nineteenth century, they have their own ensemble names such as Rent Heads, Taboons, Jeckies and Twickies. Noticeably, they have adopted the production or character's name rather than the actor's name. Seeking, perhaps, more of a performative role in the theatre, these colourful audience ensembles can be distinguished by their performances. Similar to the Forrestites of the nineteenth century,[12] the Jeckies of New York are "legendary for being zealous. They're obsessed with it and they will verbally attack anyone who doesn't agree with them" (Bonanni 2013, PI).

Interestingly, groupies, male and female, are still referred to as stage-door Johnnies by some ushers in London. Fullerlove described groups of young women she encountered after performances of *Shakespeare in Love* that displayed all the flush and enthusiasm of the early twentieth-century matinee girls: "[T]he girls hang around the stage door. I've heard at least two or three pairs of girls saying, 'This is our second time, we love it so much. We got our tickets through tweeting about it!'" (2014, PI). The groupies of New York and stage-door Johnnies of London have formed close-knit communities of audience performers who share a common theatrical language.

New houses are entering established houses and are creating quite a ruckus. A tug-of-war is occurring in the house between established audience communities and new audience communities. There are contradictory messages from theatre companies who attempt to attract new audience members through savvy marketing and programming and then impose strict rules of behaviour which marginalise and exclude the young audience members. I posit that the new audiences, through performing their expressive repertoire of actions, are working against theatre etiquette rules – or established structures – to create communitas. As Turner argues, "Structure, or all that which holds people apart, defines their differences, and constrains their actions, is one pole in a charged field, for which the opposite is communitas" (1974: 274). Communitas is synonymous with spontaneity and free will. It is still a form of structure, but one without obligation, jurality, law or constraint (Turner 1974: 49). Perhaps the gallery boys and the matinee girls who were shunned from the theatres over a hundred years ago, and who have now in their new incarnation been invited back in, will be allowed to stay.

For over 50 years, new theatre designs and darkened houses have created distances between audience members. McAuley argues that many aspects of the design of the house have "an impact on the social experience and on the function that theatre has come to fulfil in a given society" (2000: 275). In the twenty-first century, individuals have few places to physically commune with each other to feel part of a community: theatre houses have the potential to become a community space. Liz, a retired nurse from London, attends the theatre around 20 times a year. One of the changes she has witnessed over time is socialising "in the National" and other London theatres, although "there's a melee [and] it can be a bit packed, the foyers are places for social meeting" (2014, PI).

The audience space – their house – and where they have learnt to respond to performed fictitious worlds, digital or otherwise, affects their performance in the theatre. There is an inquisitiveness and need – particularly among young people – for a safe, welcoming environment where audiences can perform as part of a community.[13] I suggested that audiences only become a community, a house, when they are in relationship with each other through ensemble performances. A progressive theatre company that has been attempting to build a theatre community through both space and relationship is Signature Theatre Company.

Case Study
Signature Theatre Company: Building Communities

Signature Theatre is an Off-Broadway theatre company founded in 1991 by artistic director Jim Houghton. In 2005 Signature decided to renovate their company in an attempt to "democratise" (Houghton 2013, PI) the theatre-going experience for audiences. Signature wanted the New York "community reflected on [their] stages and in [their] audiences" (Houghton 2013, PI). To achieve this, they made two significant changes: they built a new audience-friendly theatre and they introduced a ticket initiative to make theatre more accessible.

Houghton recognised the importance of the audience and the actors "breathing the same air […] in the same space" (2013, PI), so a theatre was designed by architect Frank Gehry that democratised the theatre experience. It was the first new theatre of its scale to be built in New York in over 40 years. The new theatre is housed in West 42nd Street, Pershing Square and is 70,000 square feet, the size of a New York city block. It is a complex of three performance spaces, two rehearsal rooms, a foyer and administrative offices. In each of the theatres, two rooms of the same size sit beside each other: the stage and the house. The purpose in building the house the same size as the stage was to create a "visceral feeling of intimacy: of [the audience's] participation in that event having significance" (Houghton 2013, PI). In the Signature theatres, the playing space for the two troupes of performers, actors and audience, is of equal value.

The audience's backstage, the foyer, is a much larger room than any of the performance or rehearsal rooms. In this space, which is open-plan, there are various audience support spaces: a bar, café, lounge area, bookstore, digital wall and restrooms. Houghton argues that "what we're trying to foster is multiple invitations to multiple interests in that foyer that are open [for audiences] to commune" (2013, PI). With all the amenities of a family home – before, at interval or after the show – audience members can eat in the dining room, pick up a book from the study and read in the lounge room, use the technology in the media room or chat with other community members over a drink in the bar. To further create an ambience of home, all the materials used to build the playhouse are basic materials that can be bought at any home-improvement or hardware store. The purpose in choosing rudimentary materials was to create a familiar "home" environment for the audience. Although Houghton admits that the sense of a home environment cannot be measured and that it may work only on a subconscious level, the audience-centred motivations are obvious.

The dimensions and audience-centred initiatives of the foyer are reminiscent of the grand lobbies built round the *fin de siècle* with their adjacent smoking rooms and powder rooms. Although not as decorative and luxurious, Signature's foyer was designed with the same intentions in mind: to create an audience space that reflected the desires and mindset of those that inhabit it. In the contemporary theatre this means a comfortable, relaxing space with opportunities to explore, critique, unwind and socialise in a twenty-first-century way. A digital wall where you can have your photograph taken replaces the gold-framed mirrors of the late nineteenth century. Your image still gazes back at you, but this time from a digital screen. All of the public areas in the theatre, the performance and backstage spaces, give a clear message about how much audiences are valued. The performance space with its 50/50 shared space is undoubtedly egalitarian, and the audience's backstage, the foyer, privileges the audience.[14] The actor's backstage spaces are not as radically changed.

Part of Signature's ethos is to provide opportunities for an "intimate experience of going into these rooms" (Houghton 2013, PI) so that relationships can form that create community. The spaces in the theatre are designed so that audience members, actors and other theatre professionals not only breathe the same air, but have the opportunity to literally bump into one another. The 42nd Street front door of the theatre is also the stage door: it is the actor's door, the director's door, the usher's door, the staff door *and* the audience door. It is purposefully designed so that "everyone passes through the same space." Houghton argues that this creates a relationship between theatre professionals and audience that is "a conversation, it's a collision, it's meant to be provocative" (2013, PI). Sharing a front door also works to create more of a community amongst the two troupes of performers. After the performances, the actors often unwind at the bar or have a bite to eat in the café where audience members are welcome and invited to chat to their co-performers.[15] Whether this seemingly utopic environment is fully realised is difficult to determine. Some actors prefer to keep the character/audience relationship rather than introduce an actor/audience dynamic. Others prefer to unwind on their own. Nevertheless, the incentives and motivations for creating this environment are democratic.

The second component of Signature's company renovation was to introduce a ticket initiative to provide accessible tickets for those that could not normally attend the theatre because of inflated ticket prices. Every show in an initial run of a play costs only $25 to attend, rather than the normal $75. The other $50 is subsidised by corporate, foundation, and individual supporters who pledge funds at the beginning of each new season. This highly successful initiative has attracted a "new" audience to the theatre, one that is close to replicating Houghton's vision of Signature audiences "reflect[ing] any average subway car in New York which has [a] sense of diversity on every level, from colour to sexual preference to economic class" (2013, PI). When the Ticket Initiative was first introduced, the company were naturally concerned as to whether, if the economic barrier was overcome, people would actually still want to attend: "are people then ultimately interested?" (Houghton 2013, PI). And they were. In the first six years of the programme, over one-third of the audience members were new audiences attending Signature for the first time. Signature has invited new audiences to become part of a diverse community where the playing spaces are equally divided and the audience's backstage is a welcoming space.

To conclude, I turn to another aspect of Signature's new democratic implementations. On the digital walls in their foyers, audience quotes are often placed alongside quotes by their "Playwrights-in-Residence" such as Sam Shepard, Paula Vogel or Will Eno. Audience photographs are also displayed alongside actors' images in the photograph collage on the screens. Digitising or printing audience comments is not a new practice. Over the past decade some large-scale musicals have begun to include audience comments on billboard advertising alongside critics' comments. In the context of Signature's ethos, however, to privilege the audience in every component of theatre – house design, foyer design, accessibility – and to break down barriers of class, ethnicity, high culture and wealth, this practice is undertaken for the purposes of inclusion not simply for marketing. Representing the voice of the audience also re-casts the audience in the role of critics.

Houghton argues that Signature Theatre is "a centre that is truly made and built for the community" (2013, PI). This may sound like a platitude, but after experiencing an evening there, I have to concur.[16] In a city where the sidewalk has become the audience support space, I found Signature's backstage a sanctuary from the tumult of New York where the calm environment of the pre-show experience prepared me to enter into the fictitious world of the play. I saw the actors arrive in the house and walk up on the stage. Glowing from the contagion of laughter during the play, two audience members chatted to me in the house at interval, and another audience member invited me to join in a picture to be displayed on the digital wall in the foyer. Audience members were leafing through books in the bookshop. During the second half of the play, the houselights were raised several times on the audience community. After the performance many people stayed to critique the play at the bar or in the dining area over refreshments. By the end of the evening, having spent time with people in rooms in a playhouse that created a safe environment to play and to have some down-time, I was part of an audience that became a community. We became a house.

Notes

1 The actors I interviewed gave me numerous examples of times when they "peek" through the curtain and watch the audience enter the theatre. For many, this is an essential part of their warm-up; the audience's anticipation and excitement stirs their own.
2 See Beckerman (1970: 135), Carlson (2004: 214, 215), Lilley (2010: 35–50) and Rancière (2009: 16).
3 Most notable of these are Aston and Harris's girls' night out groups. Their delightful book (2013) documents the increase of these groups in the UK in this new millennium. Several ushers I interviewed in Sydney also discussed these "girls" communities that are not dissimilar to the girls clubs of the early twentieth century. Some of the girls groups are definitely no longer girls. An usher at Sydney's Lyric Theatre said he regularly encountered groups of "raunchy old women" (*Strictly Ballroom* usher 2014, PI) at Wednesday matinees.
4 For an example see Henslowe (1961: 6).
5 During the advent of Realism and living room drama, the "fourth wall" was firmly erected separating the two audience rooms. It is only in the last few decades that actors have begun to break down the separation and reach out more to audiences.
6 These observations are based on comments made both in the personal interviews and the questionnaires. When interviewees were asked what it means to them to "be" an audience, "shared experience" was the third most-frequent response (see Appendix 1).
7 See Carlson (1989), Mackintosh (1993) and McAuley (2000).
8 Notable examples include New York and London productions of *Once* and the 2013 Melbourne Theatre Company production of *The Cherry Orchard*.
9 The development of the subscription model in the United States is largely credited to Danny Newman. See Harlow et al. (2011: 5). The subscription model in the UK is much older.
10 I attended a Roundabout theatre company subscriber event in New York after a performance of *The Big Knife* on Broadway and was surprised how many discussions centred around programming and loyalty.
11 These comments regarding community were recorded in Sydney, Melbourne and Brisbane. They are not indicative of the tourist audiences of New York and London. Comments on community from these groups are limited to my own interviews.
12 See Chapter Two section "Followers."
13 The Public Theater emerging writer Brian Kushner argues that his students from upper Manhattan never go to plays because "the theater is not a safe space for them. They don't know what they should wear, or how much they should react to what's happening" (2012).
14 Some other New York theatre companies, such as 59E59, also try to create audience-friendly spaces in their foyers.
15 This practice is reminiscent of the practices of some nineteenth-century actors who used to join audience members in the boxes in between acts and share refreshments.
16 The play was *Old Hats*, created and performed by Bill Irwin and David Shiner.

References

Adams, Ricci-Jane, Michael Anderson, Penny Bundy, Kate Donelan, Robyn Ewing, Josephine Fleming, John O'Toole, Christine Sinclair and Madonna Stinson (2012) *The Theatre Space Project: Accessing the Cultural Conversation*. Final Report.
Aston, Elaine and Geraldine Harris (2013) *A Good Night Out for the Girls: Popular Feminisms in Contemporary Theatre and Performance*, Houndmills: Palgrave Macmillan.
Auslander, Philip (2008) *Liveness: Performance in a Mediatised Culture*, 2nd edn, London and New York: Routledge.

Beckerman, Bernard (1970) *Dynamics of Drama*, New York: Alfred A. Knopf.

Bogart, Anne (2006) "The Role of the Audience." *TCG National Conference 2006*, 9 June. Transcript.

Carlson, Marvin (1989) *Places of Performance. The Semiotics of Theatre Architecture*, Ithaca: Cornell UP.

——(2004) *Performance: A Critical Introduction*, 2nd edn, Routledge: New York and London.

Dolan, Jill (2005) *Utopia in Performance: Finding Hope at the Theatre*, Ann Arbor: Michigan UP.

Goffman, Erving (1959) *The Presentation of Self in Everyday Life*, New York: Random House.

Grotowski, Jerzy (1980) *Towards a Poor Theatre*, ed. Eugenio Barba, London: Methuen.

Harlow, Bob, Thomas Alfieri, Aaron Dalton and Anne Field (2011) "Building Deeper Relationships: How Steppenwolf Theatre Company is Turning Single-Ticket Buyers into Repeat Visitors," *Wallace Studies in Building Arts Audiences*, Bob Harlow Research and Consulting.

Hauser, Karen (2014) *The Demographics of the Broadway Audience*, New York: The Broadway League.

Henslowe, Philip (1961) *Henslowe's Diary*, 2nd edn, ed. R. A. Foakes, Cambridge: Cambridge UP.

Hildy, Franklin (2006–7) "Lessons from the Study of Historic Theatre Architecture," *Blueprints*, Vol. XXV, No. 1.

Jouvet, Louis (1936) "Success: The Theatre's Only Problem" in *Theatre Arts Anthology* (1950), eds. Rosamond Gilder, Hermine Rich Isaacs, Robert M. MacGregor and Edward Reed, New York: Theatre Arts Books.

Kushner, Brian (2012) "The Public." Available from http://publictheaterny.blogspot.com. au/ [18 December 2012].

Lilley, Heather (2010) "Vital Contact: Creating Interpretive Communities in a Moment of Reception," *About Performance*, vol. 10.

Mackintosh, Iain (1993) *Architecture, Actor and Audience*, London: Routledge.

McAuley, Gay (2000) *Space in Performance: Making Meaning in the Theatre*, Ann Arbor: Michigan UP.

Mermira, Tina (2013) *State of Play: Theatre UK*. LiveAnalytics, Ticketmaster International.

Murdoch, Alexi (2012) "Theatre Etiquette Debate on Q," *CBC Radio,* 9 May 2012. Available from http://www.cbc.ca/player/Radio/Q/ID/2232475993/?page=26 [18 December 2012].

Ostrower, Francie (2008) "Multiple Motives, Multiple Experiences" in *Engaging Art: The Next Great Transformation of America's Cultural Life*, eds. Steven J. Tepper and Bill Ivey, New York: Routledge.

Pepys, Samuel (1663) *Project Gutenberg's Diary of Samuel Pepys*, ed. Henry B. Wheatley, trans. Rev. Mynors Bright. Available from: http://www.gutenberg.org/files/4200/4200-h/ 4200-h.htm [24 May 2014].

Rancière, Jacques (2009) *The Emancipated Spectator*, trans. Gregory Elliott. London and New York: Verso.

Sartre, Jean-Paul (1976) *Sartre on Theatre*, eds. Michel Contat and Michel Rybalka, trans. Frank Jellinek, New York: Pantheon.

Strasberg, Lee (1988) *A Dream of Passion: The Development of the Method*, New York: Plume.

Turner, Victor (1974) *Drama, Fields and Metaphors*, Ithaca and London: Cornell UP.

6

AUDIENCE AS CONSUMER

It is a chilly April morning in Hamilton, New Jersey. A crowd has gathered in a local car park. At this point they are strangers to each other. Their stilted conversations and enthusiasm serve as a buffer against the biting wind. A convoy of coaches arrive. Their operators perch on the entrance steps and address the crowd: "*Assembled Parties!*," "*Orphans!*" The operators entice them to enter "this coach for *How to Succeed in Business*," and announce destinations "*Chicago*," "*Motown*." The crowd disperses and individuals and couples clamber onto the coach that bears the name of the production they have purchased tickets to see. Once enveloped in the warmth of the interiors, the strangers' dialogue is punctuated with laughter as anecdotes, tips and excitement are shared in anticipation of the forthcoming experience:

> I saw him in *Priscilla*. He was amazing!
> I bought these tickets as a Christmas present for them.
> I love musicals the most: they are feel-good.
> I went onto Broadway Box and got the tickets cheaper.
> I don't get out much so this is a real treat.

After a two-hour journey the coaches arrive in Midtown Manhattan. Individuals and couples now form into groups and continue their animated dialogue as they walk to Planet Hollywood. A free beer glass comes with the meal. "I'm going to give it to my son-in-law: he collects them." Dialogue now focuses on Broadway show memorabilia. One person is wearing a *Jersey Boys* sweatshirt, another produces a dishevelled ticket stub out of the depths of her pocket-book:

> It's from the opening week of *Phantom*; I've seen *Phantom* eight times now.
> I've seen *Wicked* twelve times: it's my favourite.
> I didn't like it, I thought it was overdone.
> What! How?[1]

The group discusses Broadway shows. On their arrival at the theatre to see this particular show, ushers invite the coach group, now audience members, to join the cast on stage. Some stand on stage and tap their feet to the music; others sit in the auditorium and devour their playbills. During interval the audience are again invited onto the stage, into the world of the show, to purchase a drink from the Dublin pub. Ushers have to limit the throngs of audience members that want to enter the stage. An audience member dances back to her seat, drink in hand: "It's a spectator experience. There aren't any spectators anymore, just experiences. Spectating is the experience." After the show some audience members purchase souvenirs: an i-phone case, a scarf, a keyring. Exhilarated but exhausted, the dialogue on the drive home is a chorus of reflections, comparisons and snoring. Souvenirs are displayed and examined. In the late afternoon, car-park warm farewells consummate the theatrical experience.

I was a fellow audience member on this coach tour to New York to see *Once* in 2013. I purchased the whole Broadway package: coach, lunch, gift and show. Theatre packages in major cities can include coach or even air transportation, accommodation, dinner, a show, and time to purchase theatrical memorabilia. As Bennett argues, in New York and London, the theatrical experience is "a premium cultural product" (2005: 408).

Kershaw documents that from the 1950s to the 1970s the audience role transformed from patron to client and then from client to customer from the 1980s to around 2000 (2001: 141). The rise of the spectacle musical in the 1980s helped herald this "customer" role, which I call audience as consumer. We have already encountered the audience as consumer in the late nineteenth century: the fashionables. The consumer practice in theatres over the last three decades can be seen as a revival of the fashionables' consumer role. Although there are new ensembles playing this role now and the purchasing habits and products have changed, the motivations for playing the role remain essentially the same. Consumption is an avenue for audiences to retain some autonomy and to extend the pleasure of the event. As argued in this chapter, it is a role embraced with much verve and enthusiasm by particular audience ensembles. In this second decade of the twenty-first century, as illustrated in the above narrative, there are many opportunities for audiences to perform the role of consumer. This chapter begins with a discussion of the audience as consumer and then considers opportunities for the audience to perform this role in the theatrical experience.

"Package," "consumer," "transaction," "exchange": theatre studies often baulk at these terms, but audience members and actors often employ this language of consumer culture:

It's all about how [the show] is packaged.

(Keith 2013, Audience member, PI)

Well for me it is a pretty standard sort of exchange with the audience.

(Owen-Taylor 2014, Actor, PI)

> The time-travel scenes [in *Somewhere in Time*] were hard to buy.
>
> *(Holly 2013, Audience member, cited in Healy 2014)*

This chapter borrows from the language of economists and arts management.[2] Rather than take the more traditionally pessimistic approach to the commodification of audience experience,[3] economic terms are employed for the purposes of describing the very palpable activity of exchange that occurs between audience and box office, audience and merchandise, and audience and concession stand. "Consumption," a term predominantly applied to an economic rather than cultural milieu, is defined for the purposes of this chapter as a process in which the purchaser of an item is actively engaged in trying to create and maintain a sense of identity through the display of purchased goods (Baudrillard 1988: 10–20). I use one of Abraham Maslow's motivating factors of individuals, the need for esteem, to explore the motivations of the audience consumer. Audience as consumer is, as the case study explores, the most self-conscious role of all those explored in this book.

Esteem

The practice of purchasing as a means for constructing identity is interrelated to the audience member's need for esteem. Maslow's hierarchy of needs progress from basic motivating factors of survival to self-actualisation: the physiological needs, the safety needs, the social needs, the esteem needs and the need for self-actualisation. The theatre, as discussed in the previous chapter, meets the social needs. Esteem needs are often met when the audience is valued as a critic and the theatre offers the potential, as seen in the subsequent chapter, to fulfil aspects of self-actualisation. The consumerism I discuss focuses specifically on the esteem needs. Maslow argues that "all people in our society (with a few pathological exceptions) have a need or desire for a stable, firmly based, (usually) high evaluation of themselves, for self-respect, or self-esteem, and for the esteem of others" (1943: 381). In the contemporary theatre, one vehicle for audiences to meet this need for esteem is through playing the role of consumer.

In contemporary theatre an audience's consumer power is far more significant than their verbal power. Maslow describes how self-esteem leads "to feelings of self-confidence, worth, strength, capability and adequacy of being useful and necessary in the world" and, if this need is not met, disempowerment leads to discouragement (1943: 382). The contemporary audience's power as a co-performer or contributor to the event is limited: they can laugh and they can applaud. Their power as a consumer is, however, manifold: they can purchase tickets, subscriptions, programmes, badges, stickers, fur toys, pens, aprons, hoodies, lip gloss, scarfs, cushions, bags, pins, hoola hoops, mugs, eyelashes, bracelets, flip-flops, nail-polish, i-phone cases, onesies, caps and t-shirts. At interval they can purchase alcohol, cold drinks, hot drinks, sweets, potato crisps, nuts and ice creams. They can purchase a theatre package with a coach, flight, meal and accommodation. The opportunities to consume are boundless; the opportunities to contribute are restricted. In the last two decades of the twentieth century, purchasing was one of the few activities available for audience members who desired to play a more participatory role in the theatre event. Purchasing was an avenue through which audiences could construct an identity to build or regain esteem. Audience members who relish the opportunity of playing the role of consumer in the theatre form the largest contemporary ensemble in mainstream theatre: the tourist audience.

The Tourist Audience

In the 2013–14 Broadway season, approximately 70 per cent of the tickets were purchased by tourists (Hauser 2014).[4] This percentage has steadily been rising in New York yearly. At the inception of the data collection by the Broadway League 16 years ago, only 39 per cent of the tickets were purchased by tourists. The millennium tourist continues practices that are similar to the fashionable audience's performance in the theatre houses in the late nineteenth century. As discussed in the next chapter, the tourists often talk during performances, are easily distracted and sometimes sleep during the performance. Around the *fin de siècle* purchasing garments worn on stage worked to construct the fashionables' identity and distinguish them as a particular audience ensemble. Purchasing tickets, packages, merchandise and wearing their own identifiable costume works to construct the identity of the contemporary tourist.

Similar to the fashionables, the tourist ensemble's repertoire of actions is more extensive and at the same time more prescribed than that of the local or subscriber audience member.[5] Because the tourist has been taken out of their quotidian lives, they often give more demonstrative performances than if they were attending a local social event. Their identity as tourist, in many ways, liberates them from normative behaviour. They employ what De Certeau calls "tactics" to "take advantage of 'opportunities'" (1984: 94) to perform and can be quite creative. Playing the role of tourist in the theatre disinhibits personalities, sanctions extraordinary behaviour and frees the "inner-actor." Yet the tourist performance is often prescribed by preconceived norms or perceived constructions of how a "world" tourist "should" perform. The most generalised character breakdown of the tourist reads: "gregarious, uses lots of large gestures, loud." The tourist costume includes athletic shoes, nylon cargo pants and a cap with a tourist destination imprint. Props are often a water bottle and camera. While this may appear trite, the tourist role is so very well developed and articulated, the dialogue, and even timbre of the voice, scripted, that some homage is due to the animated character role that the tourist plays in our contemporary auditoriums.

Esteem can be gained from playing this role well in the theatre. Similar to Benchley's scathing criticisms of the demonstrative audience's esteem building camaraderie during ovations in the 1920s, tourists are often admonished in contemporary theatres for their unrestrained and demonstrative standing ovations. The contemporary tourist performance and detailed analysis of their consumption practices are often well documented in critical reviews.[6] Apart from these pejorative remarks, and despite the tourist audience's growing numbers, there have been few accounts of this gregarious audience group in theatre scholarship until quite recently. Fortunately, accounts of tourist audiences are now materialising in theatre scholarship with occasional entire chapters dedicated to their practices.[7] We are all tourists, unknowingly or otherwise, at some time in our lives.[8]

Audience as Consumer

Every audience member plays the role of consumer on some level. The purchasing of merchandise and collection of theatre memorabilia can provide another vehicle, similar to critical commentary, to empower and build the esteem of audience members. During theatrical events, contemporary audience members naturally search for products to purchase to construct their identity, extend their pleasure and stake their share of ownership in the cultural product. Although this activity is market-driven,[9] many audience members have embraced this practice with so much unconcealed enthusiasm that it is injudicious to ignore their performance and their perspectives. Kevin goes to Broadway shows once a month because he loves "to be part of the action" (2014, PI). For Kevin this means purchasing merchandise, packages and experiences. Purchasing is part of the audience's performative role.

Audiences perform the role of consumer through the activity of purchasing tickets for the cultural product or the coach package and purchasing programmes, merchandise and refreshments at interval. With the emergence of the spectacle musical, the 1980s saw a particular proliferation of theatrical merchandise. Ownership of t-shirts, mugs, soundtracks, stuffed toys and badges emblazoned with show titles, logos and images secured a new cultural identity for the consumer. Peaking in the 1990s with merchandise guru Disney's production of *The Lion King*, entertainment retail has now become a demanded aspect of the theatrical experience. Just as consumers use clothing brand names to construct a social identity, they also use the ethereal face of Cosette in *Les Misérables* on a t-shirt to construct a cultural or tourist identity. Sometimes the social and cultural identities are imbricated when, for example, the green crooked smile of the Witch of the West from *Wicked* peeps out from the top of a pair of Converse hi-tops. The construction of identity through merchandise purchase escalated to the point that purchasing and, as Kershaw argues, "wearing the *Phantom of the Opera* T-shirt and/or a National Theatre peaked cap may be even more culturally charged than an evening in the stalls watching the show" (1994: 174).

The Pleasure of Purchasing

The purchasing of merchandise is a means of extending the pleasure of the theatrical experience. Forty–fifty per cent of audience members purchase some sort of merchandise at productions on Broadway (Bonanni 2013, PI). The cold, static piece of merchandise is instantly transformed once it is clutched tightly in the warm hands of the audience purchaser: it becomes a souvenir, a keepsake, a memento, a treasured item of memorabilia. The souvenir works to memorialise the experience for the audience member. The audience members on the New Jersey coach tour affectionately handled their souvenirs. At home the souvenir will be worn, attached to keys, filled with coffee, displayed on a wall or a shelf. It becomes a memorial. The object subsumes all the memories of the experience, which will be re-performed each time the souvenir is viewed, used or discussed.

Re-performing the experience is most potent when the souvenir is displayed to a friend and the experience is relayed through dialogue. Re-performing can also work to build esteem. This occurred on the coach and during the Planet Hollywood lunch. The ticket stub from *Phantom of the Opera* became a means for gaining the esteem of others. The object represents the experience. Talking about or wearing the souvenir not only memorialises, but can extend the pleasure of the theatrical experience because of this very association. As Bentham argues, pleasures in objects are "afford[ed], not of themselves, but merely in virtue of some association they have contracted in the mind with certain […] incidents which are in themselves pleasurable" (cited in Winter 2011: 53). The object recalls and sometimes immortalises the production for the beholders. While the initial thrill of purchasing can be seen as hedonistic, the longer-term fulfilment that the memorialised object brings is eudaimonic.

The theatrical programme, more than any other souvenir, stirs the memory of the event.[10] Some audience members cherish and almost deify their programmes. Eileen is a regular subscriber to Steppenwolf. She reads her programme cover to cover and refers to it as "the book": "The book is always there by my bed at night when I get home so I can say, wait, what was that?" (2013, PI). For some audience members, the programme subsumes all the memories of the suspended moments of the production. For Wayne it becomes "a time capsule to capture a special moment in time" (2014, PI). In the United States, the playbill, which is complimentary, is an institution. Large collections of playbills can number up to 30,000 (BroadwayWorld. com 2010). Collections of glossy souvenir programmes, often because of the high cost, are more conservative. Anita, a British financial controller, is a programme collector. She often shows the programmes to other people because she likes "to promote theatre" (2014, PI). During these times, Anita's experiences are re-performed.

At the theatrical event itself, the programme directs the gaze of the audience member. Joshua sees it as "a map to an undiscovered country" (2013, PI). Some of the gaze is directed towards the stage, the play, the actors, the other theatre professionals and the playwright, but often the gaze is directed towards consumption. Many programmes contain a strong directive on how to perform as audience members: as consumers. Conservatively, 60 per cent of the Broadway playbill is filled with directions of where to eat, park, stay, shop, bank, subscribe, holiday, worship,[11] get insured and what to buy your children for their birthdays. Advertising fills approximately 30 per cent of the comparative West End programme. Similar to the late nineteenth-century programme that emerged as a garment catalogue for the fashionables, the advertisements in the contemporary programme re-enforce the audience role as consumer. Theatre merchandise manager Bonanni can ascertain when audiences are going to purchase more souvenirs during productions on Broadway by "how well people are reacting" and how much they are enjoying themselves (2013, PI). As a product catalogue, a keepsake, a time capsule, a map or a means for building esteem, the theatre souvenir documents, memorialises and extends the pleasure of the event for audience members.

Ownership

I stated earlier that audience members cite fashion changes as the largest alteration in the audience experience over the years. The second aspect is the inflation of ticket prices (see Appendix 1). Audience members, actors, directors and other theatre professionals are beleaguered by the high cost[12] of seeing a Broadway or West End production:

> Who can afford to get a good ticket?
>
> *(Lee 2013, Actor, PI)*

> You pay a lot of money. You expect a lot of bang for your buck.
>
> *(Linda 2013, Audience member, PI)*

> The prices have gone up; they are much dearer than they used to be.
>
> *(Doreen 2014, Audience member, PI)*

> Ticket prices when you first look at them can be extremely expensive, especially when you consider we travel to London with the extra accommodation costs.
>
> *(Barry 2014, Audience member, PI)*

In 2014, standard ticket prices for a Broadway show ranged from $80 to $140, with musicals such as *The Book of Mormon* peaking at $477 during some times in the season. On the West End, tickets ranged from £12 to £152. Perceived exorbitant ticket prices affect the performance of the audience. In Chapter One I discussed how the now quotidian practice of standing ovations can be seen as corollary of audience ownership[13] because of the high price paid for the tickets. Some audience members argue that they purchase the performance rights to perform in whatever way they choose. Wayne contends, "You pay $80, $100, $200 for certain shows, you have a right to do what you want" (2014, PI). Keith, a student, emphasises, "[I]f I am paying a considerable amount of money then I want to have customer's rights."[14] This sense of entitlement is not dissimilar to the "rights" of the audiences of the first half of the nineteenth century. The ticket stub with $140 printed on one end has become a kind of contract of entitlement. That the high entrance price unfortunately excludes almost anyone that earns under a certain amount is an issue that some theatre companies, such as Signature discussed in the preceding chapter, are trying to rectify. Perhaps theatre managements are fearful of a return of the boisterous gallery gods and goddesses and their demonstrative performances should some lower ticket prices be made available.

Regardless of the inequity and the sometimes solipsistic entitlement that is associated with inflated ticket purchases, ownership of theatrical merchandise or a ticket to a Broadway or West End production is one way that contemporary audience members build esteem. Theatre-goers enjoy sharing their theatrical souvenirs and programmes with others to construct cultural identity. Purchasing tickets to a theatre production for Caroline, a school librarian, is "not an everyday transaction" but one that makes her feel she is purchasing ownership of an experience that is "a little bit special."[15]

Audience as Guest at the Theatrical Experience

Part of "feeling a bit special" at the theatre is purchasing the privilege to be a guest rather than a customer. In this new millennium, audiences are more frequently being welcomed by theatre managements as guests rather than patrons or customers (Prendergast 2008). This is an important part of esteem building for contemporary audience members. In the questionnaire, audience members identified that they would prefer to be treated as a guest more than a patron or customer in the theatre (see Appendix 2). What was more significant, however, was their reasons:

> I just feel the term guest implies that you are part of the experience.
> I want to feel like I am "at home."
> Something special, different – not an everyday thing.
> Theatre is an art of the people and for the people and I want to feel like I'm part of their family.[16]

The majority of the responses, such as these, indicated that by being identified as a guest, audiences felt a sense of community, felt special or part of the larger theatrical family or experience. This desire to belong or feel part of an experience was also a recurring motif in the interviews and is taken up in the next chapter.

As ticket purchasers, some audience members still regarded themselves as customers. Michael, an editor from Sydney, identified more as a customer because, he stated, "I think patron is condescending" (2014a, PI). Patrick, a glass fitter from London, wanted to be treated as a customer because he felt he would then get better "service."[17] As exemplified here and previously, audience members regularly employ the language of consumerism, even when purchasing a cultural experience. Ric Knowles argues that contemporary audiences "understand [themselves] to be consumers" (2004: 32). The theatrical event is packaged as a commodity precisely for this reason.

Theatrical events, in many ways, are commodity-centric: theatre companies package the commodity – the event – then ask how it affects the consumer. Some theatre companies do not even bother to ask, they just "show." The theatrical "event" can be exclusive for audience members. Conversely, the theatrical "experience" has the potential to become inclusive.

At the turn of the millennium, audience development departments in theatre companies quickly capitalised on the packaging of the experience, marketing the "audience experience" in addition to the actual event. The emergent experience mindset in mainstream theatre can also be traced to non-mainstream influences. Participatory and immersive theatre stress and privilege the experience of the spectator often by addressing the audience as guests.[18] Punchdrunk's immersive theatre experience *Sleep No More*, now in its fifth year in New York, invites audience members to join them as "guests" at the McKittrick Hotel to embark on a journey lasting up to three hours "in which audiences experience epic and emotional storytelling inside sensory theatrical worlds" (Maughan 2013: 7). The ubiquity and phenomenal popularity of immersive theatre experiences, especially for young people, herald the new age of purchasing experiences that audiences can be part of rather than events that they can watch. Over the past decades, the theatrical "experience" has superseded the theatrical "event."

Mainstream companies, such as the National Theatre in London, are capitalising on the success of companies like Punchdrunk through collaborations.[19] In arenas such as these the previous well-constructed and policed boundaries between fringe theatre and the mainstream are blurring. Examples of how this is beginning to change the participatory elements of the theatrical experience are discussed more in the proceeding chapter. Lyn Gardner believes that this blurring is driven by audiences that "crave the intimacy and connectedness that live art can deliver, but which is mostly absent" in the mainstream playhouse (2013: 84, 85). As Conner argues, audiences "don't want 'the arts,' they want the arts experience" (2013: 24). The two seemingly divergent legacies of the "experience" – one economically driven by theatre marketing, the other artistic – can be seen to work cooperatively to create a sometimes unpredictable but always memorable experience in the mainstream theatre for audience members.

Interestingly, in my conversations with audiences, interviewees used the term "experience" 57 times to describe what it means for them to be going to the theatre. "Event" was mentioned only 13 times. Katie is a senior policy researcher from London. When asked what "being" an audience member meant, she stated, "It means an experience" and then went on to describe that it is also a "sharing experience" and a "relaxing experience" (2014, PI). Many audience members described productions as "shared experiences" and "unique experiences." Other epithets included personal, emotional, natural, exciting, memorable, new, lifting, cultural, great, immersive, fabulous, enjoyable and unusual experiences.

In *The Experience Economy*, Pine and Gilmour argue that we need to re-focus on how individuals experience the using of commodities. They state that "staging experiences is not about entertaining customers; it's about engaging them" (2011: 45). When audiences are given the opportunity to perform – as critics, as community, as co-creators and even as consumers – they are engaged "on an emotional, physical, intellectual or even spiritual level" (Pine and Gilmour 2011: 17) in an experience.

Contemporary audience members desire to be engaged on many levels. To be engaged they often want to purchase more than products. When asked, "What do you most want from going to the theatre?" 68 per cent of the questionnaire respondents said, "To have a good time *and* learn something." Only 18 per cent said that their main objective was to have a good time (see Appendix 2). For some, part of the entertainment experience is consuming meaning or knowledge. Lindsay goes to the theatre around six times a year. For her, "going to the theatre is exercise for [her] mind" (2014, PI). Maggie from Canada goes to the theatre because "learning is enjoyment. Learning and enjoyment go hand in hand" (2013, PI). There were a wide range of aspects that were considered "knowledge," including knowledge gained from the dramatist, from the actor's interpretations, from the characters in the play, from the issues in the play and knowledge about the human condition.[20] Often respondents associated purchasing and knowledge consumption: "I am doing it for fun and spending money on it so I want to get something out of it."[21]

De Certeau argues that consumers do not have "any *place* in which they can indicate what they *make* and *do*" (1984: xii) with the knowledge or products they have acquired from entertainment. Audience-centred post-show discussions, discussed in Chapter Four, are one vehicle through which the consumed knowledge can be performed and also provide an opportunity for audiences to feel more of a guest at the theatrical experience. Some progressive mainstream theatres and theatre companies are beginning to understand and embrace the experience model that invites audiences to be guests at a cultural experience. For this they are indebted not only to audience development departments but also their fringe theatre cousins.

Consuming the Right to Perform

What does this experience look like in twenty-first-century theatres? Audiences as consumers purchase the right to perform. An emergent practice in mainstream theatres that is clearly experiential for audience members is audience "theming." While ushering, Fokes has observed some audience members, what he calls, "theming" productions by wearing costumes to the theatre reflecting the play or musical's themes. Audience members wear Goth gear for *The Addams Family*, tutus with boxing gloves around their necks for *Billy Elliot*, leather jackets with their hair slicked back for *Grease*, feather boas and dresses dripping in sequins for *Strictly Ballroom*, and lion onesies for *The Lion King*. Fokes explained that these colourful audience performers are not only individuals: "We had a whole group, must have been about six of them, all in Pink Lady Jackets: girls' night out at the theatre" (2013, PI). The rise of the colourful ensemble of girls-night-outers is well documented in *A Good Night Out for the Girls* (Aston and Harris 2013). Although girl groups tend to be more prevalent, some productions on Broadway are also attracting ensembles of boys–night-outers: *Rocky*, *Rock of Ages*, *Big Fish* and *The Book of Mormon*.[22] Having first issued the invitation for audiences to perform in 1981, the 2014 revamped production of *Cats* now offers audiences the opportunity of having their faces painted as cats in the London Palladium foyer as part of their experience. Cats onstage perform to cats in the audience. Through theming, audience members can be seen to not only purchase the experience, but the right to take part in the experience.

In a practice reminiscent of the decades in the late nineteenth and early twentieth century when, as Schweitzer states, "Broadway was the runway" (2009), Lord and Taylor once again in the spring of 2013 filled its window displays with fashions from the Broadway production of *Kinky Boots*. In the following spring of 2014, spring fashions from *Beautiful – the Carole King Musical* extended the experience of the production by featuring costumes from the musical. These showings were preceded by window displays of fashions from *How to Succeed in Business* in 2011 and *Promises, Promises* in 2010. Twenty-first-century audience members not only wear costumes in the audience, but, through purchasing and wearing fashions "inspired by" productions, extend the diegesis of the play into the streets of New York.

Do the audience performers in their pink or leather jackets or their costume-inspired garments begin to perform the characters they are portraying? By purchasing a "costume" have the audience purchased the right to become co-performers? It is obvious that the audience display of costumes and merchandise in the auditorium is essentially playful. During that brief suspension of disbelief in the theatre, they are playing a role that extends their pleasure and experience. This role performance of wearing costumes inside and outside the auditorium can be seen as a desire for more participation in the theatrical experience. Twenty-first-century audiences are developing novel ways of performing in the theatre through theming. They know they are part of a larger experience. Mary has been going to the theatre for over 60 years. "Being" an audience member for her means she is "part of an experience that involves an author, actors and the people around you. It's just a great experience. It's one of those things in life that you just want to keep doing. It's an art form, so you want to participate in an art form" (2014a, PI).

Audience members have long considered going to the theatre an experience, but it is often described in different terms:

> Going to the theatre has [...] become more of an occasion.
>
> *(David 2013b, PI)*

> It's the occasion, it's a night out, it's something to look forward to, it's a planned event, you have dinner before/after. It's like a big production: getting ready and getting dressed up.
>
> *(Wayne 2014, PI)*

> I like the atmosphere of it, well, the theatre of the theatre. So I think that's what I enjoy from going to the theatre, it is a sense of occasion.
>
> *(Sue 2014, PI)*

In the sense that these audience members use the term, an "occasion" is "a special ceremony or celebration; a social function; a significant or noteworthy happening; an opportunity" (OED, "Occasion"). Attending a play or a musical incorporates so much more than just the event itself for these audience members. The experience begins long before the production. It is an opportunity "to look forward to," a social function that starts with preparation for the "big production," having dinner, and then immersing themselves in "the atmosphere" of this significant or noteworthy happening. Occasion is synonymous with experience because it embraces the entire experience of the audience member. It is almost interchangeable: the "theatrical occasion." Theatrical occasions are something that are looked forward to. In this they are similar to what Maslow calls "peak-experiences" that "are life-validating, i.e., they make life worth living" (1999: 230). Interestingly, Maslow argues that in experiencing "peak-experiences, [people] are *most* their identities, closest to their real selves" (1999: 115). This is an intriguing observation in the context of the theatrical experience. The theatrical experience is, perhaps, a stage on which audience members can perform their identity.

Theatre packages, such as the coach tour described above, are pertinent examples of how the entire experience rather than just the event has traction in mainstream theatres. In the auditorium there are small but heartening "happenings" in mainstream theatre, indicating that the theatrical event is evolving into an experience. The audience member of *Once* that danced back to her seat after purchasing a drink at the onstage bar did not say, "It's all about the spectator *event*," but rather "*experience*." While there was a certain glee in her exclamation that was contagious and at the same time slightly unnerving in its entitlement, it was clear that the experience for her was participatory, inclusive and enjoyable. It was no longer about the event onstage or even the whole event-ness. It was about her experience.

All of these performances as consumer – the purchasing and wearing of merchandise, costumes and fashions inspired by productions and the experience of the theatre package – work to build the esteem of the audience member through ownership, performance and building identity. Kennedy asks if we will "ever be able to restate or refuse the commodity status of watching a spectacle?" (2009: 179). One way to answer this is to reframe the question: How can the audience experience be heightened *in* a commodity culture? Maslow argues that a central tenet of the need for esteem is "the desire for reputation or prestige" (1943: 382). In early twenty-first-century Western culture, the desire for reputation and prestige is personified through the performance of the self in selfies, Facebook, about.me, and multiple other simulacrum. To explore the fetish for performing oneself in the millennium theatrical experience, we need to journey to the venue of a para-theatrical experience that occurs before and sometimes after the production: the red stairs of Times Square. Times Square is a total theatrical consumer experience.

Case Study
Times Square: Self-Conscious Performance

Broadway carves a defiant, diagonal path across the ordered grid of New York streets. If, as De Certeau asserts, people who walk the streets of cities are practitioners whose pathways inscribe poems (1984: 93), then the narrative of many New York *Wandersmänner* concludes in Times Square. Earnest tourists, tired business wo/men and curious travellers meander down Broadway to meet in this foyer of the theatre district. Travellers are drawn to Times Square by some unconscious yearning for a sense of place: "It's a great place to be. We need to go here first when we arrive to feel like we are in New York."[23] Times Square seems to subsume all what De Certeau calls the "magical" properties that locations that are ideas more than places encompass. It is not just the effervescent lights of Times Square that bring it worldwide acclaim; it is the bearers of this acclaim, the audience that bask in the electric atmosphere. The name Times Square is "carried as [an] emblem by the travellers [it] directs and simultaneously decorate[s]" (De Certeau 1984: 104). Times Square is not an event; it is a twenty-first-century consumer experience that primes and prepares the audience for their auditorium performance.

Having arrived at this nexus of their itinerary, the tourist audience is first confronted with a set of red stairs that seem to lead to infinite possibilities: your name in lights, a good place to rest, a meeting point, a place to eat, a place to watch, a place to imagine. It is these last two aspects that I focus on. In what De Certeau calls the "spatial acting-out of place" (1984: 98), audiences perform on the red stairs of Times Square in myriad ways. They drink, eat, laugh, talk, play, kiss, embrace, listen to music, text, tweet and take photographs.

No longer wanderers, they have become *wächters*. An odd, anachronistic figure watches over the *wächters*: a statue of Father Duffy, a much decorated military chaplain from the First World War that stands at the bottom of the stairs.[24] Although the statue and the cross behind him are large and imposing, he is often invisible to the *wächters*. His presence is upstaged by the digital screens that become Joanne Tompkins's impermanent "counter-monuments" (2006: 47) projecting the seeming desires and values of those that watch.

The *wächters* have not only come to watch the digital screens that scream for their attention, they have come to watch each other perform:

> It is a great place to be, chat and have a look around and see how funny people are. You feel like you are with friends. You can see people's excitement on their faces.
> You find all sorts of people. There is a kind of camaraderie between the tourists. It's friendly.[25]

From the red-staired seating bank of their theatre, this community audience watch or window shop at the production: the vast display of super-saturated, pulsating digital images that captivate, mesmerise and offer to satisfy. The lights become the focal point:

> Everybody's bewildered by the lights and the size. Everything's larger than life.
> Something amazing. I haven't seen anything like this. It's always day. The lights are very, very bright.[26]

The dizzy, bewildering light display spectacularises not only productions on Broadway, but also spectacularises other forms of entertainment, products, services, travel destinations, the stock market, annual holidays, belief systems and conspiracy theories. Every show, product or idea that is imagined on the larger-than-life screens instantly receives celebrity status. The screens reflect back or offer for consumption the desires, needs and wants of the *wächters*.

The screens are often a reflection of the *wächters* themselves. An image of a red stair *wächter* can suddenly be projected onto a digital screen. In this early twenty-first century that trades in images, it is almost as if the *wächter's* reflection is offered as another product for consumption. During this apotheosis into a celebrity, the *wächter* becomes highly self-conscious. Since 2009, opportunities for this kind of self-conscious performance in Times Square and other public arenas have escalated. In Times Square you can "leave your mark" and have your "15 seconds of fame" with your image on a digital billboard. A picture of "your beautiful skin" that "deserves to be shared" can appear on a print billboard. On another digital sign, in a strange kind of silent-film projection, your thoughts appear above your head in a speech bubble. If you manage to clamber through the other *wächters* to the summit of the red stairs you can view a film of yourself taking a photo of yourself.[27]

Times Square is full of watching people who watch each other and watch themselves up on the screens. There is a self-consciousness endemic to this performance of the self that is often at odds with the almost trance-like state that the *wächters* embody as they are hypnotised by the overwhelming digital screams. I have watched a face previously glazed with inertia and stupefaction suddenly sparkle with excitement once they see their image captured on a screen. The *wächter* becomes extremely self-conscious and animated and begins performing large facial and hand gestures in elation. This self-conscious performance is, perhaps, one way for the contemporary audience performer to retrieve what Maslow describes as a central aspect of the need for self-esteem: the desire for reputation and prestige.

Times Square primes the Broadway theatre audience for its auditorium performance. Once inside the theatres, the self-conscious performance continues. Actor Tony Sheldon states that the primary change he has witnessed in audiences over the last decade is not only their increased responsiveness but also their self-awareness. He observes that twenty-first-century audiences "are more responsive, but in a very self-conscious way" (2013, PI). Interestingly, this self-consciousness is not a source of embarrassment; it is an avenue for performing the self. Various young audience members interviewed described their practice of watching theatre in terms of a consciousness of themselves or their experience. Sarah, a British department store buyer, emphasised that "in the theatre, you feel like you're conscious of where you are when you're watching" (2014, PI). Lottie explained that she was very "conscious watching the theatre tonight" (2014, PI), then went on to explain how important consciousness was to her in all her activities.

An integral part of self-conscious performance in any activity or at any event is the selfie. Of the over 40 productions I saw in 2013 and 2014, there was rarely a performance when I did not witness a selfie being taken by an audience member, before, after and sometimes during the show; *wächters* taking photographs of themselves watching. Similar to the counter-monument screens in Times Square, the selfie is an impermanent souvenir that works more to build esteem than extend the long-term pleasure of the experience gained through purchasing merchandise. Taking selfies is the early twenty-first-century iteration of the fashionables' late nineteenth- and early twentieth-century practice of seeing and being seen at the theatre. In addition to purchasing merchandise, photographing images of the self or aspects of the production is a distinguishing practice of the audience consumer at the contemporary theatrical experience.

Taking a selfie in the theatre "draws attention to yourself," a practice that we have seen was frowned upon in the second half of the twentieth century. So many of what would have been considered backstage performances such as taking a selfie have now become frontstage performances in the new millennium. In self-conscious performance contemporary audiences, especially younger audience members, can satisfy their esteem needs. Self-conscious performance is practised regularly in everyday life and these practices are brought into the playhouse. Self-conscious performance can take myriad forms in the theatre that are, however, not only digital (explored in the next chapter). The theatrical experience, by its very nature, is a fertile environment for self-conscious performance for actors and audiences alike.

The theatrical performance has spilt out of the theatres on Broadway into the consumer culture of Times Square itself. Or has the Times Square culture permeated the theatre auditoriums? As the *wannersammner* walk and the *wächters* stare at screens and stages, purchasing products inside and outside the theatres, the margins of theatre and square meld to become one vast theatrical/tourist/consumer experience. In the congenial buzz and whirl of Times Square the *wächters'* esteem is elevated onto mega-screens, heightening the anticipation of their forthcoming auditorium performance as self-actualised co-creators.

Notes

1 I recorded these comments and the above during a Starr Broadway shows coach tour on 27 April 2013.

2 Academic research has frequently eschewed the work of arts management and audience development, and for good reason. Yet recent developments in this field are now espousing a more relational approach and considering the experiential rather than the transactional. For a comprehensive discussion of this new approach see Glow et al. (2013).

3 Christopher Balme argues that "public and scholarly consciousness since the beginning of the twentieth century" has considered commodification and its related terms in a negative light and has "not yet acknowledged [theatrical commodification] as a theoretical approach to theatre" (Balme 2005: 2).

4 This percentage includes domestic and international tourists who were not residents of New York City or its greater suburbs. Comparative statistics are not available for the West End as the Box Office Report definition of "tourist" differs. The numbers of tourists in West End theatres do, however, continue to rise as significantly as on Broadway.

5 It is important to note here that the "local" can become a tourist in her/his own town.

6 There are numerous examples of criticisms against tourist demonstrative behaviour in theatre critics reviews, online postings by other audience members and tweets. For examples see Gardner (2000) and Prescott (2005).

7 I would like to acknowledge Susan Bennett's trailblazing work in this area. Through early conversations I had with her and her subsequent articles on the tourist audience,

my own unfolding focus on mainstream audiences was clarified. For chapters and articles on the tourist audience see Schechner (2013), Kennedy (2009), and Bennett (2005).

8 Increasingly, the lines are becoming blurred between tourist and theatre regular. For example, Bennett argues that theatre scholars are "avid cultural tourists" (2005: 209).

9 Maurya Wickstrom describes how the American public constructs and performs their identities through "brandscapes" such as Disney, Nike and American Doll. Wickstrom argues that this identification with brands is destructive and works more to support global capitalism than fulfil individual needs (2006: 104).

10 For a deeper analysis of how audiences perceive the theatre programme see Heim (2008).

11 The Church of Jesus Christ of Latter-day Saints began posting advertisements in the *Book of Mormon* playbill in 2012.

12 The actual increase in cost over time in ticket prices is very difficult to gauge.

13 Anne Bogart refers to ownership as a disease: "[P]eople have spent so much on tickets [they] feel like they own it" (2013, PI).

14 Comment taken from London questionnaire, July 2014.

15 Ibid.

16 On the questionnaire, audience members were asked to identify why they had written "guest." This list is a small but indicative sample of the reasons written.

17 Comment taken from London questionnaire, July 2014.

18 Performance artist Sylvia Mercuriali refers to the audience, for example, as "guest-performers."

19 Punchdrunk originally collaborated with the National Theatre on *Faust* in 2006, then *The Masque of the Red Death* in 2007 and *The Drowned Man: A Hollywood Fable* in 2013.

20 Topics taken from respondents' answers on questionnaires.

21 One respondent's comment on questionnaire who selected "have a good time *and* learn something."

22 There are no specific records of male gay-night-outers, but, as McCollum states, "gay men are a core part of the Broadway audience" (cited in Healy 2014).

23 In August 2014 I interviewed 22 people sitting on the red stairs in Times Square. This was one comment recorded.

24 Australian architects John Choi and Tai Ropiha actually designed the steps, which were erected in 2008 to draw attention to the Francis Duffy monument (Hynes 2009).

25 Comments from August 2014 interviews (see Note 23).

26 Ibid.

27 These are just four examples of digital screens and print billboards that have projected images of "ordinary" people in Times Square since 2009.

References

Aston, Elaine and Geraldine Harris (2013) *A Good Night Out for the Girls: Popular Feminisms in Contemporary Theatre and Performance*, Houndmills: Palgrave Macmillan.

Balme, Christopher (2005) "Selling the Bird: Richard Walton Tully's *The Bird of Paradise* and the Dynamics of Theatrical Commodification," *Theatre Journal*, vol. 57, no. 1: 1–20.

Baudrillard, Jean (1988) *Selected Writings*, Cambridge: Polity Press.

Bennett, Susan (2005) "Theatre/Tourism," *Theatre Journal*, vol. 57, no. 3: 407–28.

BroadwayWorld.com (2010) "Extremely Large Playbill Collection." Available from: http://www.broadwayworld.com/board/readmessage.php?thread=1018843 [1 December 2014].

Conner, Lynne (2013) *Audience Engagement and the Role of Arts Talk in the Digital Era*, New York: Palgrave Macmillan.

De Certeau, Michel (1984) *The Practice of Everyday Life*, Berkeley and Los Angeles: California UP.

Gardner, Lyn (2000) "Just Sit Down and Shut Up," *The Guardian*, 14 October.

——(2013) "There is Something Stirring," *Programme Notes: Case Studies for Locating Experimental Theatre*. 2nd edn, eds. Lois Keidan and C. J. Mitchell, London: Oberon.

Glow, Hilary, Katya Johanson and Jennifer Radbourne (eds.) (2013) *The Audience Experience: A Critical Analysis of Audiences in the Performing Arts*, Bristol: Intellect.

Hauser, Karen (2014) *The Demographics of the Broadway Audience*, New York: The Broadway League.

Healy, Patrick (2014) "In Audiences on Broadway, Fewer Guys among the Dolls." 29 March. Available from: http://www.nytimes.com/2014/03/30/theater/in-broadway-seats-few-guys-among-the-dolls.html [27 November 2014].

Heim, Caroline (2008) "The Theatre Programme: A Public Discourse at a Staging of Maxwell Anderson's *Anne of the Thousand Days*" in *Being There: Before, During and After*, Proceedings of the 2006 Annual Conference of the Australasian Drama, Theatre, and Performance Studies, ed. Ian Maxwell, The University of Sydney.

Hynes, Ruth (2009) "TKTS Booth and Father Duffy Square by Choi Rodiha, Perkins Eastman and PKSB Arts," *De Zeen Magazine*, 26 November. Available from: http://www.dezeen.com/2009/11/26/tkts-booth-and-father-duffy-square-by-choi-ropiha-perkins-eastman-and-pksb-architects/ [15 October 2014].

Kennedy, Dennis (2009) *The Spectator and the Spectacle: Audiences in Modernity and Postmodernity*, Cambridge: Cambridge UP.

Kershaw, Baz (1994) "Framing the Audience for the Theatre" in *The Authority of the Consumer*, eds. Russell Keat, Nigel Whitely and Nicholas Abercrombie, London and New York: Routledge.

——(2001) "Oh for Unruly Audiences! Or, Patterns of Participation in Twentieth Century Theatre," *Modern Drama*, vol. 42, no. 2: 133–54.

Knowles, Ric (2004) *Reading the Material Theatre*, Cambridge: Cambridge UP.

Maughan, Tallie (copy ed.) (2013) *Punchdrunk's Sleep No More*, 23 April 2013, programme, McKittrick Hotel: New York.

Maslow, Abraham H. (1943) "A Theory of Human Motivation," *Psychological Review*, vol. 50.

——(1999). *Toward a Psychology of Being*, 3rd edn, New York: John Wiley.

OED "Occasion". Available from: http://www.oed.com/view/Entry/130114?rskey=ApEJGU&result=1#eid [21 March 2014]

Pine, Joseph and James Gilmour (2011) *The Experience Economy: Work is Theatre and Every Business a Stage*, Boston: Harvard Business School Press.

Prendergast, Monica (2008) "From Guest to Witness: Teaching Audience Studies in Postsecondary Theatre Education," *Theatre Topics*, vol. 18, no. 2: 95–106.

Prescott, Paul (2005) "Inheriting the Globe: The Reception of Shakespearean Space and Audience in Contemporary Reviewing" in *A Companion to Shakespeare and Performance*, eds. Barbara Hodgdon and W. B. Worthen, Malden: Blackwell.

Schechner, Richard (2013) *Performance Studies: An Introduction*, 3rd edn, Abingdon: Routledge.

Schweitzer, Marlis (2009) *When Broadway was the Runway: Theatre, Fashion and the American Culture*, Philadelphia: Pennsylvania UP.

Tompkins, Joanne (2006) *Unsettling Space: Contestations in Contemporary Australian Theatre*, Houndmills: Palgrave Macmillan.

Wickstrom, Maurya (2006) *Performing Consumers*, New York: Routledge.

Winter, Sarah (2011) *The Pleasures of Memory: Learning to Read with Charles Dickens*, New York: Fordham UP.

7

AUDIENCE AS CO-CREATOR

> Sometimes they are sitting there laconic; sometimes they are really into it. You can feel it. It's like electricity: an electric, tactile thing that you can feel. It's a participatory thing, a dialogue with the audience. It's all part of the live experience. That's what makes it so amazing … or horrible.
>
> (Paul Schoeffler 2013, Actor, PI)

In the liminal space between the auditorium and the stage, there is a phenomenon that occurs that charges the air with electricity so visceral that audience and actors alike often gasp in awe at the sheer wonder of it. This is the dynamic experience of co-creation that only occurs in live theatre. As Gadamer contends, "The spectator is manifestly more than just an observer who sees what is happening in front of him, but rather one who is a part of it insofar as he literally 'takes part'" (1987: 24). In this electric air of live theatre, audience and actor co-creation can be so potent that the audience often have what I call a moment of recognition when they realise they are playing an integral part in the performance:

> I'm very naive when I go to the theatre. […] The kids will come out and say, "Did you see this, and did you see that?" No, I was just there in the story, I was part of it.
>
> (Sue 2014, PI)

> Anything I watch at the theatre, whether it is a straight play, Shakespeare or musicals, I personally feel like I am part of it.
>
> (Judith 2014, PI)

> You really *felt* everybody on the stage – you were absolutely part of it. You were part of something great.
>
> (June 2014, PI)[1]

Ushers enjoy observing this moment of recognition: "[Y]ou can see them becoming part of what's happening and sitting on the edge of their seats. Or you see the tear, or the hand over the mouth as something's happening on stage" (Fokes 2013, PI). Leaning forward, sitting on the edge of their seats, the audience play a part in what transpires onstage, they actively contribute to the creation as co-creators.

In this chapter, we return to our two troupes of performers. Actors and audience members do not perform autonomously, their movements are often synchronised. There are times when the actors lead this alliance, and others when the audience lead. The reciprocity between actors and audience members is a conversation, each troupe contributing to the style and creativity of this synergy. When the two troupes are aligned, they breathe as one.

Co-creation takes numerous forms in the playhouse. One of the most discussed in theatre scholarship is cognitive co-creation through meaning-making. I am more concerned with the gestural, verbal and paralingual performance of co-creation. Verbal co-creation often occurs in the progressive contemporary post-shows that I discussed in Chapter Four.[2] The first half of this chapter introduces three phases of co-creation – participation, collaboration and transformation – and their relationship to reciprocity, leading and following, and breathing. The second half of this chapter details specific examples of emergent twenty-first-century participations and collaborations that occur during the production itself. Before I describe the synergy of co-creation, I consider the fertile environment necessary for this sometimes intimate performance of co-creation to occur: the electric air of the theatre.

The Electric Air

Unsurprisingly, in over half of the interviews undertaken for this book, unprompted, audiences used the word "live" to explain either their experience of theatre, the reason they attend theatre or to differentiate their experience of attending theatre from that of cinema. In the playhouse the live presence of two ensembles provides myriad opportunities for co-creation to occur. Much has been written about the "presence" of actors.[3] An actor is often considered to have a "strong presence" or "not much presence." Audiences too have a presence that changes in strength from night to night. This is often reflected in backstage comments such as, "Hello, is anybody out there?" and, "They are really with us tonight." In the former example, it is almost as if the audience are, in the words of Blau, "absent," even when they are there (1990: 5). Being "with" the actors is synonymous with the audience having a strong presence. In the context of co-creation, this can be best described as a co-presence.[4] The two performing troupes are present for each other, available, ready to collaborate, to collude, to conspire; ready to accept the impossible, to imagine the uncanny into being. When the doors are first opened and an audience makes their way into the auditorium, the stage manager will announce backstage that "the house is live." The audience are not absent, they are fully a-"live." Oakleigh believes the role of the actor is "to keep the audience alive. Without them there is no show" (2014, PI). In this liveness, created by the actor's and audience's co-presence, the air is electric, brimming with possibilities for co-creation.

It is difficult to describe or quantify the electric air of live theatre. In her book *Stage Presence* Goodall describes it as an energy, a "special charge in the air" (2008: 122). While some actors argue that "the energy that comes from the audience is not ethereal, it is a real, dynamic, palpable thing" (White 2013), I would argue that it is ethereal and palpable, loud and silent. It gives some audience members goosebumps (*Shadowlands* 2010), while others feel "there's a light buzz about it" (Carson 2014, PI). When the two troupes of performers come face-to-face in the theatre a transformation of the atmosphere can occur: as "the Other's gaze touches me across the world [it] is not only a transformation of myself, but a total metamorphosis of the world" (Sartre 2010: 293). In the theatre, the actor's and audience's gaze reaches across the footlights and not only casts each other in a role, but also transforms the corporeality of the playhouse into another realm. The diegetic world of the play or musical spills into the auditorium.

The metaphor of electricity to describe the actor's and audience member's live, magnetic performance used widely in the nineteenth century continues in this twenty-first century. Now, however, the entire atmosphere of the theatre is considered electric. Audience members and actors take pleasure in basking in the electric air of this transformed environment:

> Ah the energy, […] the energy in New York theatres is not like anything I've ever seen. And I've been to London, I've been to West End and seen musicals and dramas there. The theatres of New York just have a different electricity […] It's live, that's the operative word.
>
> *(Mary 2014a, PI)*

> It is this energy electricity that we get from [the audience], rather than it just being about what you hear. It is definitely more to do with what you feel as well. It makes you spark.
>
> *(Fullerlove 2014, PI)*

It is because the electric air is charged with the live presence, expectations and anticipation of the audience and the actors that co-creation can transpire.

Audience as Co-creator

There are phases in co-creation that can best be described in Sartrean terms as participation, collaboration and transformation. While Sartre's concept of participation in his essays about theatre was predominantly related to meaning-making, he argued that in the theatre, "If you 'participate' […] then you change what you participate in" (1976: 73). When an audience member, consciously or otherwise, laughs, sighs or comments on the performance, they participate in the production and their performance has the potential to change the theatrical experience. When asked what it means to "be" an audience, Ron asserted that, for him, to go to a play is something that's spontaneous. And even though [the actors] have a track that they're going to follow, it's going to be different each night based on what the audience does, based on what the actors do.

(2014, PI)

"What the audience does," their participation, is their verbal, gestural and para-lingual performance. Gareth is a journalist and has seen *The Book of Mormon* three times:

[E]ach time, although it has been largely the same cast, you can totally tell what the audience is engaging with and it changes [the actor's performance] from a sardonic sarcasm to a high cartoonish sort of caricature depending on which way the audience applaud each night.[5]

(2014, PI)

Participation leads to collaboration or is, more often than not, collaborative. As can be seen from Gareth's observations, not only does "the audience write the play quite as much as the author does" (Sartre 1976: 68), during collaboration the audience writes the play quite as much as the actors. Sartre goes on to argue, "It is at such moments that an audience comes to collaborate with an author [or actor]: when it recognises itself, but in a strange guise as if it were someone else; *it brings itself into being*" (1976: 74). Sylvie, a French teacher from London, describes this recognition as a self-actualising experience: "I feel like a 'new' me after a performance and I leave smiling" (2014).[6] This moment of recognition[7] can be quite extraordinary. Audiences recognise that they are not only a part of the performance, but they are *playing* a part. Not surprisingly, after a performance of Sartre's *No Exit* in Sydney an audience member described the recognition moment as such: "I got the same feeling watching the play that I get when I go to the hairdresser: of looking in front of me in the mirror and looking at the back of me in another mirror" (Heim 2011).

Similar to the metamorphosis of the playhouse realm, collaboration through participation can be transformative. Sartre argues that it is "the audience that works with the author to bring about the transformation" (1976: 67). Through this collaboration, the Other's gaze reaches the audience across the footlights and a transformation occurs. Audience members desire and almost expect to be transported to another realm outside of the quotidian: "I like being totally absorbed in something other than my daily routine"; "To be temporarily removed from daily life"; "[O]ne enters the theatre carrying the day with them, they experience the moment, and leave with a new perspective."[8] The theatrical experience is often expressed in terms of timelessness: "For a couple of hours you are completely engrossed in something else" (Judith 2014, PI) where "[y]ou completely forget about everything, the normal worries. You can lose yourself completely" (Anne 2014, PI). The theatrical experience has a timeframe all of its own. Houghton (2013, PI) calls theatre an "analogue" experience for this very reason.

Some theatre-goers actively seek transformation from the theatre, and the majority believe that theatre is transformative.[9] Margaret and Mike go to the theatre around ten times a year. For Margaret the theatre has regenerative qualities: "If we are feeling really low we see a play. It's a 24-hour rejuvenation. It gives you energy and life" (2014b, PI). When Judith went through a divorce she went to the theatre because it helped her to "step outside what is happening and forget" (2014, PI). Anne stated that she always "comes away" from the theatre "slightly changed" (2014, PI). In all of these cases, transformation is cathartic. It is only in the electric air of live theatre that audience members have the opportunity to, as Sartre argues, "work with the author" and collaborate with their onstage co-performers to be transported out of their daily life into an engrossing and meaningful world for a few hours. This is transformation. Transformation is difficult to divorce from participation and collaboration as it is the consequence of both. The rest of this chapter concentrates on the more conspicuous and performative aspects of co-creation: participation and collaboration. Audience participation in the theatre is not a self-contained performance, but is reciprocal.

Reciprocity

In his later philosophical writings, Sartre discussed the praxis of individuals and argued that when individuals form a collective their individual praxes become positively reciprocal[10] (Boileau 2000: 115). In response to what the actors perform, audience members desire to "give back" something to the actors: "[I]t gives them a boost if you're there and enthusiastic and reactive, laughing when you're supposed to laugh, reacting when you're supposed to react and coming out thinking" (Sue 2014, PI).[11] In the theatre, the individual audience member's praxis, their performance, is reciprocal with their co-performers the onstage actors. Actors[12] and audience members describe this reciprocity as an interchange:

> It's great when the audience are really into it. It's a back and forth thing. We take their energy and they take ours in a dialogue.
>
> *(Schoeffler 2013, Actor, PI)*

> You can feel the connection across the edge of the stage – it's coming to you and you're giving back. It's wonderful that. And the more you give back, the more they give forward.
>
> *(Mike 2014a, Audience member, PI)*

> I honestly believe it's such a two-way thing and if it's not working, then I think we've got to look at what we're doing.
>
> *(Tenney 2013, Actor, PI)*

The process of reciprocity is so instinctive, immediate and contagious that actors describe it in terms of "feeding." This term was spoken so frequently in the interviews that it is impossible to ignore. As Fullerlove emphasises,

> I think we are fed by the audiences. Yes, and I think we feed on their energy. It's a circular thing: we put our performance out there, we hope to get the responses, and when you get the responses you feel something inside and it cranks up your performance that little bit more, and then you give them something. There is this rotation of energy and it comes to us, from the audience, in the form of laughter or response.
>
> *(2014, PI)*

Audience member Fiona, from London, also describes reciprocity in terms of feeding: "You get some performances where there is quite a lot of audience response, whether that is humour or tragedy, and you can see that the actors are feeding off that" (2014, PI). John works in costumes in film, he loves theatre because the "actors are feeding off the crowd and their reactions" (2014c, PI). Maggie went so far as to describe "being part of a theatre audience" as "nourishment" (2014, PI). Perceiving reciprocal exchange in such a somatic context emphasises the co-dependent relationship of the actors and audience who feed off each other's performances.

One germane example of the reciprocity of co-creation occurs when audiences complete the dialogue of their onstage co-performer. In a 2013 Sydney production of *Rapture, Blister, Burn*, Tenney described a moment when the following dialogue transpired:

AVERY: Well, that's terrible, why don't you go out drinking with them?
GWEN: Well I can't go with them because I don't have a …
AUDIENCE MEMBER: Babysitter.

Tenney described how at every performance one audience member, unprompted, would finish her dialogue (2013, PI). Often the entire audience ensemble completes lines. In the premiere season of David Williamson's 2014 play *Cruise Control* in Sydney, the character Sal, a dentist, asked another character: "What do I know better than anything?" Invariably before the actor had a chance to reply the audience spoke his line: "gums." The congenial laughter that followed revealed how gratifying this collusion had been. While this kind of exchange was a common practice in pre-twentieth-century theatres, contemporary audiences, "taking part" in the action, fully absorbed in the transformed world, occasionally co-create in this way.

There are times, however, when audiences do not comprehend the vital role they play in co-creation and, sometimes deliberately, withhold their performance by refusing to participate. As Owen-Taylor describes:

> It is a give and take thing and sometimes audiences don't quite get that and they will never reach over. That is when the mark doesn't work. A lot of

audiences will pay their money but they don't think they have to [give back]. An audience is going to participate anyway whether physically [or otherwise] ... but sometimes when we don't make that connection it is because there is not a willing transfer of energy, a communal energy. It is not a wanky thing it is just [that] people can give you energy or they can suck it in. We feed each other.

(Owen-Taylor 2014, PI)

This is a different kind of withheld energy or performance than the restraint imposed because of theatre etiquette or negative empathy discussed in Part I. It can be a conscious decision on the part of an audience member who argues, "I've paid my money, I expect to sit back and be entertained."[13] Interestingly, this audience member describes the lean back in their seat as a part of their withheld performance. Other audience members notice this kind of stasis. Patricia is perturbed when others seem to "have their hands under their seats. No-one's moving, no-one's clapping" (2013, PI). It often affects other audience members' spontaneous performance. Max Herrmann argues that audience members can curb the enthusiasm of each other because they cannot empathise with the aesthetic object (cited in Fischer-Lichte 2008: 36).

Some are seemingly unaware of just how much their performance contributes to creating the theatrical experience or how dependent actors are on audience performance. Laughing, crying, mimesis and other paralanguages are all reciprocal, feeding the actors the essential energy that they need to "ride the wave" (Schoeffler 2013, PI). Some performances of laughter or applause can, however, be forced and inauthentic when audience members over-act. Maggie finds this very distracting: "[T]here is facile laughter at things that are not particularly funny and the atmosphere is damaged for probably both the audience and for the performers" (2014, PI). The enchantment of authentic co-creation is broken. Reciprocity is an essential part of collaboration. It is fundamentally any form of unmediated, back and forth, two-way communication: a concordant empathic exchange between actors and audience members.

Leading and Following

In reciprocity there is often one performing troupe that leads the other. Actors speak their lines, and the audience respond. Many actors concur that "when you first get an audience it's an absolute joy to hear the reactions" (Fullerlove 2014, PI). When the actors direct the audience they often "work extra hard to make them smile, make them want to giggle" (Henry 2013, PI). It is often a very conscious and prescribed direction:

We don't want to exhaust [the audience]; even with laughing you can exhaust a crowd ... so it is in the pacing of a show. You step back a bit, you lower your vocal strength so they actually have to start participating physically, and then you slowly come together.

(Owen-Taylor, PI)

Actors can also give bad direction when leading. Grubb described a performance in *Strictly Ballroom* in Sydney where he accidentally smothered an audience laugh. After a "bit of business" when his character prevents the leads from dancing in a competition, "one woman [in the audience] yelled out 'no!' and [he] broke in on her and said 'cut that out!' [He] knew immediately [he] went too hard because the audience didn't laugh, and they usually do" (2014, PI).

This returns to my original concept of granting permission, an important aspect of leading and following. It is not only the audience that needs to be given permission to perform, but the actors also need permission. Audiences give permission through their responses. When audiences "have responded positively, it allows [actors] to float, to soar. It is about confidence: knowing you will be caught, you will be supported" (Grubb 2014, PI). From this perspective, audiences carry quite a responsibility for catching what is given to them from the stage, and have a vital role to play in supporting the actors by performing their response. If the audience allow the actors to fall, "if they are not interested, they just drop away" and the production "can drop completely" (Owen-Taylor 2014, PI). Tacit consent given by actors and audiences is essential to create a productive environment for co-creation to occur. Permission can be extended in multiple ways: in an actor's pause, an audience's spontaneous laugh or a more explicit invitation from the stage. If permission is given generously and joyfully, the enchantment of theatre can be transformative for the audience *and* the actors

Once face to face in the playhouse, actors argue, it is often the audience that directs *them*. In rehearsals, the "actors have worked really closely with the director, and have got [the play] to a great place, but then [the audience] will tighten that direction ever so much" during performances. Through "the sounds they make and the moments they pipe up in […] they give you your marks [to] hit" (Henry 2013, PI) and "they teach [you] by their reactions" (Oakleigh 2014, PI). "You are using the audience to polish your performance up" (Danby 2014, PI). "You often have to take your cue from the audience" (Schoeffler 2013, PI) because "every gauge the actor has of his work comes from the audience. The audience is your map or your gauge to get from here to there" (White 2013).

As described by the actors above, it is surprising how regulative and immediate this direction is. The cues the actors receive from the audience are the verbal and paralingual "sounds": the audience's performance.

Some actors, however, find it demoralising to allow audiences to lead. Gielgud argued, "If you once allowed them to order you about […] audiences can make you rather vulgar as an actor" (cited in Funke and Booth 1963: 30). Tenney emphasises that often there are "waves of laughs, and they can sometimes get out of control, so you have to put a lid on it" (2013, PI). These are times when an audience performance can upstage the actors and is referred to as "stopping the show." While the show can be stopped by audience interruptions, actors predominantly use the idiom to describe times when the audience is so overwhelmed by a particular moment in the onstage performance, their applause, cheering or laughter is so loud, demonstrative, excessive and usually prolonged, that they stop the show from continuing for a time.[14]

Audience members can participate with their onstage co-performers and ride the crest of the wave together or keep their hands under their seats. Whether leading or following, the audience works collaboratively with the actors to create the theatrical experience. If the actors' performances change because of the audience's performance, then the onstage scripted performance, what Ron above called the "track," is also changed. The co-created performance is going to be different every night.

Breathe as One

Reciprocity and leading and following can be described in terms of expiration and inspiration: an exchange of breath. As discussed above, when the lights first illumine the stage in the electric air of the playhouse there is often a moment of inspiration as the audience breathe in the possibilities of the imaginary world. During the production, the actor's performance is the expiration that meets this expectation, and this reciprocity continues throughout the performance in a form of unlimited symbiosis. Bogart argues that "ultimately, all of us want that incredible circular relationship where the audience changes breathing with the actor" (2006).

At times it becomes an actual rather than a metaphorical inspiration or expiration. In a climactic point in the 2013 *Jekyll and Hyde* on Broadway, the audience performed a sharp intake of breath, a gasp, when one character was stabbed. White, a performer in the production, explained that this inspiration "fuels the performer, it informs the performer how far to go, when to step back when to move on. It informs the pace, it informs the drama, it informs everything. It is essential" (2013, PI). In this example the actors were clearly "taking their cue" from the audience.

In those moments when an actor has hit his/her mark, when the audience is leaning forward, part of the utopian performative, the audience can breathe as one. When the onstage and auditorium performance is aligned,

> the audience breathes as one sometimes. The audience sigh. In *Death of a Salesman* [on Broadway] the audience were as one, you could breathe together. That kind of energy is thrilling. It is important to an actor, to the success of a piece.
>
> *(White 2013)*

When the audience breathe in and out as one they are conspiring in the true meaning of the word.[15] In the electric air of the theatre, the possibilities for co-creation are myriad. Audience and actors intuitively and consensually collaborate as co-performers and sometimes co-conspirators to create a performance that exists for only a few but fully charged hours. Because they have performed verbally and physically, because they have been part of the live and lived experience of the theatrical event and have been co-conspirators exchanging breathing, the audience has the potential to be "transformed into whatever that world is for two hours" (Stephen 2014, PI).

Twenty-First-Century Audience Co-creation

What does theatre co-creation look like in the twenty-first century? Audience performance is continuously evolving: partly due to the introduction of so many new technologies in the auditorium, and partly because of audience behaviour that has been acculturated from watching and interacting with screens. Throughout this book I have recorded examples of theatre practices in this new millennium that are part of the audience's co-creative performance: the use of screens for critical response, the wearing of themed costuming and post-show discussions, among others. Some of these practices are revivals of nineteenth-century audience performance, some are adaptations, and others are completely novel. In my audience interviews, one of the most frequently discussed changes noted was the increased responsiveness of audience members (see Appendix 1):

> I think they're more enthusiastic. They stand up, they cheer. I think they're enthusiastic and appreciative.
>
> *(Mary 2014a, PI)*

> They are much more responsive. Now people get up and cheer and you hear "Whoo wee." […] I think it's a good thing.
>
> *(Kay 2014, PI)*

Interestingly, actors also cited increased responsiveness as a significant change they had noted in audiences over time, often framing it as audiences participating more in the theatrical experience. Actor Lois Weaver has observed that in the contemporary theatres "mainstream fear of audience participation that started in the seventies has broken and people are not so afraid" (2012, PI). Actors interviewed had worked in the theatre from 8 to 53 years, so it is noteworthy that even the younger actors noticed the change in responsiveness over the last decade. I focus here on audience participation as it is the twenty-first-century audience's participative response that works to cast them as co-creators.

Some of the participation that is discussed in this section is reminiscent of the theatre of participation that began in the 1960s, noted in my introduction, although on a much smaller scale. In twenty-first-century mainstream performances, onstage participation is often a single event rather than an essential component of the entire performance. These isolated performances are, however, fast becoming conventional in Broadway and West End productions. In my interviews, audience members and actors rarely differentiated "onstage" participation and participation that I distinguish as "communal performance." Communal performance occurs when audience members are invited, usually by an actor, to perform jointly as an ensemble in the auditorium.

At the opening of his book *Audience Participation in the Theatre*, White contests, "There are few things in the theatre that are more despised than audience participation" (2013: 1). Some of the audience members I interviewed would heartily agree. David is a chartered accountant who attends around eight performances in London a year. He is inimical to participation of any kind: "I don't like it at all – I won't participate" (2014a, PI). Actors working in mainstream theatre are often very sensitive to this reticence to participate. In productions that include some kind of participation or communal performance they can gauge when audience members "don't want to feel kind of foolish, they don't want to feel humiliated" (Owen-Taylor 2014, PI) and adjust their invitation accordingly. Shirley and Maree are retired bankers that go to the theatre together in Glasgow. They have antithetical and strong opinions on audience participation. At the conclusion of her interview, Maree, similar to David, ensured that her hostility towards audience participation was recorded: "I have to add another thing: I am *not* an audience participation person – you know the way they wave their hands. I would rather just sit and watch" (2014, PI). Her theatre companion felt otherwise:

> Well I am different: I like getting involved, I want to clap my hands. And if I have to throw my hands in the air, I will throw my hands in the air. I have even got up and danced in the aisle, but that wasn't asked for. I like getting involved with it, I must admit, it is part of my enjoyment. It is not my enjoyment to just sit and watch. Part of my enjoyment is getting involved as part of a group.
>
> *(Shirley 2014, PI)*

In addition to her obvious enthusiasm for communal performance, what is interesting is Shirley's comment regarding the invitation. Shirley's performance "wasn't asked for" but was, rather, volunteered.

White's categories of overt, implicit and accidental participation invitations are useful here. Overt invitations are issued from the stage. An onstage performer invites an audience member to participate and describes the performance expected of the participant. When audiences intuitively understand what kind of performance is expected, though uninvited, this is considered an implicit invitation. Moments in the theatre when an uninvited and sometimes undesired performance is given by the audience are considered accidental or uninvited participations (2013: 40–42). Shirley's dancing, which was "not asked for," is one such example. Accidental participations, which sometimes are a cause of consternation for the onstage actors and other audience members, are at other times so spontaneous and liberating from theatre etiquette strictures that they are contributions rather than interruptions to the performance. The following is a summary of audience performances that are now regularly witnessed in the twenty-first-century mainstream playhouse that, because of their responsive, participatory elements, construct the audience as co-creators.

Youth Theatre

The lights go down at a theatre on Broadway and around one-third of the audience scream. A Hollywood star makes her/his first appearance on stage, the audience applaud and catcall. A hit song is belted out while the audience wave lit mobile phones over their heads. The star actor comes out to bow, the audience scream again, stand and applaud, whistle and catcall. This is one of the most demonstrative performances in twenty-first-century theatre auditoriums and is predominantly initiated by younger audiences.[16] As Owen-Taylor has observed from the stage, "younger people are more inclined to participate" (2014, PI). Attendance at any Hollywood or rock star-billed production, juke-box musical, movie adaptation or cult-following show is almost guaranteed to be an interactive audience experience.

The majority of these performances are musicals. Some, especially those including stars, are plays. The number of Hollywood stars in lead roles on Broadway and the West End has escalated in this second decade of the new millennium. In the 2013/14 Broadway season, for the first time, the primary motivating factor for play selection was "to see a particular performer in a show" (Hauser 2014: 41). Many star-dominated productions are attracting not only younger audiences, but new audiences that have never before entered theatres.[17] Many of these performances are designed to attract a young audience for marketing purposes. At different times throughout the productions, the auditorium is pulsating with a cacophony of shrill sounds, the patter of slapped hands, high-spirited vocalisations and flashes of light. Sheldon argues that this kind of responsiveness has affected the exchange between audience and actor: "[T]he whole give and take has changed. Audiences have become very vocal. In *Pippin* and *Kinky Boots*, audiences start screaming like it was a rock concert. It's a young person's thing" (2013, PI). During this very vocal performance the audience troupe are leading the dance of reciprocity and often stop the show with their performance of applause or cheering.

An interesting part of youth theatre performance is public demonstration of affection. Kissing and massaging shoulders during performances, considered backstage activities in the second half of the twentieth century, are sometimes observed by ushers and sometimes actors in the frontstages of theatre houses. Couples are often amorous in the seating banks, and one adventurous couple recurrently booked private boxes in West End theatres in 2011 for the purposes of making love in the electric air of performances.[18] Although none of these enactments are confined to youth audiences, ushers have noted that the majority of these performances are given by young people replicating their screen watching and rock concert performances in theatre auditoriums.

The most obvious rock concert behaviour is the mobile phone wave. During one of the hit songs in *Jekyll and Hyde* on Broadway, the audience, cued by some tacit collective knowledge, extended their lit devices in the air and slowly waved their arms in unison. The electric air of the auditorium glowed with hundreds of bright globes and almost a kind of meditative reverence settled over the audience. This was a heightened moment of ritualised co-creation. Only a century and a half before this time, audiences were waving hats in the air expressing similar approbation of peak experiences performed onstage. Twenty-first-century audiences provide, however, their own lighting.[19] One of youth theatre's central objectives is to give young people the opportunity to express themselves through the creative arts. The youth performances occurring in audiences of many Broadway and West End theatres are expressive, uninhibited and gregarious.

Immersive Theatre

There have been small but significant imbrications of the seemingly contrary genres of immersive theatre and traditional, mainstream theatre over the past decade.[20] In The Royal Shakespeare Company production of *The Two Gentlemen of Verona*, groups of audience members were ushered onto the stage set of a café and given ice-creams from a vendor. In the Broadway production of *Motown*, select audience members were invited onstage to chat and sing with "Diana." In the Broadway play *The Testament of Mary*, audience members milled around the stage before the performance and took photographs of Fiona Shaw as Mary and multiple props and set pieces including a live vulture. Audience members felt this experience was "Breathtaking" and "So moving."[21] In *One Man, Two Guvnors*, two audience members were invited onstage to lift a heavy trunk. These moments of onstage audience performance took place over 2013/14 and had their antecedents in productions such as *Cats* in 1981, *The 25th Annual Putnam County Spelling Bee* in 2005, *Spring Awakening* in 2006 and *Hair* in 2009. Audience onstage immersion in mainstream productions has escalated over the last five years. In these productions individuals or groups of audience members were invited onstage to immerse themselves in the fictitious world of the production. Many of these audience participations were, however, single incidences from visionary directors.

Onstage encounters between audience members and actors are approaching the objectives of immersive theatre where the audience is "thrown [...] into a totally new environment and context from the everyday world," which is "outside 'everyday' rules and regulations" (Machon 2013: 27). The audience performers participate in what has come to be known as the core of immersive theatre: the "one-to-one" encounters with their onstage co-performers, the actors. In March 2014 *Rocky the Musical*, billed as an "immersive" theatre experience for audiences, opened on Broadway. It was directed by Alex Timbers, whose immersive theatre production of *Here Lies Love* at The Public theatre had achieved much success. Consider the audience comments at interval:

> How you going, you ready? It's 1979!
> I'm gonna be cheering Rocky, you? He's gonna go for Apollo.
> I want to be part of the action.

I'm sure going to be cheering as if it was real.
You excited?
I'm tuning up my voice: hmm, hmm.[22]

The audience were anticipating their performance and warming up for their ringside event. In the final 20 minutes of the production, 111 audience performers left their seats and joined their co-performers onstage. They entered into the production's *fabula* and sat on ringside bleachers where they were immediately interpellated as boxing fans as the boxing ring swung out into the audience. They screamed and cheered with their fellow characters. They beat their fists in the air and chanted for Rocky and booed at Apollo. The auditorium audience watched the onstage audience watch. Fully embracing and revelling in their role as co-creators, the audience performers improvised and yelled encouragements. As Rocky left the ring he threw his towel into the crowd and high-fived an audience performer. The performer jumped up and down in fervour.

As the production ended, the audience members who performed onstage were euphoric: "[Y]ou feel like you want to run five miles and do push ups because your adrenaline is just pumping." Talia works in IT in libraries and has attended *Rocky* for the second time for another round of performing for the "adrenaline rush" and because she feels like she is "involved as an audience member" (2014, PI). This is not dissimilar to the "mix of adrenaline and exhaustion" (Oakleigh 2014, PI) that most actors feel after a performance. *Rocky* audience members responded to the overt invitation to play a role in the drama, to co-perform, and experienced the same rush of exhilaration as their co-performers. They were not, however, spent after their performance. Some audience performers who I had interviewed at interval sought me out, eager to share their experience with me. A post-show discussion would have given them the opportunity to de-brief, reflect on and share their experience.

The immersive experience of *Rocky* for audience members is an apposite example of Sartre's perceptions of the transformation of worlds and selves. Audience theming occurred at every performance. The auditorium was scattered with audience members already in costume. Many were robed in gym wear inscribed with the names of famous and infamous boxing rings or wore Italian Stallion t-shirts.[23] Not only was there a transformation of the world of the playhouse as the set moved into the auditorium, but the audience enthusiastically embraced their roles, keen for this opportunity to actively contribute as co-creators. They recognised themselves in Sartre's strange guise as characters in the production. As one audience performer enthused, "You felt like you were right there. You were part of it" (2014, PI). Audience performers at *Rocky* immersed themselves in the diegesis of the play. They not only experienced authentic one-to-one encounters with their onstage co-performers, they collaborated with them to create the final scene of the musical. Participatory twenty-first-century audience performance has evolved significantly since *Cats* in the 1980s when audience members were startled and at times embarrassed by the invitation to co-perform onstage. Twenty-first-century audience performers often arrive at the theatre warmed up, in costume and enthusiastically await their onstage co-creation.

Communal Theatre

Performance involving the entire audience that is directed from the stage often works to create a community in the theatre. More audience members are willing to join in communal performance than go onstage (see Appendix 2) in productions like *Rocky*. The precursor of contemporary communal performance is not only demonstrative nineteenth-century performance, but also cult-following productions such as *The Rocky Horror Show*, which opened in the West End in 1973, was subsequently made into a film, and is revived in many capital cities worldwide each year. Communal performance is an essential part of each *Rocky Horror* performance. Any form of communal performance where the audience sings, dances, recites[24] or performs gestures in unison are what I posit as communal theatre.

Singing is an almost obligatory audience performance at all juke-box musicals. *Let it Be, Thriller, Mamma Mia, Jersey Boys, Motown* and *Dirty Dancing* audiences lift their voices in unison throughout the performance. Singing, particularly communal singing during juke-box musicals, is an example of an implicit invitation; the audience who are familiar with the songs "join in" (White 2013: 41). In *The Lion King*, which has been playing since 1997, the audience regularly joins in singing the familiar "Hakuna Matata." This kind of co-creation works to build community. Actor Owen-Taylor argues that people sing the Australian well-known 1970s song "Love is in the Air" at *Strictly Ballroom* in Sydney and Melbourne because "it is a communal thing, and people really respond because we all want to be a part of something" (2014, PI). In some musicals, audiences are encouraged to sing solos or give requests: "You can shout your requests out. I know it's weird," encourages the actor playing George Harrison in the 2014 production of *Let it Be* at the Garrick Theatre in London.

Over the past decade, dancing and other kinetic performance often accompanies singing. In *Motown* and *Mamma Mia* audience members hold hands and sway side to side. In *Rock of Ages* jazz hands are fluttered throughout the auditorium. In *Let it Be* audiences are encouraged to "rattle their jewellery." In *Legally Blonde* audiences Mexican wave in the dress circle. Dancing is almost *de rigueur* in *Strictly Ballroom*. By the end of the show there is strictly no theatre etiquette as the audience weave a conga line onto the stage for their curtain call dance to "Love is in the Air." JJ Silvers asks the remaining auditorium audience members to applaud "the most important people in the show – our audience" (Luhrmann 2014). Audience dancing is so emotionally contagious in *Strictly Ballroom* that audience members sometimes take their dancing out onto the street after the show and can be seen "twirling on the road" (Owen-Taylor 2014, PI). The sense of community created inside the theatre spirals into the outside community as passers-by gaze and wonder at the promenading dancers.

Dancing in the aisles or onstage is not for everyone. But for some, all that is needed is an invitation to surprise themselves. Grubb regularly encounters elderly ladies at *Strictly Ballroom* that throw caution and decorum to the wind, exclaim "oh damn it" and join Tina Sparkles in the conga line. They are tickled that "someone is asking them to go and dance. They surprise themselves, they surprise their friends. And then their friends say 'oh bugger it, if she is doing it, then so am I.' They are proud of themselves" (2014, PI). This is a pertinent example of what Ridout calls "the pleasure of embarrassment" (2006: 79). Often in these self-conscious performances, the surprise is one of self-recognition, and it can be extremely pleasurable. All collective audience performances, but particularly singing and dancing, work to create a community in the theatre. Some of the charisma and spontaneity of audience performance that was lost in the darkness of the twentieth century has been regained in the twenty-first.

One-Person Show

A pertinent example of the uninvited participation is what I call the one-person show, where one audience member delivers a line out loud during the production. Actor Nicholas Bell recalled an incident during Pinter's *Betrayal* at the National Theatre in London where "suddenly from the back of the auditorium this plummy voice shouted out 'you fucking hypocrites'" (2013, PI). While this was a common and accepted performance during the nineteenth century, it clearly transgresses the boundaries of propriety in contemporary theatre.[25] Although it can disrupt the flow of the action onstage, there are times when the one-person show contributes an extra layer of meaning to the production, and when used effectively by actors rather than ignored, works to strengthen the reciprocity of co-creation. In *Newsies* the musical in New York two actors embrace onstage. At one performance a child in the orchestra yelled out "She kissed him!" The audience erupted in laughter, which stopped the show for such a long time that the actor onstage took off his hat and looked at the child in a quizzical fashion, which continued the audience laughter. The actor was feeding off the audience in the circular process of reciprocity described by Fullerlove above.

Not dissimilar to the dialogue that was thrown back to the stage in the nineteenth century, audiences at *Strictly Ballroom* regularly became so involved with the production that they delivered encouragements such as "c'mon Dougy" and "good on ya son" back to the stage. This kind of participation can become almost immersive when the actors walk in the aisles of the auditorium providing a fertile environment for one-to-one encounters. During one performance an audience member tugged the sleeve of the character Doug as he walked by: "[Y]ou have got a good boy there Dougy" (Owen-Taylor 2014, PI). This audience member was clearly performing in the world of the play and the auditorium was transformed into another room in the production.

A different kind of one-person show occurs on the stage when an actor improvises outside of the script. This often transpires when actors "corpse," a term used in the actor's lexicon to describe a moment when an actor makes another actor laugh, or when an actor "starts to laugh of his or her own accord, sometimes inexplicably"

(Ridout 2006: 131). If the audience is alerted to this improvisation, reciprocity usually occurs. In a performance of *The Book of Mormon* on a hot balmy evening in July 2014, Jared Gertner delivered a seemingly improvised line to his co-star Gavin Creel. Creel stared at Gertner then corpsed. The audience burst into laughter. Creel then improvised, "It's *so* hot!" The audience went wild: they clapped and laughed and whistled for an extensive two minutes stopping the show.

These happenings can often be the most pleasurable moments in theatre, not just for the "inside joke" that audiences have conspired with, but also because of the collaboration that occurs and that can only occur in live theatre. Audience members seek these moments. The two troupes of performers intuitively understand what occurs when the audience empathises not only with the character onstage, but the actor:

> They love it when something goes wrong. It makes us real, human.
>
> *(Bell 2013, Actor, PI)*

> That moment when they get out of character, they connect with the audience. Those moments make it feel a little more real for me.
>
> *(Gint 2014, Audience member, PI)*

During these one-person shows, the actors and audience co-create a performance text together that is born in the electric air of theatre existing for just that performance. As Sue emphasises, "[I]n the theatre it's the people, and the interaction with the actors that make it. Somebody's fudged it and you can see the smile. I enjoy it" (2014, PI). In this complicity of reciprocity, audience members may recognise themselves, in a strange guise, as co-creators.

The Soliloquy

An uninvited performance that is more often than not disruptive for other audience members is the audience soliloquy. Audience members speak their thoughts aloud, often to their partner:

> She told him to put on his suit!
> I love that Chinese dress she's wearing.
> Look at the ship at the back!
> I used to be able to do that.
> I've seen him somewhere before.
> I can't believe it!
> Amen to that![26]

Audience members who engage in this kind of performance usually have no malice in their responses, they are simply so engaged with the production that they desire to share their thoughts. Edie and Ron are regular theatre-goers and confessed chatterers who use techniques to quell their impulse to soliloquise:

RON: Edie and I will talk to each other during the play.

EDIE: We're bad.

RON: Which disturbs people around us.

EDIE: Because we are so spontaneous, "Look at that, look at that! Oh can you see how they did that?" Or "Can you believe that person? Do you recognise that person?" I take notes. Part of that is to shut me up, because I think of things and I want to talk about it right away. I'm just too excited. I take notes so I'm not disturbing other people.

RON: We are shushed all the time. Well, we are pretty interactive.

(2014, PI)

Actor Fullerlove makes concessions for these chatterers: "[T]hey're so used to watching the story unfolding and speaking at the same time, you can tell when it's not an audience educated in theatre etiquette. They are definitely engaged in their own way! It's just a bit off-putting" (2014, PI). Fullerlove is here alluding to the concurrent watching and talking that is a regular occurrence in the television room.

There is no doubt that this performance can be incredibly distracting for other audience members and actors alike. For the audience performers themselves, however, spontaneous, improvised, impulsive soliloquies such as those listed above are one way for the audience to feel part of the theatrical experience. They are often expressed during times of recognition, during utopian performatives, during moments when actors have hit their mark. As such, they have a small part to play in co-creation for that individual performer in the theatre.

All of the above audience performances – youth theatre, community theatre, the one-person show and the soliloquy – whether responding to overt, implicit or even accidental invitations, are contributions to the theatrical event often emerging as profound moments of co-creation for our two troupes of performers. Because the moments have been embodied or vocalised as part of an audience performance and because they are often pleasurable experiences, this not only works to bring about transformation, but also augments the potential for remembering the experience. The production has not only been a watched experience for the audience, it has been performed.

Creating a Scene

While I have been writing my treatise on twenty-first-century audience performance, I have been very conscious of a character standing behind me in the guise of Frances Trollope from the nineteenth century (introduced in Chapter Two). I am sure she would find the behaviours of some of these "posture masters" of the new millennium excruciating. There are many trollopisms performed in contemporary theatres that interrupt, distract from and break the enchantment of theatre. Trollopisms are easy to distinguish. Twenty-first-century audience activities that are contributions to the onstage performance such as singing, dancing, waving mobile phones and playing a character onstage work to shut out the outside world. Trollopisms such as the mobile phone ring, conversations unrelated to the performance, falling asleep and snoring,[27] web-surfing, rattling food packaging or having an argument in the seating banks bring in the outside world. These are intrusions, not contributions. They disengage audiences from the theatrical experience and sever the relationship between stage and audience and between audience members.

Goffman argues that "a new scene is created by such disruptions," colloquially referred to as "creating a scene" (1959: 210). Scenes are a performance in themselves, but one that turns the attention and often the gaze of the audience from the stage to the auditorium. These performances are often met with angry glares from other audience members, polite or impolite entreaties, verbal, or sometimes physical arguments as a new scene is created. David likes to confront the scene-makers:

> [W]hen they have a nasty habit of bringing their meal in, or popcorn, or are talking, I often get involved in stand-offs with people: "I have come to the theatre to watch the performers, why have you come for your evening meal?" It tends to settle things down. It can spoil our enjoyment – eating popcorn and talking, telephone lights going on, texting – especially when you're paying 65 pounds.
>
> *(2014a, PI)*

Actors sometimes become embroiled in these disputes. They have been known to engage in polite or heated dialogue with the offender, order detractors to leave the theatre, throw phones against walls, or have confrontations with audience members during intervals. Similar to the one warning policy implemented in some theatres in the early twentieth century, audiences at *Rock of Ages* on Broadway are given a generous three-warning policy. Three scenes and you are escorted out of the theatre.

Audience members not only find the scene a distraction for themselves, but have sympathy for the actors:

> Someone starts talking behind you or shuffling with crisps or popcorn and firstly it is distracting me as a member of the audience, but what irritates me more is it distracts the actors; they are not respectful of the actors. The actors are trying to create another world for us and we ought to be respecting that. We ought to be trying to enter into that.
>
> *(Susan 2014, PI)*

> People have spent hours and hours of time and effort to do something for you to watch, you are supposed to be respectful.
>
> *(Wayne 2014, PI)*

> I totally disagree with technology in the theatre and I don't like people rustling crisps; people should respect the performers on the stage.
>
> *(Doreen 2014, PI)*

Offended audience members find numerous ways to admonish the disruptive scene-makers. In Goffman's terms, the miscreants are "ridiculed, gossiped about, caricatured, cursed, and criticized. [...] Plans may be worked out for 'selling' them, or employing 'angles' against them, or pacifying them"[28] (1959: 170). Cursing, criticism and plans for expelling scene-makers from mainstream theatres are ubiquitous online. One such plan for containing trollopisms is Richard Gresham's Theatre Charter, which was launched in July 2014. UK theatre-goers are asked to agree to police trollopisms: "[T]o quietly 'shhh' the offender during the performance; to politely ask them to stop during an appropriate applause moment or at the interval and to request an usher to take action" (Gresham 2014). Comparative attempts to regulate these behaviours are regularly initiated. Similar to the high-hat law of the late nineteenth century, in 2003, New York theatre owners successfully passed a law which would fine theater-goers 50 dollars for mobile-phone use in theatres. The law remains un-enforced today. All scene-making is uninvited, interrupts the flow of the onstage narrative and abrogates any co-creation that is occurring. Let us consider a contemporary venue that has borrowed from the past to create an environment where co-creation can thrive: Shakespeare's Globe.

Case Study
Shakespeare's Globe: Extending the Invitation

London 2014: I am standing in a hooded opaque plastic bag, dripping wet, with rose petals and strips of shiny cellophane plastered all over my costume watching a performance of David Eldridge's *Holy Warriors* at Shakespeare's Globe. More rain falls from the clouds and more cellophane floats down from the gods. People sitting under shelters divide their attention between the bedraggled cellophane figures in the yard where I am standing and the action on stage. Beside me stands Siobhan who has just got off a plane and made her way directly here because she wants "an event, something special, with action taking place all around" (2014, PI) her. Alex and Meg, standing in front of me, like being "out in the fresh air in a thunderstorm" (Alex 2014, PI). Onstage some strange rituals are performed and there are heated conversations, some fights and much arguing. It is rather splendid to watch, but I, like others, am rather distracted by the well-lit facial expressions and gestures of those sitting under the shelters. At the end of three hours the performers onstage and those in the yard break into a little jig, clap, then leave. We have all witnessed a performance onstage and a performance in the audience.

There was certainly much electric air, of the meteorological kind, during this audience experience I had in July 2014. I was not one of the Globe groundling groupies who line up for sometimes an hour before each show to stand compacted against the stage in the coveted first-row yard positions. I was, however, still able to play the role of an Elizabethan groundling standing at the back of the yard. The audience experience was not dissimilar to what Carlson describes as a "living history" (2004: 3) performance. Indeed, nearly all the audience members and actors I interviewed that had performed at the Globe, seemingly by default, proceeded to give me a history lesson on Elizabethan audiences. There was a self-conscious role-playing in the yard. Some audience members felt the need to play the role of demonstrative groundling, others only performed when invited by the actors.

Fullerlove argues that "there is more willingness to respond [at the Globe] because the very space they're in has a history of giving the audiences permission to respond" (2014, PI). Globe audiences perform in response to sometimes overt but predominantly implicit invitations from the actors and from what can be seen as a more intuitive "historical invitation." Actors interpellate their audiences as courtiers of Caesar's palace, members of the British army and citizens of Rome, encouraging them to shout out dialogue such as "down with Caesar!" The bifurcation of the Globe house into yard and stalls casts the audience as different types of performers: "The yard can be laughing while the watchers in the gallery sit stony-faced" (Carroll 2008: 42).

The historical invitation makes audience members less inhibited because, as regular Globe audience member Katie stated, "you are actually living it as [the Elizabethans] would have" (2014, PI). Audiences in the yard can be asked to carry sacks over their heads, they can have their backpacks raided and can be tickled, kissed by actors, have water dripped on them and confetti sprayed over them from the gods. One-person shows, communal performances and soliloquies are more frequent at the Globe than possibly any other mainstream contemporary theatres. In *Two Gentlemen of Verona* (1996) a man in the audience told Proteus to "go on give her [Julia] a kiss." *King Lear* when choosing between his daughters was advised in a 2001 production to "have them both." Audiences were invited to sing in *The Merchant of Venice* (1998) and many yard members join their onstage co-performers in the now customary closing jig. Community clapping during the production is often encouraged.

Natural lighting, proximity to other audience members, exposure to the elements and physical endurance impacts the audience performance. The day-lit audience space naturally influences the actor/audience interaction. The actors can actually see the audience performances, even facial expressions, providing many opportunities for the circular exchange of leading and following. Alex stated that "you can see the nuances of the actors more" because of the "intimacy" of the space (2014, PI). Here, people watch each other in close confines leading to a different and, perhaps, more self-conscious performance than that given in Times Square (discussed in the preceding chapter). This heightens the experience: "[T]he audience can see the rest of the audience. [In] *Julius Caesar* people [were] experiencing shock and horror – you could see it on their faces" (Katie 2014, PI). Similar to the pre-First World War lit auditoriums, because audience members can read the visceral responses of their audience co-performers, emotional contagion is pronounced. Reciprocity is much more palpable in the "contained, and cosy" (Meg 2014, PI) intimacy of the Globe, creating a plethora of opportunities for co-creation.

The elements naturally contribute much to audience performance. Rain buckets down from the heavens, and the scorching sun causes some to faint. Groundlings sometimes faint not just from dehydration, but from exposure to overwhelming gore onstage in plays such as Lucy Bailey's *Titus Andronicus* (2014). The physical discomfort from standing and exposure to the elements often makes it a more engaging and certainly self-aware and physically demanding experience. Audience members particularly relish the opportunity to move around in the yard rather than sit still (Carson and Karim-Cooper 2008: 121). Audience members are also free to leave the theatre enclosure whenever they wish. This permission to be selectively inattentive (Schechner 1988: 229) liberates the young audience members. Director Ralph Cohen has taken many groups to the Globe and has found that the play is more pleasurable for those that stand rather than sit (2008: 225).

Bailey's 2010 production of *Macbeth* could only be described as an immersive experience for the groundlings. A huge black cloth covered those standing in the yard with slits for the groundlings heads. The groundlings were buried in a landscape reminiscent of Dante's Hell becoming the extended set. The three witches began their performance in this eerie terrain running underneath the cloth, tugging at surprised and terrified audience members. In an interesting inversion, Fullerlove, who played one of the witches, stated that she felt "part of the audience" (2014, PI). She was wearing the same kind of tunic, although much distressed, worn by the Globe stewards (ushers), which added another layer of meaning to her "audience" role. At the conclusion of the performance the witches collaborated with the groundlings to lift Macbeth up through the cloth. This was a fascinating moment for Fullerlove, who made eye contact with the groundling performers, "gave them a glimmer," colluding with them as actor/character to co-create one of the climaxes of the production (2014, PI).

The lit space, the exposure to the elements, the opportunity to stand or sit or come and go, the intimacy of the space and the historical invitation offers our two troupes of performers the opportunity to re-write the rules of not only the audience/actor relationship, but what it means to "perform." Christie Carson argues that actors and audience members had to "re-learn their roles and their relationships" (Carson and Karim-Cooper 2008: 124) at the Globe. Actors at the Globe have learnt to play *with* rather than *to* their audiences. This has taken some time. Mark Rylance observed in John Dove's production of *Measure for Measure* in 2004 that the actors felt they had reached a point where they "were creating with an audience, not recreating" (Carson and Karim-Cooper 2008: 110). Similarly, Globe audiences have learnt to play more *with* the actors than playing *to* each other.[29]

Audiences have noticed and welcome the more demonstrative performances given by actors at the Globe:

> I like the way they engage with the audience. They bring the humour out in the plays a lot more. Other times when I've seen Shakespeare it doesn't really absorb me very much. The [Globe performances] make me feel interested and excited. They seem to reach out more to people. The actors were ad-libbing and they talked more to the audience.
>
> *(Fran 2014, PI)*

> I have always stood in the yard: any excuse to stand in the yard! The actors are usually closer to you and it is just a bit more of a lifting experience. The actors interact with the audience more, particularly because of the lighting.
>
> *(Katie 2014, PI)*

The historical invitation which is taken up by actors and audience members ultimately assists the process of co-creation giving the audience permission to perform demonstrably.

The Globe has been pejoratively described as a Disney tourist attraction or a contemporary sports stadium (Prescott 2005; Worthen 2003) that replicates the original building accurately, but does not allow for appropriate homage to be conferred upon the bard: a hushed, contemplative reverence. Audience performance is considered to be too demonstrative. Whether denigrating or approbating the audience, it is refreshing to witness a revival of critical reviews discussing audience performance, a common practice in the nineteenth century. Audience reviews online are replete with comments of audience performance. Audience reviewers are sometimes so affected by the co-creation that transpires that the reviews often focus on audience experience rather than the plays themselves. Journalist Georgina Brown noted in a 2000 review that "if you sit in the stalls, there's a lot of drama to take in before you come to the stage itself" (cited in Prescott 2005: 362). There is much drama in the yard, but it is, predominantly, welcomed from the stage.

There may be more trollopisms performed at Shakespeare's Globe than in indoor theatres. The distinction between audience performances that bring in and those that shut out the outside world is often blurred in this anachronistic space. This blurring is much more pronounced when a twenty-first-century aircraft streaks above, a pigeon lands on the stage, or rock, pop, funk or soul music wails from party boats on the Thames. Similar to performances when actors improvise during audience one-person shows, these forces of technology and nature often add extra layers of meaning to the performance when actors skilfully incorporate them into the play's *fabula*.

Groundlings feel liberated to perform from the historical invitation that seems to emanate from the very walls of the playhouse itself and from the invitation from the actors onstage to join them in co-creation. Their performance may not conform to what is considered appropriate contemporary Shakespearean reception. The invitation to give a demonstrative, authentic performance is, however, offered generously and provocatively, and it is extended to the audience *and* the actors.

Notes

1 So many audience members described "being part of" the theatrical experience that it was difficult to limit my selection to three quotes.
2 For specific examples of co-creation through the post-show discussion see Heim (2012).
3 For different perspectives on an actor's presence see Philip Zarilli (2012), Jane Goodall (2008), Joseph Roach (2007), Joseph Chaikin (1991) and Bert O. States (1983).
4 Zarilli (2012) and Fischer-Lichte (2008) discuss co-presence in theatre in more detail.
5 During *The Book of Mormon* the audience applaud throughout the performance not just at the conclusion.
6 Comment taken from New York/London questionnaire.
7 This moment of recognition shares some features of Aristotle's *anagnorisis* when a character in a play has a moment of recognition described as a change from ignorance to knowledge. *Anagnorisis* usually results in the recognition of some person or persons.

In Sartre's recognition, the audience member suddenly recognises *themselves* in a strange guise.

8 These comments are taken from another questionnaire I distributed to regular theatre-goers after I delivered a public lecture on theatre history in the United States in February 2014. The question asked "What do you want most from theatre?" There were 41 respondents.

9 In the New York/London questionnaire when asked "Do you think theatre is transformative?" 95 per cent of the respondents said "yes" (see Appendix 2).

10 Positive reciprocity is the desire to give back in a cooperative manner.

11 When asked the question "Do you think your responses affect the actors?" every audience member interviewed responded positively, often detailing how they perceived the reciprocal process.

12 Co-creation was the topic that actors were most excited to talk about, eager to share their understandings of what happens and to acknowledge the audience as vital and equal accomplices in creating the theatrical experience.

13 This comment was spoken by an anonymous audience member to me after a performance in Britain in June 2014.

14 In one celebrated example, during the infamous rivalry between American Edwin Forrest and British Charles Macready that culminated in the Astor Place Riots of 1849, when Edwin Forrest delivered Macbeth's line, "What rhubarb, senna, or what purgative drug, would scour these English hence?" at the Bowery Theatre in New York, 3,000 Americans rose and cheered for America for what was anecdotally reputed to be six minutes, stopping the show.

15 "Conspire" derives from the Latin conspirare, "to breathe together" (OED, "Conspire").

16 Older audience members revisiting their youth in juke-box musicals such as *Jersey Boys*, *Thriller* and *Let it Be* also engage in demonstrative performance.

17 A notable example was the appearance of Martin Freeman in *Richard III* at the Trafalgar Theatre in London in July/September 2014, which attracted a much younger group of fans. See Hastings and Hen (2014).

18 Although the couple have never been identified, several actors and ushers confirm these incidences.

19 Waving lit phones, which were first noted in rock concerts in 1998 (Strauss 1998), are a legacy from cigarette lighters that were waved in concerts in the 1960s.

20 For many years immersive theatre lived in Off-Broadway, Off-West End environments and beyond.

21 These were comments I heard and noted while on the stage at *The Testament of Mary* on 20 April 2013.

22 This includes a combination of interval comments I heard and noted during the interval of *Rocky the Musical* on 1 August 2014 as I sat with my co-performers ready to go up onstage for the final scene of the musical.

23 When the show opened, so many audience members were wearing their own "Italian Stallion" t-shirts to the production (purchased when the film debuted in the 1970s) that the merchandise managers decided to produce and sell a quantity of these t-shirts (which were not part of their original merchandise inventory). The t-shirts sold out nearly every performance.

24 Audience recitation of familiar passages, particularly of Shakespeare, occasionally occurs in mainstream theatres worldwide. In the 2013 production of *Hamlet* at Belvoir St Theatre in Sydney, an audience member, uninvited, recited Hamlet's exhausted soliloquy "To be or not to be" along with Toby Schmitz. This is, more often than not, an uninvited participation.

25 Again I need to reiterate that this practice is more accepted in European theatres, and I am referring to English-speaking Western countries. For examples of audience one-person shows in Germany see Heim (2012).

26 This is a small list taken from the numerous audience comments I overheard and recorded while watching productions in New York, London and Sydney.

27 I would like to add, though, that snoring can sometimes be a critical response.
28 Although Goffman here describes service specialists (ushers) as undertaking this kind of denigration, fellow performers – what Goffman would term "team members" – regularly share stories of trollopisms.
29 Much has been written about Shakespeare's Globe actors and audiences. See particularly Carson and Karim-Cooper (2008) and Worthen (2003).

References

Blau, Herbert (1990) *The Audience*, Baltimore: Johns Hopkins UP.
Bogart, Anne (2006) "The Role of the Audience," *TCG National Conference 2006*, 9 June. Transcript.
Boileau, Kevin (2000) *Genuine Reciprocity and Group Authenticity: Foucault's Developments or Sartre's Social Ontology*, Maryland: University Press of America.
Carlson, Marvin (2004) *Performance: A Critical Introduction*, 2nd edn, Routledge: New York and London.
Carroll, Tim (2008) "Practicing Behaviour to His Own Shadow" in *Shakespeare's Globe: A Theatrical Experiment*, eds. Christie Carson and Farah Karim-Cooper, Cambridge: Cambridge UP.
Carson, Christie and Farah Karim-Cooper (eds.) (2008) *Shakespeare's Globe: A Theatrical Experiment*, Cambridge: Cambridge UP.
Chaikin, Joseph (1991) *The Presence of the Actor*, New York: Theatre Communications Group.
Cohen, Ralph Alan (2008) "Directing at the Globe and the Blackfriars" in *Shakespeare's Globe: A Theatrical Experiment*, eds. Christie Carson and Farah Karim-Cooper, Cambridge: Cambridge UP.
Fischer-Lichte, Erika (2008) *The Transformative Power of Performance: A New Aesthetics*, Milton Park: Routledge.
Funke, Lewis and John E. Booth (eds.) (1963) *Actors Talk About Acting*, New York: Avon.
Gadamer, Hans Georg (1987) *The Relevance of the Beautiful and other Essays*, ed. Robert Bernasconi, trans. Nicholas Walker, Cambridge: Cambridge UP.
Goffman, Erving (1959) *The Presentation of Self in Everyday Life*, New York: Random House.
Goodall, Jane (2008) *Stage Presence*, Milton Park: Routledge.
Gresham, Richard (2014) *Theatre Charter*. Available from: http://theatre-charter.co.uk/ [3 October 2014].
Hasting, Chris and Peter Hen (2014) "Applause! Applause! My Kingdom for Applause: But are Overexcited Hobbit Fans Ruining Martin Freeman's Richard III for Shakespeare Purists?" *Daily Mail*. Available from: http://www.dailymail.co.uk/tvshowbiz/article-2681878/Applause-Applause-My-kingdom-applause-But-overexcited-Hobbit-fans-ruining-Martin-Freemans-Richard-III-Shakespeare-purists.html [22 December 2014].
Hauser, Karen (2014) *The Demographics of the Broadway Audience*, New York: The Broadway League.
Heim, Caroline (2011) *No Exit* post-show transcript, facilitator Warwick Middleton, Sydney Convention and Exhibition Centre, Sydney, 25 August.
——(2012) "'Argue with Us!': Audience Co-creation through Post-Performance Discussions," *New Theatre Quarterly*, vol. 28, no. 2: 189–97.
Luhrmann, Baz (2014), director and writer, *Strictly Ballroom the Musical*, Sydney, Lyric Theatre: Global Creatures.
Machon, Josephine (2013) *Immersive Theatre: Intimacy and Immediacy in Contemporary Performance*, Houndmills: Palgrave Macmillan.
OED "Conspire". Available from: http://www.oed.com/view/Entry/130114?rskey=ApEJGU&result=1#eid [17 December 2014].
Prescott, Paul (2005) "Inheriting the Globe: The Reception of Shakespearean Space and Audience in Contemporary Reviewing" in *A Companion to Shakespeare and Performance*, eds. Barbara Hodgdon and W. B. Worthen, Malden: Blackwell.

Ridout, Nicholas (2006) *Stage Fright, Animals and Other Theatrical Problems*, Cambridge: Cambridge UP.

Roach, Joseph (2007) *It*, Ann Arbor: Michigan UP.

Sartre, Jean-Paul (1976) *Sartre on Theatre*, eds. Michel Contat and Michel Rybalka, trans. Frank Jellinek, New York: Pantheon.

——(2010) *Being and Nothingness: An Essay on Phenomenological Ontology*, trans. Hazel E. Barnes, Abingdon: Routledge.

Schechner, Richard (1988) *Performance Theory*, 2nd edn., New York: Routledge.

Shadowlands Survey (2010) "Your Response." Available from: http://survey.qut.edu.au/site/ [12 October 2010].

States, Bert O. (1983) "The Actor's Presence: Three Phenomenal Modes," *Theatre Journal*, vol. 35, no. 3: 359–75.

Strauss, Neil (1998) "A Concert Communion With Cell Phones; Press 1 to Share Song, 2 for Encore, 3 for Diversion, 4 to Schmooze" *The New York Times* 9 December. Available from: http://www.nytimes.com/1998/12/09/arts/concert-communion-with-cell-phones-press-1-share-song-2-for-encore-3-for.html?pagewanted=all&src=pm [14 November 2014].

White, Gareth (2013) *Audience Participation in the Theatre: Aesthetics of the Invitation*, New York: Palgrave Macmillan.

Worthen, W. B. (2003) *Shakespeare and the Force of Modern Performance*, West Nyack: Cambridge UP.

Zarilli, Phillip (2012) " … presence … as a etc" in *Archaeologies of Presence: Art, Performance and the Persistence of Being*, eds. Gabriella Giannachi, Nick Kaye and Michael Shanks, New York and London: Routledge.

CONCLUSION

New Possibilities

There's something really joyous about that exchange between actors and audience. It is sad that you only get to look them in the eyes and say hello in a funny sort of way at the end of it.

(Fullerlove 2014, PI)

Theatres are places for performance. Conventionally, the performance is considered to occur on the stage performed by a troupe of actors. This book has considered that in the playhouse there is another troupe of performers in the auditorium: the audience. During the theatrical experience the two troupes encounter each other, perform for each other, critique each other's performances and co-create fictitious worlds into being. The audience text and embodied actions of the audience performers are a crucial part of the theatrical experience which inform the actor's performance and experience.

Research into the role of the audience as performer is in its nascent stage. In this book, "The floodlights have moved away from the actors who possess proper names and social blazons […] settling on the mass of the audience" (De Certeau 1984 n. pag.). Most of the audience members I interviewed for this book not only watched the actors' performance but were often preoccupied with watching the social blazon and colourful performances of other audience members in the floodlights of interval and sometimes during the onstage performance. The actors' and audience's detailed descriptions of audience performance were intriguing, humorous, pejorative and enlightening: the laugh that is contagious, the walk-out that bristles, the scream that thrills, the phone ring that deafens, the dialogue that effuses, the purchasing that memorialises, the singing that celebrates. The audience's repertoire of actions is expanding in this new millennium.

Theatre audiences play diverse roles in the twenty-first century. There are audience members that perform as critics in post-shows and through multiple forums in the virtual air. Audiences can become a pseudo community when they perform in the house adjacent to the stage of the actors. Much pleasure is gained from playing the colourful role of consumer through purchasing mementos or through costume theming. When the fourth wall is shattered and audience members play a co-creative part in a production with their onstage co-performers, the electric air of theatre proliferates with new possibilities for audience performance. All of the theatrical spaces discussed in my case studies are environments where audience members can have Fullerlove's "joyous exchanges" with actors or with each other. Steppenwolf's emancipated critics, Signature's democratic communities, Times Square's self-conscious consumers and The Globe's playful co-creators become emancipated audience communities because they are given permission to perform in relaxed environments that privilege audience creativity.

Everything Old is New Again

This book has documented some examples of what it means to "be an audience" in the nineteenth, twentieth and twenty-first centuries. Demonstrative audience performances have been encouraged or constrained, or both simultaneously at different periods throughout theatre history. The performance of the audience for most of the nineteenth century was gregarious and uninhibited. During the twentieth century the demonstrative audience performer became an endangered species. Expressive audience performance can be seen as cyclical. By the time we reach the second decade of the twenty-first century, new audience practices and ensembles have emerged that are reminiscent of the nineteenth-century performances and performers. To understand some of what it means to be an audience in this new millennium I shared the perspectives of over one hundred ordinary audience members and two other groups of fans of audiences: actors and ushers.

A number of corollaries have emerged from my study suggesting that audiences are becoming more demonstrative. The audience are bringing new modes of not only performing into the playhouse, but new modes of talking about and criticising productions. Due to the explosion of new technologies in the arena of social media a corresponding new set of possibilities of audience performance is emerging. Given the flexible nature of ever-changing technologies, this orientation could turn in a different direction or even reverse. Future research on audience performance will need to take into account the opportunities for audience performance that new technologies invite in the playhouse.

As we have seen, much theatre audience performance in the twentieth-first century is acculturated behaviour from television watching, rock concert attendance and presence at some fringe events such as immersive theatre. This book, borrowing from Frances Trollope's nineteenth-century signature monograph, could well be re-titled *Domestic Manners of the Twenty-First Century Audience Member*. Some of the more domestic performances now seen in theatre houses are re-enactments of television viewing behaviours where continuous partial inattention has replaced selective attention. The more effervescent auditorium performances have been traced to their beginnings in rock concerts and the more venturesome to fringe theatre events.

The technology-savvy twenty-first-century audience members are also bringing new approaches to criticism into the theatre. Many of these practices have been rehearsed in various platforms online. Different ways to discuss productions are emerging such as innovative post-show discussions, focus groups, tweeting and online reviews. These platforms for audience criticism are currently increasing exponentially. As Rylance asserts, "Audiences want to have something more happen than they did twenty years ago. I do not think they are happy to sit quietly in the dark and admire us with their minds" (cited in Carson and Karim-Cooper 2008: 108). This happening is the corporeal, verbal and often very playful performance of the audience. After a hiatus of over one hundred years, the audience is bringing some demonstrative performances back into the playhouse.

The creativity of twenty-first-century audience members is only limited by the constraints imposed by etiquette strictures. The trammels of theatre etiquette that have introverted demonstrative performance for the last century are, however, loosening. They are loosening out of necessity in response to the more tenacious and expressive performances that are being brought into the theatre. As we saw in Chapters Six and Seven, in some cases they are not being loosened, but are being trampled by the more entitled audience members.

A peek inside the twenty-first-century auditorium reveals old and new audience practices. Groups of matinee girls attired in blossoming pink and sparkles are taking selfies, screaming their delight at star actors or singing out of tune to familiar songs pulsating from the stage. The b'hoys of the gallery have re-appeared, lurking in the dress circle. They are no longer cracking peanuts, but have a new bag of tricks: their mobile phones. They share quips from websites while laughing too loud in all the wrong places in the play. A couple in the front row effuse over souvenir flip-flops they have bought for their grandchildren. Audience critics engage in heated discussions as they carry their drinks back to their seats. A "stall-ite" surprises themself by clambering onstage to be costumed in a flamenco skirt and salsa in a chorus dance as another audience member roars "Amen to that!"

You could say that this twenty-first-century audience performance is reminiscent of eighteenth- and nineteenth-century audience responses. However, the flash and lure of the i-devices that blind actors onstage and tweet and twirp criticisms to the performance were not around a century or two ago. The contemporary audiences are performing to a much wider virtual community as they take selfies, tweet their reviews, capture their image on digital walls in foyers or download the production's soundtrack from i-Tunes to share with virtual friends.

Although this is a wonderland for some and a dystopia for others, these performances, not usually enacted concurrently, are now an integral part of twenty-first-century mainstream theatrical experience. Each of these performances from new twenty-first-century ensembles – the tourists, the girls/boys night outers, the critics, the consumers, the groupies – are small but significant enunciations of audience authority, liberation and pleasure. Audience members are discovering new ways to perform in the theatre in this twenty-first century which are often remarkably evocative of nineteenth-century performances.

Emerging Questions

Do audience members actually want to perform in or contribute more to the theatrical experience? From my encounters with audiences over the past two years I believe that they do, particularly in playing the role of critic. Audience members eagerly accept any invitation to contribute their critical responses in the twenty-first-century playhouse. No one I approached before, during or after productions refused an interview. This alerted me to the strong desire audience members have to share their ideas. Most, although often initially apologetic, had much to contribute. I was handed impressions of theatre-going scrawled on the backs of programmes during intervals or torn out of precious "theatre memory notebooks" that audience members carried with them to each production. One audience member wanted to bequeath me a sizeable collection of playbills. In the post-show discussions I have facilitated, up to two-thirds of audiences have attended the discussions to play critic, and I have too often had to prematurely conclude post-shows that were in full flight because of time restraints.

Audience oral and written critical reviews of plays are ubiquitous. In this second decade of the twenty-first century, audience word of mouth has the most significant impact on ticket sales, far surpassing the authority of the traditional theatre critic.[1] Word of mouth has always swayed audience opinion to some extent. With the emergence of new digital technologies we are now, however, documenting what were formally only oral reviews and have evidence of the large, insightful repertoire of criticisms offered by the armchair critic. Criticisms delivered through word of mouth can be ignored or forgotten. Audience word-of-tweet, online reviews, filmed or recorded responses are far more tangible and, therefore, potent. As detailed in Chapters Four and Five, theatre companies and productions are turning to these reviews to record ordinary audience members' responses and because audiences listen to audiences. Audience members play the role of critic in all of these forums not only to share their critical responses, but to connect with others. The contemporary theatre world is rife with opportunities for audiences to play the role of critic, and many audience members are taking up this new role with much unbridled enthusiasm and pleasure.

Lynne Meadow has been artistic director of New York's MTC since 1972. When I asked her if she had witnessed audiences change over that time, she articulated the following paradox: "[W]e've watched attention-spans shrink, and we've also watched people have a greater and greater appetite to be in the presence of something that is not in a hurry" (2013, PI). This is consonant with my own observations. When I observe the buzz and whirl of the frenetic twenty-first-century audience performer that tweets and screams and sings and clamours for more from the theatrical experience, I can well imagine that this is an audience member with an ever-shrinking attention span. I have also witnessed this same audience member craving an analogue, timeless experience in the theatre. This is a curious phenomenon and further research is needed to explore how this affects and shapes audience performance and how theatre companies respond to these needs. Audience members strive to "live in the moment"[2] of the theatrical experience; something that only a real-time experience with real people performing beside you and onstage can satisfy. Can these seeming cross-purposes be fulfilled in the twenty-first-century playhouse? We will see in the decades to come. It is going to be an interesting but challenging journey.

New Possibilities

However you have read this book – a documentation of audience performance in mainstream theatres – it is my hope that it has been received in the spirit it was intended: as a celebration of audience performance. There are many geographic, intercultural and generic frontiers that future research could traverse. Although not all audience members even desire to perform in the theatre and countless may be aghast at the thought of performing onstage with the actors, many emboldened, vivacious and uninhibited twenty-first-century audience members are ready to perform. In this, audience members are performers. Even some veterans are adopting new practices. Mike, an accountant from London, goes to the theatre 16 times a year and has embraced new performatives to express his appreciation to the actors:

> I'm not frightened of applauding. Not the "whoop" and the "holler" bit, but the cheers and the "heigh-eigh": a bit of that, especially at the end. You've got to do that. You've got to let them know they're doing a good job.[3]
>
> *(2014, PI)*

As this book has demonstrated, audience performance always encourages, feeds and thrills actors. Actor Tandy explains, "You don't expect the audience to perform for you, but you love it when an audience is actually *with you*: it creates a lovely warm atmosphere" (italics mine, 2013, PI). Permission from the onstage actors is ultimately the key to reviving demonstrative audience performance for those that enjoy participating. Contemporary audiences have been told to sit still for so long that it takes an overt, playful and almost mischievous invitation to break through the barricades that theatre etiquette has constructed. Actors, because "they have an open, playful side that has an innocence to it" (Fullerlove 2014, PI) can achieve this. As Gadamer contends, "The player receives back from the onlooker what he has dared to do and inversely we, the onlookers, receive from the daring presentation of the players new possibilities of being that go beyond what we are" (1987: 64). In daring to take up the invitation from the actors to perform in the twenty-first-century theatre, new possibilities for "being" an audience member emerge.

When I was part of an acting troupe I often pondered the audience: the role of the audience, their performance, their contribution and what a crucial difference they made to my performance. Interestingly, now as an audience member, I ponder the actors onstage and what a difference they make to my performance as an audience member. As an actor, if I felt the audience were *with me* – that they were hanging on my every word, reacting to everything I gave them, experiencing the emotions my character portrayed – then, as an actor, I would work to live more in the moment and allow myself to become more vulnerable and spontaneous onstage. I would give them more. Now as an audience member if I feel that the actors are *with me* and are reacting to what I give them – that they are hanging on my every response, that they are listening to me listen – I will laugh more, I will cry more, I will applaud more. I will give them more. In either troupe I am a performer.

As this book has shown, the contemporary audience performer does not perform alone but performs in the gregarious community of fellow critics, consumers and co-creators *and* with their co-performing troupe, the actors. The essence of theatre is the encounter between two troupes – actors and audience members:

> The audience can actually carry us through the play. It's like a wave, the audience just erupts in laughter. It's a wonderful feeling between audience and actors when that happens.
>
> *(Tenney 2013, Actor, PI)*

> When it really gets you, when it really comes to life, it makes you either cry or laugh or whatever. *That* is theatre, that is it, isn't it?
>
> *(June 2014, Audience member, PI).*

Notes

1 In the 2013/14 Broadway season, theatre-goers reported personal recommendation as the most influential factor affecting ticket purchase. 48.4 per cent of audience members were influenced by personal recommendations and 29 per cent by critics' reviews (Hauser 2014: 39). In my own questionnaire when asked "Whose opinion about a show are you most likely to listen to?" 79 per cent said a friend or relative and 21 per cent said a critic (see Appendix 2).

2 This is an actor's term employed by Sanford Meisner. Sanford Meisner, a Method acting advocate who developed a technique of acting based on Stanislavski's methods, used the phrase "being in the moment" to describe the actor living in the temporal world of the play responding spontaneously to the stimulus given to him/her from the other actors onstage by "living in the moment" they happen. See Meisner and Longwell (1987).

3 Interestingly, Mike has gathered up the courage to perform a "heigh-eigh" for the actors, the signature dialogue of the b'hoys of the nineteenth century.

References

Carson, Christie and Farah Karim-Cooper (eds.) (2008) *Shakespeare's Globe: A Theatrical Experiment*, Cambridge: Cambridge UP.

De Certeau, Michel (1984) *The Practice of Everyday Life*, Berkeley and Los Angeles: California UP.

Gadamer, Hans Georg (1987) *The Relevance of the Beautiful and other Essays*, ed. Robert Bernasconi, trans. Nicholas Walker, Cambridge: Cambridge UP.

Hauser, Karen (2014) *The Demographics of the Broadway Audience*, New York: The Broadway League.

Meisner, Sanford and Dennis Longwell (1987) *Sanford Meisner on Acting*, New York: Vintage.

CONTRIBUTORS

Note: Quotations derived from these personal interviews are indicated throughout the book with the initials "PI" in accompanying parenthetical citations.

Audience Members

Agnes (2014) Personal interview, 27 July.
Alex (2014) Personal interview, 20 July.
Alexander (2014) Personal interview, 27 May.
Alice (2013) Personal interview, 20 April.
Anita (2014) Personal interview, 24 June.
Anne (2013a) Personal interview, 5 October.
Anne (2013b) Personal interview, 29 November.
Anne (2014) Personal interview, 24 June.
Barry (2014) Personal interview, 24 June.
Bill (2014) Personal interview, 19 July.
Billy (2014) Personal interview, 24 June.
Carson (2014) Personal interview, 22 July.
Cheryl (2014) Personal interview, 6 June.
Chevonne (2013) Personal interview, 12 March.
Christian (2014) Personal interview, 18 July.
Clay (2013) Personal interview, 9 Febuary.
David (2013a) Personal interview, 14 March.
David (2013b) Personal interview, 24 April.
David (2014a) Personal interview, 24 June.
David (2014b) Personal interview, 19 July.
Dawn (2014) Personal interview, 27 May.
Dick (2014) Personal interview, 18 July.
Don (2013) Personal interview, 1 May.

Doreen (2014) Personal interview, 6 June.

Edie (2013) Personal interview, 31 January.

Eileen (2013) Personal interview, 1 May.

Elaine (2014) Personal interview, 10 September.

Ellen (2013) Personal interview, 1 May.

Fiona (2014) Personal interview, 18 July.

Fran (2014) Personal interview, 21 July.

Gareth (2014) Personal interview, 17 July.

Gina (2014) Personal interview, 24 June.

Gint (2014) Personal interview, 19 July.

Hedda (2013) Personal interview, 5 October.

Ian (2014) Personal interview, 24 June.

Janet (2013) Personal interview, 20 April.

Janet (2014) Personal interview, 20 July.

Jean (2014) Personal interview, 24 June.

Jenita (2013) Personal interview, 1 May.

Jenny (2014) Personal interview, 20 July.

Jim (2013) Personal interview, 19 April.

Jim (2014) Personal interview, 27 May.

Joan (2014) Personal interview, 1 August.

John (2014a) Personal interview, 27 May.

John (2014b) Personal interview, 27 July.

John (2014c) Personal interview, 1 August.

Joshua (2013) Telephone interview, 30 April.

Joyce (2013) Personal interview, 9 Febuary.

Judith (2014) Personal interview, 23 June.

June (2014) Personal interview, 27 July.

Kat (2014) Personal interview, 18 July.

Kate (2014) Personal interview, 18 June.

Katie (2014) Personal interview, 21 July.

Kay (2014) Personal interview, 27 May.

Kaye (2014) Personal interview, 27 May.

Keith (2013) Personal interview, 15 March.

Kevin (2014) Personal interview, 1 August.

Linda (2013) Personal interview, 5 October.

Lindsay (2014) Personal interview, 24 June.

Lisa (2014) Personal interview, 18 July.

Liz (2014) Personal interview, 17 July.

Lois (2013) Personal interview, 27 April.

Lottie (2014) Personal interview, 20 July.

Lynda (2013) Personal interview, 5 October.

Maggie (2013) Personal interview, 15 March.

Maggie (2014) Personal interview, 27 July.

Maree (2014) Personal interview, 18 June.

Margaret (2014a) Personal interview, 1 February.
Margaret (2014b) Personal interview, 24 June.
Marjorie (2014) Personal interview, 24 June.
Mark (2013) Personal interview, 17 April.
Mary (2013) Personal interview, 5 October.
Mary (2014a) Personal interview, 1 February.
Mary (2014b) Personal interview, 2 February.
Meg (2014) Personal interview, 20 July.
Melanie (2013) Personal interview, 19 April.
Michael (2014a) Personal interview, 27 May.
Michael (2014b) Personal interview, 19 July.
Mick (2014) Personal interview, 27 May.
Mike (2014a) Personal interview, 15 June.
Mike (2014b) Personal interview, 24 June.
Morgan (2014) Personal interview, 1 August.
Natalie (2014) Personal interview, 19 July.
Pam (2013) Personal interview, 5 October.
Patricia (2013) Personal interview, 14 March.
Paul (2013) Personal interview, 29 November.
Rachel (2013) Personal interview, 29 November.
Rachel (2014) Personal interview, 20 July.
Ray (2014) Personal interview, 24 June.
Ron (2014) Personal interview, 31 January.
Rosemarie (2013) Personal interview, 29 November.
Roy (2014) Personal interview, 2 February.
Sara (2013) Personal interview, 29 April.
Sarah (2014) Personal interview, 18 July.
Shirley (2014) Personal interview, 18 June.
Siobhan (2014) Personal interview, 20 July.
Stacey (2014) Personal interview, 18 July.
Stephen (2014) Personal interview, 24 June.
Sue (2014) Personal interview, 29 January.
Susan (2014) Personal interview, 24 June.
Talia (2014) Personal interview, 1 August.
Terry (2013) Personal interview, 24 March.
Till (2013) Personal interview, 29 April.
Tom (2013) Personal interview, 12 March.
Tom (2014) Personal interview, 1 February.
Wayne (2014) Personal interview, 29 January.

Actors

Bell, Nicholas (2013) Personal interview, 1 August.
Danby, Trevor (2014) Personal interview, 18 June.

Fullerlove, Janet (2014) Personal interview, 20 July.
Grubb, Robert (2014) Personal interview, 13 September.
Hauck, Steven (2013) Personal interview, 29 April.
Henry, Andrew (2013) Personal interview, 29 November.
Lee, Sondra (2013) Personal interview, 15 April.
Liebhaber, Bernard (2013) Personal interview, 20 April.
Oakleigh, Helen (2014) Personal interview, 18 July.
Owen-Taylor, Mark (2014) Personal interview, 13 September.
Schoeffler, Paul (2013) Personal interview, 28 April.
Shaw, Peggy (2012) Personal interview, 1 August.
Sheldon, Tony (2013) Personal interview, 25 April.
Sullivan, KT (2013) Personal interview, 18 April.
Tandy, Steven (2013) Personal interview, 19 June.
Tenney, Anne (2013) Telephone interview, 5 December.
Weaver, Lois (2012) Personal interview, 1 August.
White, Richard (2013) Personal interview, 29 April.
Young, Lee (2013) Personal interview, 29 November.

Ushers/Front of House Managers/Merchandise Managers

Bonanni, Marc (2013) Personal interview, 26 April.
Conte, David (2014) Telephone interview, 8 August.
Fokes, Kevin (2013) Telephone interview, 27 November.
Jersey Boys usher (2014) Personal interview, 18 July.
Let the Right One In usher (2014) Personal interview, 18 July.
Payne, Jodie (2013) Telephone interview, 20 June.
Spiderman usher (2013) Personal interview, 18 April.
Strictly Ballroom usher (2014) Personal interview, 13 September.
Testament usher (2013) Personal interview, 20 April.
Tom (2014) Personal interview, 20 July.

Directors/Producers/Other Theatre Professionals

Bogart, Anne (2013) Personal interview, 29 April.
Carter, Aaron (2013) Literary Manager Steppenwolf Theatre Company, personal interview, 1 May.
Houghton, Jim (2013) Personal interview, 25 April.
Lavey, Martha (2014) Telephone interview, 13 November.
Meadow, Lynne (2013) Telephone interview, 30 May.
McCollum, Kevin (2013) Personal interview, 29 April.

APPENDIX 1

Audience Interviews

Method

The author undertook 106 semi-structured interviews with audience members in New York, London, Sydney, Chicago, Toronto and Glasgow in 2013–14. The interviews ran from 5 to 60 minutes with an average interview time of 20 minutes. Participants were aged 18 to 84. Sixty-two per cent were female and 38 per cent male.

Five standard questions were asked:

In what ways have you seen audiences change over time?
What does it mean to you to "be" an audience?
How would you describe the atmosphere of theatre?
Do you think your reactions give something to the actors?
What do you talk about at interval or after the performance?

Results

In what ways have you seen audiences change over time?	
Audiences dress less formally	20%
It costs more to attend*	10%
There is more technology in the audience	10%
Audiences are more responsive	8%
Audiences are louder/noisier	6%
Audiences shuffle and fidget more	6%
There is more eating and drinking in the seats	6%
Audiences are inattentive	5%
Demographics have changed	5%

(continued)

In what ways have you seen audiences change over time?

Audiences are older	5%
Audiences are younger	3%
Audiences act like they are in their living rooms	3%
It is more of an occasion*	3%
It is less of an occasion*	2%
Audiences are more critical	2%
Audiences are less critical	2%
Audiences are more disrespectful	2%
Audiences are apathetic	2%

Although not directly answering my question, these were responses given.

What does it mean to you to "be" an audience?

Interaction with actors	10%
An emotional experience	9%
A shared experience	8%
Showing appreciation	8%
A privilege	7%
Participation	7%
An experience	6%
Being part of the atmosphere	6%
Enjoyment	6%
A mind exercise	4%
It changes me	4%
Entering a different world	4%
Relaxation	3%
I envy actors	2%
Escape	2%
Entertainment	2%
Feeling involved	2%
Feeling good	2%
An ephemeral experience	1%
Play	1%
Inspiration	1%
Pleasure	1%
Getting something out of it	1%
A spellbinding experience	1%
Nourishment	1%
A treat	1%

How would you describe the atmosphere of theatre?

Live	22%
A place where the unexpected can happen	18%
Exciting	14%
A place to share an experience with others	13%
Feeling part of something great/big/amazing	9%
Pleasurable	8%
A special occasion	6%
An immediate experience	6%
A buzz	4%

Do you think your reactions give something to the actors?

Yes	100%
No	–

What kind of reactions?

Laughing	27%
Applause	23%
Feedback	23%
Eye contact	9%
Listening	9%
Emotions	5%
Enthusiasm	5%
Catcalls	5%
Singing	5%
Dancing	5%
Crying	5%
Enjoyment	5%

What do you talk about at interval or after the performance?

The acting	24%
The staging	12%
The costumes	10%
The interpretation	8%
Issues in the play	8%
The story	8%
The singing	6%
Improvements that could be made	6%
The sound design	6%
Can we hear it	6%
The characters	6%
The emotions it evokes	6%
Was it good or bad	4%

(continued)

What do you talk about at interval or after the performance?

The audience	4%
The casting	4%
The diction	2%
Interactions between characters	2%
The pace	2%
The actor's timing	2%
How it can change your life	2%
The humour	2%
The truth of the play	2%
The comfort of the seats	2%
The pathos and bathos	2%

APPENDIX 2

Questionnaire

Respondents: 62
Age: 25–65+
Gender: Female 60 per cent   Male 40 per cent
Locations: London Questionnaires: Henry V (2014) Groundlings Theatre Company, The Rose Theatre, London, 17 July.
New York Questionnaires: *Leave it to Jane (2013) Musicals Tonight, The Lion Theatre, New York, 26 April.*

What do you most want from your theatre experience?					
To have a good time and learn something	To have a good time	To escape from my everyday life	Other	To laugh and/or cry	To learn something
68%	18%	10%	3%	1%	–

Do you ever watch other people?		
Never	Sometimes	Often
25%	63%	12%

Do you most often go to the theatre...		
With one special friend or family member	With a group of friends or family members	Alone
62%	24%	14%

How would you best like to be treated at the theatre? As a ...

Guest	Patron	Customer
42%	32%	26%

Do you moderate your behaviour according to etiquette "rules"?

Never	Sometimes	Often
8%	30%	62%

Do you like audience events?

Yes	No
69%	31%

Which of the following do you like?

Post-show talks	Backstage tours	Audience invited to sing, clap, cheer along	Subscriber events	Audience invited up on stage
65%	60%	55%	35%	26%

Whose opinion about a show are you most likely to listen to?

Friend/relative	Critic
79%	21%

Do you think theatre is transformative?

Yes	No
95%	5%

INDEX